Six Summers
in Paris
1789-1794

By the same author

EYE-WITNESS

1815: AN END AND A BEGINNING

Six Summers in Paris

1789-1794

JOHN FISHER

HARPER & ROW, PUBLISHERS

New York and Evanston

This book was originally published in England under the title "The Elysian Fields."

Cause première de tout être
Auteur des vertus et des lois
Sois toujours notre unique maître
Venge-nous des crimes des rois.
Ils ont usurpé ta puissance
Pour faire oublier tes bienfaits
Mais la chute du Palais,
Nous annonce encore ta présence

HYMN TO THE SUPREME BEING SUNG BY THE
CITIZENS OF TULLE (CORREZE) AND PRESERVED
IN THE ARCHIVES NATIONALES OF THE FRENCH
REPUBLIC

Contents

Illustrations

Georges-Jacques Danton (1759–1794), engraved by W. H.
Mote (*Radio Times Hulton Picture Library*)

Four typical revolutionaries (1793–4): A member of the Commune, a jailer at the Temple Prison, an agent of the Committee of Public Safety and a Section leader summoning a
general assembly (*Radio Times Hulton Picture Library*)

A Republican Belle—a British view of a French woman in
1794, cartoon by Cruikshank (*British Museum*)

A street in Paris during the Reign of Terror 1793. Drawn by
G. Durand for *Quatre-vingt-treize* by Victor Hugo (*Radio Times
Hulton Picture Library*)

Louis (de) Saint-Just (1767–1794), from the portrait in the
Musée Carnavalet, Paris (*Mansell Collection*)

Queen Marie Antoinette on her way to the guillotine, sketched
by Louis David. In the Musée Carnavalet, Paris (*Archives
Photographiques, Paris*)

Queen Marie Antoinette (1755–1793), in the Musée Carnavalet,
Paris (*Archives Photographiques, Paris*)

In the Text

INTRODUCTION

I F, as Napoleon said, history is a myth that men agree to believe, then the history of the French Revolution has never yet been written. For there is no final agreement as to what occurred.

Adolphe Thiers and François-Auguste-Marie Mignet, both liberally minded, wrote before the age of documentation and scientific analysis. Thomas Carlyle, in a Calvinistic frame of mind, excelled himself in demolishing the achievements not only of the French monarchy but of the whole of the eighteenth century and almost succeeded in justifying the Terror. Jules Michelet glorified 'the people' without defining who they were. Hippolyte Taine, horrified by the Paris mobs of 1871, poured scorn and disdain on those of a century earlier. Alphonse Aulard, among the first historians to make use of modern methods of research, emphasized political developments, Jean Jaurès, labour relations and Albert Mathiez, economic problems and Robespierre.

Even contemporaries failed to understand the events they were witnessing. Eighteenth-century observers, for example, expected the Revolution to follow the pattern of the American rebellion

1

witnessed by them some ten years earlier, which had led to a United States Constitution established by men of education and discretion.

New doubts have sprung up. And just as the glitter and gleam of some ancient spire alters from moment to moment in the changing light of the sun, so the events of the Revolution take on fresh significance from one decade to the next. Fifty years ago it could never have occurred to anyone to wonder whether the French Revolution, which was unloosed by the bourgeoisie and completed by the mob, set the pattern for the Bolshevik Revolution which also had its bourgeois and proletarian phases.

Today, scholarly and penetrating studies are in circulation on this very subject, and analogies are drawn between French attempts to export a revolution to other countries and the Russian plans for a Communist International.

Also, now that we can look back over a perspective extending over a century and three quarters, we may, perhaps, be allowed to raise further questions which might previously have been too nebulous to contemplate. For example, we may ask whether the Revolution, destroyed the literary and artistic glories of France to any permanent extent; and we may wonder whether these glories were not dimmed more effectively by Napoleon's murderous campaigns.

There are other respects, too, in which we are entitled to review, and perhaps to revise, former presentations of the historical scene. This is because as each year goes by it grows harder and harder to relive in imagination the physical events of the past. A greater effort has to be made to reconcile the increasing contrast between our prejudices, our ways of thought and our behaviour and those of other days. Our views on education, health and the use of leisure, conception of what, or who, is beautiful, our preferences in food, and clothes, our standards of living, our tastes in architecture and in the theatre—all these have changed to an extent which makes it difficult to cast our minds back even ten years, still less a century and three-quarters.

As recently as a generation ago it already required some imagination to picture a revolution achieved in times when the fastest way of conveying news was to urge a galloping horse along an unmetalled road.

Today it is harder still to conceive a national revolution without radio to carry the voices of its leaders, without even loud-speakers, without television, without photographs to make them recognized or telephones by which to make an appointment or pass on a warning, and without reliable newspapers to counteract the force of rumour.

Even appearances tell. Visitors to Paris as they wait for the traffic lights to change at the Place de la Concorde can hardly be expected to reflect that they are re-visiting the chief showplace of the guillotine . . . or to recall that Pigalle, Malesherbes, Boissy d'Anglas, Daunou and Carnot, whose names are to be found in the Paris Street Directory, were real people who lived in the century when the tricolour flag first flew.

And so a fresh attempt to return to those days of savagery and eloquence, of bloodshed, bravery, treachery and ignorance, and to draw what lessons we can from them may be harder than the task could have been even a few years ago. One of the most difficult problems, when translating 'then' into 'now', is to represent the livres of two hundred years ago, or francs as they afterwards became, in terms of today's pounds or dollars. For example one might argue that since in bygone days it need only x francs to provide for the needs of a typical French family and since it now needs perhaps ten times as many francs, therefore the old franc was worth ten times as much as the new.

But in practice any such comparison between the two households is fallacious, for the luxuries of one generation are the necessities of the next. And the requirements of typical families change for psychological reasons. Where could you find today a family able, for the purposes of an economic comparison, to wash their clothes in the brook and walk about in home-made clogs, divesting themselves of the use of street-cleaning services for which they pay directly or indirectly? And where could have been found a hundred and fifty years ago a family discontented because they 'needed' a telephone or new bicycle?

Equally the value of money has changed for other reasons than that more of it has been minted. In fact it is possible to argue that the old pre-Revolution franc was worth more simply because there was less to buy with it and therefore less inducement to part with it. The fashion of the time was to knock up something rather than buy it and to mend and make do rather than throw away. Throughout much of the eighteenth century obsolescence was still primarily a human weakness, design was relatively static and money represented not so much cash for spending or even capital for investing but was akin to pure treasure to be hoarded for its own sake. It needed a revolution to transform the society which derived its wealth primarily from inherited land to one based mainly on movable wealth owned by the bourgeoisie.

All this makes it hard to convert francs or livres of those days into modern money with any certainty that the rate of exchange is reasonable.

We know, however, that disregarding seasonal and local variations, a typical semi-skilled worker such as a carpenter or locksmith could expect, in the years shortly before the French Revolution, to earn about ten livres per week, which it might be reasonable to compare with a bare subsistence rate of four pounds weekly in the United Kingdom today. This would give the pre-Revolution livre a value of eight shillings or slightly more than a dollar, a figure also in sympathy with the prices charged then and now for household necessities. It is on this basis that conversions have been made here for British readers. American readers need do no conversion sums but should merely read dollars instead of livres.

The list of books given at the end is very much a personal choice. It includes mainly those works which are stimulating as well as instructive and a few others which, though not so readable, can't be overlooked. For those with interests beyond books, I would strongly recommend visits to the Carnavalet Museum and the National Archives Museum in Paris, both of which have fascinating galleries packed with souvenirs of the French Revolution.

Chapter 1

PRELUDE

THE Court at Versailles changed for ever in May 1774 when the smallpox carried off King Louis XV. The new Louis, only nineteen years old, left the Palace of Versailles with his Queen, Marie Antoinette, still younger, in the customary journey which followed a royal decease, and took up residence in the Château de la Muette in Paris.

But the courtiers, for whom there was no place, had to be left behind and the King was completely cut off from his former ministers, condemned as they were to six weeks' quarantine for their contacts with the late monarch. There were other changes too. For more than twenty-five years Jean-Frédéric Phélypeaux, Comte de Maurepas, had remained in exile on his estate at Bourges, among the châteaux of the Loire, banished there by King Louis XV for composing a scandalous rhyme about the King's mistress, Madame de Pompadour. He had almost forgotten the days when, as a young man in his twenties, he was Secretary of State in charge of the Royal Household as well as Minister of the Marine and for the Colonies. And now, suddenly, at the age of seventy-three he received a letter from the new King.

'My certainty of your rectitude and of your profound knowledge of affairs, leads me to ask you to help me with your advice,' it read. 'Come, therefore, as soon as possible.' It was a sign, one of several, that the days when the King's mistress could have a royal Counsellor dismissed were over.

The King decided to dispense with his Comptroller of the Royal Menus Plaisirs (minor pleasures, i.e. amusements other than the chase). He renounced the levy known as the Gift of Joyous Succession and Queen Marie Antoinette said that she would not accept the contribution known as the Droit de Ceinture which was paid nominally to fill the purse carried on the Queen's girdle. 'Who wears girdles nowadays?' the Queen exclaimed.

The young couple sought to break down some of the barriers between themselves and their people. While in Paris the King threw open the gates separating the Château de la Muette from the Bois de Boulogne and took walks in the park. Later he asked that the custom by which the city of Rheims was smothered with bunting for every coronation should not be followed in his own case. 'I wish,' said Louis XVI, 'that there should be nothing between my people and myself to prevent our seeing each other.'

This direct method of communication between a King and his subjects was understandable perhaps in the days when no other simple or effective way existed, except on currency, of projecting the royal image. But Louis XVI had, in addition, a reason for showing himself to his people. He had the fatal weakness (for a King) of wanting to be liked and among his courtiers he had found neither affection nor esteem. As a boy he was too shy to speak to the royal Counsellors and learn from them.

His features showed no nobility of expression. His laugh was heavy and lethargic his face lifeless, his appearance slovenly. At the age of eleven he had lost his father, his elder brother died soon after, then his mother. He had learnt almost nothing from his grandfather. He was short-sighted, overgrown, shy and awkward. An ambassador at the Court reported that he was 'as wild and rustic as if he'd been brought up in a wood'. He liked to work with his hands and had a forge installed in the grounds of Versailles. He was never happier than when working with the masons on a new courtyard or terrace for the palace or in rearranging his rooms. He delighted to make his own locks and keys. His only other interest was hunting and as King he spent so much time on horseback that he would fall asleep afterwards during important conferences. When out with the guns nothing was overlooked. Thus on 31 March 1780 the King noted that three squirrels had been dispatched and in November 1784 another. On 28 June that year two hundred swallows had been killed. In 1789 when the King came to work out for himself what he had been doing since 1775, the year of his marriage, he reckoned that he had attended 400 wild boar hunts, 134 stag hunts and 324 other expeditions accounting for 1,562 days devoted to the chase.

The elegant society of the Court offered him nothing. He had nothing to contribute to it, and soon came to despise it. He had the countryman's graceless walk, his voice at times rose to an undignified squeak and he hated dancing. Marie Antoinette, aged sixteen when she married Louis, was already a woman; he as yet but half a man. Historians have noted that though he kept a diary he wrote in it one word to describe the day after his marriage: '*Rien*'. (He probably meant there was no hunting.)

This King had inherited great powers. All that he lacked was the self-confidence, energy and perseverance needed to make use of them. King Frederick the Great thought him a sheep among wolves. 'He'll be lucky to escape them,' the King prophesied. 'He'll need to have some wonderful ministers.'

Marie Antoinette, daughter of Maria Theresa, Empress of Austria, was chosen as a bride for Louis and not by him, and as must often have happened with such arranged marriages, the bridegroom faced his future with some indifference. And indifference was something new to the young girl. For her slim and graceful appearance, flawless complexion, blue eyes and delicately burnished golden hair had made her the spoilt child of the Court at Vienna. She could not but be disappointed at being married to the only man at the French Court who was not only disinterested in women as a sex, but incapable of concealing the fact behind a screen of elegant politeness.

The young bride had never been an intellectual or even shown any desire for learning. She was not fond of books nor, despite having played with the young Mozart, enthusiastic about music. Consequently when Louis went hunting, as he did whenever opportunity served, Marie Antoinette looked round for the more light-hearted and frivolous among those at Court with whom she could agreeably pass her time.

She seldom missed the masked balls at the Opera and loved to amuse herself by talking to guests whom she thought did not recognize her, though for decorum's sake she was invariably accompanied by a lady-in-waiting and a member of the royal bodyguard. As an outstandingly attractive woman she must have been exposed to many temptations, and at least one courtier, the Duc de Biron, claimed in memoirs published after his death on the guillotine that he had attempted to make love to the Queen without success. In public she remained faithful to her husband, and indeed rather despised the promiscuous morals of the day.

When first she came to France she had been told nothing about the custom by which the French King kept a *Grande Maîtresse* and for months she completely ignored Madame du Barry. There was a sensation in Court circles when, after much pressure from both the Austrian Ambassador and her father-in-law she was prevailed upon to offer to Madame du Barry the striking observation, 'What a lot of people there are at Versailles today.'

Marie Antoinette's tongue was unguarded—to the point of foolishness—among people whose main industry was the manufacture of gossip. She longed for a life of perpetual carnival. But her attitude changed considerably after the birth of her first child, a daughter, born in 1778. The event not only gave her a new interest, it bestowed on the King a personal reassurance of his success as a husband and bound him to her as its source. From this time on he came to depend more and more on her judgement. She in turn and as a consequence of her growing influence began to make more and more enemies among those of the King's relatives who hoped one day to push him aside.

It was not too difficult to stir up trouble for the Queen. In the first place, however moral she might be, she hardly resembled the self-effacing wives of some of the previous French Kings. And, of course, with her German accent she remained a foreigner. Worse, she became, 'Autrichienne' associated by her countrymen with the Austrian alliance which proved so unfortunate and expensive for France.

She was disliked by the Princes of the Blood, the Comte de Provence with his delicacy of language, the Comte d'Artois with his longing for the good old days of Louis XV and the Duc d'Orléans, the King's cousin and later his rival. She was equally disliked by their followers who formed an impenetrable barrier between the Queen and her subjects.

It would be hard in the whole course of history to find a pheno- menon to match the French Court. In earlier times the Court was a gathering of warriors in the field who, in return for their feudal privileges, fought the King's battles for him, shared as comrades the hardships of his campaigns, and served him his food round the camp fire. This agglomeration of nobles of the sword (whose an- cestors had won their titles perhaps in the Crusades), of the nobles of the robe (who had bought their titles and offices) and other hangers-on had been assembled by Louis XIV in a very simple way. He seldom if ever conferred favours upon those who absented themselves from Court. *'Cet homme, je ne le connais pas,'* he would say of anyone who resented squandering his fortune and living in the overcrowded garrets of the palace in order to be near the royal presence. Thus, already, before the end of his reign the barons were cut off from their followers in the provinces with whom, but for their absence at Court, they might have plotted some resistance to the royal will.

French estates became neglected and the worst fate that could become a nobleman was to be banished to his own home. The splendour of Versailles marked the end of the power of the aristo- cracy. But if the nobles had to stay at Court, the King, too, had an obligation to perform. It was to maintain their privileges there.

Versailles was the most usual meeting place of the Court, and at Versailles the leading families maintained permanent establish- ments. To the right of the palace lay the private houses of such families as de Bourbon, de la Trémoille, de Noailles, de Broglie, de Maurepas, de Bouillon, de Livry, de Villeroy, d'Ecquevilly, and to the left lay the pavillon d'Orléans, the hôtel de Chevreuse, the hôtel d'Antin, de Pontchartrain and a host of others.

The King disposed of grace and favour quarters for two thousand people and the streets of the town were lined with the houses of Court officials and storehouses for the royal possessions. Space had to be found in the town for surplus royal furniture and for the English-style garden of the King's brother. There were workshops and stores for the scenery and decorations for the royal entertain- ments, there was a store for the two hundred and seventeen royal coaches and a space for the royal vegetable allotment which stretched over twenty-nine separate gardens. Such an establishment could not be run without staff. There were billets for the men who tended the palace fountains, for the light horse of the King's Guard. The Master of the King's Wolfhounds had a house to himself. So did the Grand Falconer.

Scores of almoners, chaplains, confessors, clerics, choristers, composers and copiers of sacred music were employed in the Chapel Royal. Forty-eight doctors including physicians, surgeons, apothecaries, occulists, manipulators and bone-setters supervised the King's health. Forty-three men tended the royal bookshelves.

The King's Guard which included infantry, light horsemen, gendarmes, sentries and Swiss Guards, amounted to more than nine thousand men. There was never a shortage of people willing to serve the royal Sire.

The Bishop of Metz was the King's Grand Almoner, the Count des Cars was the Chief Maître d'Hôtel, the Duc de Brissac was Chief Pantryman, the Marquis de la Chesnaye was Carver-in-Chief, the Duc de Richelieu was one of the four Gentlemen of the Bed-chamber, the Duc de la Rochefoucauld-Liancourt was Grand Master of the Wardrobe, the Marquis d'Ecquevilly was Master of the Royal Bear Hunt, the Marquis de Dreux-Brezé was the Grand Master of Ceremonies, and so on down the line.

To serve the King as doorman or valet was a privilege for which people paid vast sums even in 1789. Each evening the King gave special directions as to who was to receive the honour of removing the golden candleholder, by the light of which the King had said his evening prayer. It took one hundred and ninety-eight valets of various kinds to see to the King's clothes, his armour and his washing. Men were appointed to comb the royal hair and to dry the monarch in the bath.

Two noblemen were allotted the task of handling the royal perforated chair, an article of toilet still to be found perhaps in the attics of some ancient country houses, if not in museums. The chair-carriers who were said to be paid twenty thousand livres year (eight thousand pounds), appeared every morning clad in velvet, to examine and empty if necessary the receptacle for which they were responsible. This continued until comparatively late in the eighteenth century, when some highly unreliable forms of water closet began to appear.

More often than not the King got up twice each morning. Once privately and later semi-publicly at his Levée. For this ceremony five classes of people were admitted to his bed-chamber to pay their respects. In the first batch came his close relations, his own children, Princes and Princesses of the Blood, the Chief Physician, the Chief Surgeon and other indispensable royal servants. The second entrée included high officials such as the Great Chamberlain, the Grand Master and the Master of the Wardrobe, the First Gentlemen of the Bed-chamber, the Duc d'Orléans and the Duc de Penthièvre, a few specially favoured noblemen, the Queen's Maids of Honour and some less exalted servants. The King's hands were than bathed in toilet water offered to him on a golden dish. He made the sign of the cross and offered up a short prayer. Then he got out of bed, put on his slippers and the Great Chamberlain and the First Gentleman handed him his dressing-gown. He put it on and sat down in the armchair in which he intended dressing. At that moment the door of the ante-chamber opened once more and a third group composed of those who had purchased the right to be present at the cere-mony, flocked into the room together with assistant physicians and surgeons, the directors and producers of the royal entertainments and those responsible for the perforated chair. At the moment when the officials of the Wardrobe approached the King to dress him, the First Gentleman of the Bed-chamber, warned by the door-keeper, went to tell the King the names of those waiting outside. This group, more numerous than the preceding ones, included nobles with the honour of carrying the King's arquebus, the Grand Almoner, the local Almoner, the Master of the Chapel Royal, the colonels and captains of the Guard, the masters of the various royal Hunts, the Grand Provost, the Grand Master and the Master of Ceremonies, the First Master of the Household, the Grand Pantry-man, Foreign Ambassadors, Secretaries of State, Marshals of France and other nobles and bishops. The doorkeepers saw that the crowd was properly disposed and called for silence if necessary. Meanwhile the King washed his face and began to take off his clothes. Two pages removed his slippers. The Grand Master of the Wardrobe took the right sleeve of his night-shirt and the First Valet of the Wardrobe the left sleeve and the two of them handed it over to an officer of the Wardrobe, while a valet of the Wardrobe brought the King's day-shirt within a white taffeta jacket. The presentation of the King's chemise marked the climax of the cere-mony. The honour of presenting it to him belonged to the heir to the throne or his heirs and in their absence to Princes of the Blood or

those declared legitimate or, failing these, to the Great Chamberlain or the First Gentleman. But in fact it was rare that the Princes
dared to stay away from the royal Levée. After the chemise had
been presented to the King, a Valet of the Wardrobe took away the
night-shirt. The First Valet of the Wardrobe and the First Valet of
the Bed-chamber took the clean shirt one by the left sleeve and the
other by the right while two other valets held the King's dressing-
gown as a screen. With the shirt on his back the King settled down
to complete his toilet. One Valet of the Bed-chamber held a mirror
before the King and two others provided extra light if need be with
the aid of candles. The Grand Master of the Wardrobe passed the
King his waistcoat and jacket, and fixed the royal blue riband and
the sword. Several cravats were offered in a basket and the Master
of the Wardrobe tied the one which the King had chosen. Then the
valet in charge of handkerchiefs brought in a selection of three
arranged on a saucer and the Grand Master of the Wardrobe
offered this for the King to choose from. Finally the Master of the
Wardrobe presented the royal hat, gloves and stick to the King.
Before leaving his bed-chamber the King sank to his knees by the
bedside and uttered another prayer. He got to his feet, announced
the programme for the day and then passed with his chief advisers
into his private rooms where he sometimes gave audiences. The rest
of the company waited in the ante-room in readiness to accompany
the King to Mass. The same kind of ceremony would take place
when the King put on his boots to go for a walk, took them off after
hunting, dressed for dinner or went to bed.

But it was at the royal table that the King really came into his
own with his three hundred and eighty-three Officiers de Bouche
including noblemen serving as pantrymen, cup-bearers and carvers.
There were spit-roasters, table-setters, cup-minders, vintners,
pastry cooks, warmers-up and every imaginable kind of specialist
serving the King's own table and the two lesser royal tables linked
with it. Twenty or thirty people attended to the dish set before the
King and supervised the glass that he drank out of. It needed four
people to serve him with a glass each of water and wine.

Every Sunday he had to suffer what was called the Grand Cou-
vert or Big Table. This involved a formal procession to the table,
followed by the arrival of the Nef, a golden boat-shaped salver in
which were placed some scented sachets and, between them, nap-
kins for the royal fingers. The Ceremony of the Assay followed. In

it the Gentlemen and Officiers de Bouche examined each dish before it was set before the King. The same procedure was followed in the case of the King's drinks. These occasions could be witnessed by the general public without distinction.

Apart from Versailles the King had palaces of one kind or another at Marly, the favourite palace of Louis XIV; at St Hubert, the hunting lodge in the Forest of Rambouillet; Fontainebleau, where Louis XIV began his passionate love affair with Louise de la Vallière; at St Cloud on the far side of the Bois de Boulogne, and at Rambouillet where Louis XVI set up a model dairy for his Queen. Each palace had its own Governor, Comptroller, its own parks and hunting reserves and its own host of gardeners, hedge-trimmers and landscape designers.

It was a sight to remember when the King moved from one palace to another. Four heralds with trumpets went ahead of the cortège and four followed it. The Swiss Guards were to one side and the French Guards to the other stretched as far as the eye could see. The Swiss Hundred, a special company dressed in sixteenth-century costume with halberds and plumed hats, marched ahead of the horses. The gilded uniforms of the military bands and drummers made the scene dazzling to the eyes. The bodyguards with their blue and white uniforms and red breeches surrounded the royal coach.

And, of course, the King's own establishment was only one of many. As soon as a prince or a princess came of age, a separate establishment was set up for them, each with its own stable, its own hunt, chapel, wardrobe, cellar, bakery, provision store and group of medical advisers. Each of the high-ranking nobles had their own minor courts; and, just as all those who had been presented were invited by the King to dine at the Palais-Royal after the Opera, so all who went, for example, to see the Duc de Penthièvre at Chateau-vilain were invited to stay for dinner. The Duc de Gèvres, First Gentleman of the Bed-chamber, Governor of Paris and of the Ile de France as well as of Laon, Soissons and Noyon Crespy and le Valois held a big dinner every evening to which ministers and even Princes of the Blood came. His house in Paris and his apartment at Versailles were never empty from the time he woke up to the time he went to bed.

Five times a week at ten in the evening the Maître d'Hôtel of the Duc de Choiseul cast an eye round the vast gallery and the various

salons of the duke's mansion to decide whether to have sixty places
laid for supper or eighty.

Women of high rank had their own separate establishments.
They had their own house or at least their own suite of apartments.
They had their own servants, their own receptions, their own particular circle of friends. Madame Cour d'Epinay, wife of a partner in a
tax-collection syndicate, relates how she would wait to get up until
she received a message brought to her by a maid on instructions
from her husband. When she had dressed she—who was thin
enough as she said to pass through the eye of a needle—would
find both the double doors thrown wide open for her by two lackeys
(not only one, as would have been the case with a not-so-important
guest), so that she could proceed to meet her husband and when she
reached the ante-chamber to his room, two footmen announced,
'*Madame, Messieurs, voilà Madame!*'

And just as husband and wife kept separate establishments so
they followed separate careers. The husband had his post in the
Government or the preferment he hoped to obtain at Court. And
the wife too had her career which she pursued by the same means
used by her husband, namely, a capacity for pleasing those with influence. There was hardly a woman at Court without means of obtaining promotion in the Army or other privileges for her followers.

Great ladies of the Court knew, like royalty knew, the art of
greeting friends and acquaintances in such a way as to distinguish
those who merited but a slight lowering of a single shoulder from
those who deserved a respectful obeisance made with downcast
eyes fit for a King.

Attendance at Court had other attractions apart from the advancement to be obtained there. The company was select. In
theory at least, a man in order to hunt with the King, or a woman to
be presented to him, had to establish with documents to the satisfaction of a qualified genealogist that the family enoblement could
be traced back to the year 1400 through four paternal ancestors.

The setting was elegant, as we see captured in pictures by
Watteau from the north of France and Fragonard from the south.
The desire to please, the grace of every movement, the tenderness
of each smile, the allure of musical voices, the glimpse of a delicate
arm peeping from a lace sleeve, of dainty hands, faces and figures,
the grace with which a fan was opened or closed, the pose and
the poise, all this was part of the atmosphere of the Court. The

conversation was witty. To be gay and perhaps flippant was not only a social obligation, it was the surest way then as now to please women of influence, and the rhymester was probably right when he wrote:

> Ne soyez point époux, ne soyez point amant
> Soyez l'homme du jour et vous serez charmant.

It was best to be light-hearted about everything under the sun. An opinion—even a declaration of love—was in bad taste if strongly expressed. A *tête-à-tête* conversation amounted to an act of selfishness since it placed a constraint on those who witnessed it. Horace Walpole remarked that one needed great cleverness or extreme curiosity to discover any liaison between the sexes, since the language of love seemed as much forbidden as at first sight the rites appeared to be.

At Versailles there were three 'spectaculars' and two balls every week and two Grand Suppers on Tuesday and Thursday. Sometimes the rehearsals for the special dances to be performed took up a large part of the week.

In general the Court was more light-hearted when away from Versailles. At Fontainebleau for example there would be gambling on Sunday and Friday, a concert staged by the Queen on Monday and Wednesday, French comedians on Tuesday and Thursday and Italian actors on Saturday.

At Choisy the courtier would find himself dining at one in the afternoon, gambling until six in the evening, watching some entertainment till half past nine, after which there was supper and more play until one or half past one in the morning.

In a typical fête the young and beautiful Duchesse de Bourbon, dressed as a voluptuous water nymph, guided the Comte du Nord in a gilded gondola across the canal at Chantilly to the Isle of Love. At le Vaudreuil the ladies were warned in advance that they were to be 'kidnapped'. Dressed up as Vestal Virgins they repaired to a Temple in the park where they were later seized by three hundred Turks and carried off down the illuminated gardens on palanquins.

No wonder the courtiers sometimes longed for the simple life. No wonder it pleased the Queen to hold a mock fair in the Petit Trianon where she acted the part of a lemonade girl in a café.

Fêtes and balls were given not only by the King and Queen but by the great hosts and hostesses of the day. There were amateur theatricals, picnics, fireworks. Fabulous silks, satins, gossamer-like muslins and a prodigality of diamonds helped to make a *grande toilette* for the great ladies. The hair, elevated into an imposing hoop supported by scaffolding, was decorated with flowers, tinsel or any other small object which could serve to illustrate a chosen theme such as Spring (flowers peeping out from a snow-field), the Shepherdess or Victory in the Field. Every step taken was an act of grace and women like courtiers learned to progress in such a manner that they appeared to glide from place to place almost as if they had been on wheels. The dances performed to the sound of a hundred violins were slow and measured as befitted the dresses worn but unsurpassed as a spectacle of grace and precision. The men's jackets decked with gold or silver were hardly less magnificent. The background, the décor and the lighting were unmatched, and often the enchantment of the scene was multiplied by the reflections of a score of mirrors.

Small wonder that the Emperor Joseph II of Austria after visiting his sister Marie Antoinette wrote to his mother, 'I left Versailles with sorrow, really devoted to my sister; I found there the charm of life which I had renounced and for which I see that the taste had never left me; she is pleasant and charming. I spent hours with her, without noticing how quickly they flew . . . I needed all my strength to tear myself away.'

Yet for the courtiers life was not all pleasure. The well-trained courtier had to learn to slide over, rather than step, on the parquet flooring of the palace and when he wished to enter a room it was considered more polite to scratch on the door than to knock on it. There were the hours of hanging about in the round ante-room outside the royal suite. Hours during which a courtier must maintain his air of respectful attention and discreet contentment as if it were his pleasure as well as his duty to endure such an existence. Many a courtier of eighty must have spent forty-five years on his feet in the royal ante-room, facing the door through which the King might enter.

'There are only three things you must do,' said one such veteran to a newcomer. 'Speak well of everyone, ask for everything that is likely to fall vacant and sit down whenever you can.' There was not much room to sit down. Sometimes the King's receptions or the Queen's gambling parties were so crowded that it was impossible to do more than talk to one's immediate neighbours. When the King gave a reception for foreign ambassadors between four and five hundred guests would be invited to fill fourteen salons. It was hard then to find one's friends.

The King himself was constrained. He was forced to cultivate the manner of Louis XIV who, as St Simon said, was naturally so polite that he was perfectly at ease when taking off his hat to a chamber-maid even though he recognized her as such. He had to imitate Louis XIV, who never made an inappropriate gesture and whose step, carriage and expression were invariably suited to the occasion. He had to learn the art of maintaining his own self-respect without destroying that of others, of performing gallantries without cheapening himself, of combining dignity with tact and with the art of putting things clearly in a language which has so many shades of meaning.

For Louis XVI, always at a loss for words, such a task must have been torture. Yet throughout his waking life he must never allow himself to lose that royal air of dignity combined with affability. He must never day-dream, or appear bored or absent-minded. He had to converse not only at receptions but on the way to his devotions, getting into his coach, or in between the drives when he was out shooting.

When he entertained, the crowd of courtiers was larger still because of the flock of duchesses and other women sitting on folding stools, or standing around the table. Women often followed the hunt together with the young people of quality who came out two or three times a week. And the surgeon, the bone-setter, the wine-master, the man to carry the royal mantle and the bearer of the King's fire-arms were present on every occasion. And at the end of the day no matter how tired he might be he had to endure the same long-drawn-out ceremony when going to bed in public with the same deliberation with which he had left it twelve hours earlier.

Frederick the Great, when he heard about the way things were run, said that if he succeeded to the French throne, his first edict would be to appoint another King to take his place at Court.

But the Court with its luxury, its elegance and its boredom was only a small part of France. In those days there were between twenty-five and twenty-six million Frenchmen, counting dependents, and at least a million of them were serfs forbidden to bequeath property. Five million were day labourers; more than eleven million shared what they grew with their landlord, to the great impoverishment of the land; five million or so were tenant farmers or smallholders; two million were non-agricultural workers; and a million were bourgeois (civil servants, professional men or wealthy businessmen who, unlike the lawyers, played relatively little part in the Revolution, or petit bourgeois (tradesmen, workshop managers, etc.). All these classes, making up what was called the Third Estate accounted in one way or another for all but half a million of the total.

The Second Estate consisted of the nobility which apart from the Noblesse de l'Epée and Noblesse de la Robe included a couple of hundred thousand poverty-stricken country squires and Lords of the Manor. We should not be far wrong if we put the numbers of the nobility at four hundred thousand.

Finally there was the First Estate consisting of titled bishops (there were a hundred and thirty-four bishops and archbishops of France), parish clergy, monks and—nearly as numerous—nuns, and unbeneficed clerks in holy orders. They numbered about a hundred and thirty-five thousand.

Perhaps this precarious structure could have been preserved under an efficient dictatorship but France was not that. In theory of course, the King's power was absolute. His powers came theoretically from God and, at his accession he had sworn to preserve them. He could banish any of his subjects by sending them a sealed letter (*lettre de cachet*) as old de Maurepas had once been banished. He could overrule opposition by passing decrees at a Lit de Justice. He could choose and dismiss the ministers of his royal Council. He decided which of his ministers should attend his special committees on Foreign Affairs, Defence, and Finance. The King alone sold the offices conferring privileges on those who bought them. The Army was the King's Army and the national revenues were almost indistinguishable from the moneys coming into and going out of the privy purse, In each of the thirty regions of France the King had his own personal representative, the Intendant, who combined the duties of a Lord Lieutenant with those of Military Governor and Collector of Direct Taxes.

But in practice the King was hampered on every side. To begin with, France was still not a united nation but a collection of provinces, some of which, notably Brittany, the south of France and Flanders, were still called 'foreign'. These were days when it mattered a great deal whether you came from Picardy or Bearn. Away from Paris, which held only a thirtieth of the French nation, the central Government, which appointed the main officials in all large cities, was distrusted and feared. Most of the provincials spoke a patois scarcely understood a hundred or so miles away. They wore distinctive traditional costumes and headgear.

Except for a few of the main highways built with forced labour, the roads were little better than tracks and it was quicker to send goods by canal—though there were few of these in France. Each province was or tried to be self-sufficient in agriculture. There was little point in growing a surplus which could be distributed only with difficulty. Nor in bad seasons was there much hope of getting supplies from anywhere else.

Trade between one part of the country and another was hindered by internal customs barriers and tolls were payable to cities or even private property owners if goods were moved over their land. A large part of the population made a living by smuggling goods. Weights and measures varied between one district and another. All these obstacles had to be swept away before France could become a trading nation.

The power of the Crown was also limited by agreements that had been made by earlier French Kings. Indeed some provinces of the country were treated as foreign territory as far as customs dues were concerned.

The Church, of course, had been given the monopoly in primary education and had been endowed with vast domains and the right to collect tithes. They also had a monopoly on the sale of all coffins and made only voluntary offerings to the national exchequer. But most of the Church offering came from the hard-working priests rather than from wealthy bishops or monastic foundations.

Then there were the nobles. Some of the Noblesse de l'Epée had earned their privileges centuries ago by providing men for the King's Armies. Now the King had his own Army; but the privileges of feudalism remained. Indeed they were needed, for, over many years, the Loi de Dérogeance had forbidden a man of noble birth to neglect his obligations by engaging in commerce. Nevertheless the aristocracy was cordially hated long before the Revolution by the newly emerging class of businessmen and factory owners.

The Noblesse de la Robe, who had bought their appointments as magistrates in the so-called French Parliaments, constituted a second section of the aristocracy. They had the right to hear appeal cases and also to register the King's edicts. They were united as a

class, eager for power, and unscrupulous in their determination to get
it if necessary by posing as defendants of the public interest against
royal tyranny. As guardians of the law they claimed the right to
remonstrate against measures of which they did not approve, to
investigate scandals which they alleged to exist and to use every
crisis to increase their grip on the levers of power. They regarded
themselves as greatly superior to common officials, merchants and
property owners. Once having bought their office they were im-
movable. They were also numerous. For example, Vounevil-Sur-
Vienne (Poitou), a town with a hundred and fifty inhabitants in the
town itself and another one thousand one hundred and fifty in the
surrounding countryside, was endowed with thirty-one Notaries
Royal.

The country seigneur also formed part of the nobility and still
received payments in lieu of labour which the peasants had in
former times performed on land no longer cultivated. Frequently
he possessed the local monopoly in milling, baking or wine production, so that all local grain, flour or grapes had to be brought to
his mill, his oven, his wine-press. There was rent of course, and
hunting rights (which meant incidentally that peasants were forbidden to shoot roe deer that feasted on their peach trees, to fire at
the voracious pigeons from the lordly dovecote that ate their grain
or to clear the stubble off the cornfields lest it disturb the young
partridges). And there were succession duties and transfer charges
which the peasant had to pay on land which he inherited or bought
or sold, despite the fact that for all practical purposes he might be
the owner.

Taxation, of course, was the most arbitrary and irrational of all
the burdens which the Third Estate had to bear. There was income
tax of a sort levied in the north on personal income and in the
south on income from land. But no proper taxation survey had
ever been made of the capacity of the different provinces to pay
what was levied. Instead the total amount required from direct
taxation was decreed by the royal Council and apportioned by
them over the provinces and to some extent over the individual
areas of these provinces.

The amount payable by each parish was arbitrarily assessed by
notables of the parish according to the style of living and presumed
prosperity of the taxpayer. Thus it paid to look poor and not to
repair that hole in the roof.

The nobility and clergy were exempt from the Taille, a species of income tax which, shortly before the Revolution, produced an amount equivalent to more than thirty-seven million pounds (ninety-one million livres) and indeed it became a mark of social distinction to avoid paying.

The Vingtième raised on many other types of income was no more successful.

Prominent among the national burdens was the capitation or poll tax raised on each household in proportion to the social standing of the payer. For this purpose France was divided into twenty-two social classes from the first, which included only the Dauphin, assessed at eight thousand pounds, to the meanest labourer who paid eight shillings. Most of the nobility succeeded in getting exemptions on one excuse or another and are said to have paid only one-eighth of their due share. The clergy bought themselves out.

The peasant paid all these dues and, in addition, had to give unpaid labour to the construction of roads in his district or in later days a money contribution in lieu. He could be called upon to serve in the militia selected each year by lot. He also paid tithe to the clergy—including abbots who in turn often sold the rights to laymen.

Everything possible was done to see that the taxes were collected. The local collectors were personally responsible for producing the money due from their districts and did not hesitate to seize the peasants' tables, chairs, cooking pots and even their bedding when ready cash was not forthcoming. In addition, until shortly before the Revolution, if a district failed to meet its assessment, the more prosperous citizens could be called on to make up the deficit, after which a new assessment was made in order to pay them back their loan.

But curiously enough it was an indirect tax, the Gabelle, which was the most unpopular of all. This tax was levied on every grain of salt eaten by the inhabitants of the kingdom. The rate was lower in those parts of the country where salt was produced and higher round Paris, where of course there were fewer means of finding any. Like other indirect taxes it was farmed out to a syndicate and collected on the assumption that everyone over the age of eight years ate about six-tenths of a gallon of salt per year. In fact they were compelled to buy their allotted ration—and treated as suspected smugglers if they did not. Officially, taxed salt was sold only through authorized merchants or traders. Everything possible was done to prevent free salt being obtained. The housewife was not allowed to use sea water for cooking, and her good man was forbidden to feed cattle on salt marshes (which, as anyone who has visited Brittany knows, leads to perfectly flavoured mutton that needs no salt). Drinking at salt springs was prohibited. Some citizens, rather than pay the tax, let butter and meat go bad. Others risked buying uncustomed salt. It took fifty thousand officials and agents to enforce the Gabelle. In the year 1783 alone agents swooped on four thousand homes and raided the larder. More than ten thousand people, many of them children, were arrested. And although the tax yielded twenty-four million pounds, a third went away on the cost of collection.

Justice was as confused as the system of taxation. Since the Middle Ages every landowner of consequence had been charged with the duty of holding a feudal or manorial Court of Justice for his tenants. The municipalities claimed the right to do the same. There were also Church courts which operated on the principle that sin was automatically illegal. Thus the single city of Le Mans contained twenty-three judicial courts and the parish of Gueugnon in Burgundy counted fourteen.

The King too had his own courts. His bailiffs tried minor offences against the Crown and heard appeals from the smaller manorial courts. Certain crimes such as treason, highway robbery, coining and murder were automatically reserved for royal justice, and State prisoners were outside the jurisdiction of the thirteen Parliaments in France which heard other major appeals.

To add to the confusion there were different codes of law. In the south of France various types of Roman Law held good but in the north these principles had been modified by the custom of Paris. Elsewhere there were codes midway between the two. One authority reckoned that there were more than three hundred different law codes in France under which a single case could be tried.

Up to within a year of the Revolution it was still permissible to use torture on criminals condemned to death in order to obtain information about their accomplices.

Until 1787, Protestants were still regarded as infidels and were denied official records of their births, deaths and marriages; they had to worship in private.

All public meetings of a political character required the permission of the authorities. In towns and villages, meetings were summoned by the tolling of a bell, the tocsin or touch-bell, which also gave warning of impending storms. The villagers were locked, albeit for their own good, within the walls at night. Their responsibilities were limited to managing the commonly owned land. They needed the consent of the Grand Master of Waters and Forests if they were to cut a few standards of timber for the repair of their church.

There have been different views about the hardships suffered by the French peasants during the eighteenth century. Certainly they could not claim pensions or sick-pay benefit. Often their work was seasonal. There was unemployment and it was reckoned that one in ten of the rural population depended on begging for at least a part of his income. Even the peasants who owned land were compelled to earn extra money by working on fields belonging to someone else. Some had to cultivate their lands by moonlight.

Arthur Young, the Suffolk squire who made several journeys to France to report on the state of agriculture there, was certainly not impressed by the good fortune of the French peasant. He wrote:

> Pass Payrac [in the Department of Lot], and meet many beggars, which we had not done before. All the country girls and women are without shoes or stockings; and the ploughmen at their work have neither sabots nor feet to their stockings. This is a poverty that strikes at the root of national prosperity; a large consumption among the poor being of more consequence than among the rich: the wealth of a nation lies in its circulation and consumption; and the case of poor people abstaining from the use of manufactures of leather and wool ought to be considered as an evil of the first magnitude.

A little further south he writes of an inn at St Geronds in the Department of Ariège:

> It could give me nothing but two stale eggs. . . . Spain brought nothing to my eyes that equalled this sink, from which an English hog would turn in disgust. But the inns all the way from Nismes are wretched, except at Lodève, Gange, Carcassonne, and Mirepoix. St Geronds must have, from its appearance, four or five thousand people. Pamiers near twice that number. What can be the circulating connection between such masses of people

and other towns and countries, that can be held together and
supported by such inns? There have been writers who look upon
such observations as rising merely from the petulance of travellers, but it shows their extreme ignorance. Such circumstances are
political data. We cannot demand that all the books of France
should be opened in order to explain the amount of circulation in
that kingdom: a politician must therefore collect it from such
circumstances as he can ascertain; and among these, traffic on
the great roads, and the convenience of the houses prepared for
the reception of travellers, tell us both the number and the condition of those travellers; by which term I chiefly allude to the
natives who move on business or pleasure from place to place;
for if they are not considerable enough to cause good inns, those
who come from a distance will not, which is evident from the bad
accommodations even in the high road from London to Rome.

Again at Montauban (West Brittany):

The poor people seem poor indeed; the children terribly
ragged, if possible worse clad than if with no cloaths at all; as to
shoes and stockings they are luxuries. A beautiful girl of six or
seven years playing with a stick, and smiling under such a bundle
of rags as made my heart ache to see her: they did not beg, and
when I gave them anything seemed more surprised than obliged.
One-third of what I have seen in this province seems unculti-
vated, and nearly all of it in misery.

A population explosion had taken place in Europe during the
eighteenth century, possibly because of new methods of farming
and because new crops—particularly maize—introduced from the
New World had increased the expectation of life of all who could
cultivate them.

In France alone the population had increased from about
eighteen million in 1715 to twenty-six million towards the close of
the century. The result, however, was to produce surplus millions
for whom there were no new jobs, since the industrial development
of France failed to keep pace with the growth in population. The
guilds limited the numbers of those who could enter the trades
which already existed, and under the medieval laws, controlling
not only commercial life but labour relations, it was hard to raise
capital for new industries.

Unemployment, open or concealed, therefore existed particularly among the poorer classes, and helped to account for the leading part which they played, from start to finish, in the Revolution. Thus people, the raw material for violence, were to be found in abundance ready to hand.

The increase in population also affected the shape of France's 'life pyramid', and an increasing proportion of the population was made up of young people. More than three-quarters of the French people were younger than forty and more than one-third under twenty. This is not the climate in which patient negotiations are built up.

Conditions, too, were favourable to combinations between different sections of this surplus population; for new concentrations of population in large cities led to shortages and high prices and all had suffered to some extent during the twelve months preceding July 1789. In 1788 the grain crops had been very poor and a freak hailstorm had destroyed many of the fields in the Paris region. The winter that followed was the severest for eighty years. The Seine was frozen over and there was public skating on it. Public transport here, as on the canals, was held up and unemployment and shortages increased. A mail courier died of cold on the box of the coach; wine bottles burst in the cellars of Burgundy; windmill sails had to be doused with warm water to take off the ice. One-third of the olive trees of Provence were killed and most of the rest were incapable of bearing fruit during the coming season. Then the snow melted and there were floods which, in the Rhône Valley, lasted for two months. A drought followed in the summer of 1789. It spoilt the wine harvest and dried up the streams which turned the grindstones of the mills. Windmills failed to work in the calms of the summer.

The price of bread rose and in July 1789 reached twice the usual level. Much of what was offered, having been made from mouldy rye or sprouting barley, was inedible. According to an eyewitness, the bread was 'generally blackish, earthy and bitter, producing inflammation of the throat and pain in the bowels. I have seen flour of detestable quality at the military school and other depots. I have seen portions of it yellow in colour and with an offensive smell; some forming blocks so hard that they had to be broken into fragments by repeated blows with a hatchet'.

Soup and rice had to be doled out for public relief. In the provinces every market day became a riot. Bands of householders appeared and compelled farmers to sell their grain at cut prices. Women ripped open the sacks of grain with their scissors and made off with what fell out. At Fougères they drove away customers from the neighbouring community of Ernée, who wanted to buy 'their' wheat. Elsewhere the people of the smaller villages tried to hold back grain going to the larger cities such as Aurillac and Limoges. At Chantenay, a miller was prevented from taking away the grain that he had already bought. At Bagnols (Languedoc), the peasants, armed with cudgels, assembled to the sound of a drum to see justice done. At Montdragon, a grain dealer was stoned. Grain convoys were waylaid and robbed. At Thiers, the workmen harvested the grain themselves and kept it. Bread had to be sold as if it had been money through a wicket gate with armed guards in attendance; sometimes the guards merely looked on while the customers ran away without paying. Monasteries were broken into and their stocks of grain pillaged.

Long before the National Assembly came into being the citizens of Ploermel refused to pay their taxes saying that the King was about to consider their *cahier* calling for the weight of such burdens to be shared equally and that therefore they were merely carrying out his wishes in refusing to pay as much as before. Feudal rights were attacked too. Ugly crowds compelled the owners of grist mills to hand over their title deeds to the village commune; those who refused found, one fine day, that someone had cut the dykes bringing water to the mill. At Agde, a crowd pursued the bishop in the street and made him sign a renunciation of half his mill rights. A mob surrounded the coach of the Bishop of Sisteron and dug a ditch into which, it was intimated, his body would be flung if he continued to disregard the welfare of his flock. The Bishop of Toulon had to flee in disguise while his coaches were flung into the sea.

For some people, the pursuit of justice in the company of their fellow men became almost a full-time occupation and mob leaders were soon demanding payment for their followers and themselves for time lost 'in the service of the public'.

The State machinery was thrown into even greater confusion by floods of rumours that periodically circulated throughout the country. Peasants refused to pay their taxes on the hearsay that they had not been officially authorized. The citizens of Lyons circulated reports that it was no longer necessary to pay local customs dues on food entering the city. Where possible the mobs seized and burnt official records of the rates and taxes for which they were liable. Four regiments of infantry and two of cavalry under a Marshal of France had to be sent to deal with the troubles at Rennes. Thus is some ways the ferment of pre-revolutionary unrest had reached a more advanced state outside Paris than in.

In the provinces the peasants, having to pay more for their bread, now had even less to spend on manufactured goods such as furniture, or pots and pans. And a recently signed commercial treaty allowed goods from Britain to compete on equal terms with the French, already a generation behind in their methods of production. The lace-makers of the north and the silk-workers of Lyons found it particularly hard going. Britain, too, retained the markets which France had hoped to find in the United States after the American Revolution.

This was the scene to which the famous French writers of the eighteenth century, nicknamed the Philosophers, had addressed themselves. Many of them wrote for a publication, the *Encyclopedia of Human Knowledge*, which appeared in instalments from 1750 onwards and to which the most respectable people subscribed. Its chief contributors were rationalists who discussed the merits of government as an exercise in the theory of political science. But they maintained the revolutionary idea that governments should exist for the benefit of those governed rather than for the rulers. Throughout their writings the illusion persisted that an ideal constitution existed, one that could be sought and found by a simple process of reasoning and then set up in place of the unnatural apparatus of government which in fact existed.

Among the leading philosophers was Jean-Jacques Rousseau, ex-servant, ex-music teacher, ex-Surveyor to the King of Sardinia, ex-Secretary to the French Ambassador to Venice, lover of nature and of the ex-waitress Thérèse le Vasseur, pet of the aristocrats in whose houses he passed most of his literary life. (To the Duc de Luxembourg, who had just done him a favour, he said, 'Ah, Monsieur le Maréchal, I hated the great before I knew you, and I now hate them all the more since you have made me understand so clearly how easy it is for them to make themselves beloved.')

Rousseau taught that all private property must originally have been acquired by force. He argued that the first man to enclose a field by force was thereby able to persuade his neighbours that it was his by right. And what applied to property applied also to authority. He wrote in his *Social Contract* published in 1762:

> Since no man has any natural authority over his equals, and since force produces no right to any, all legal authority amongst men must be established on the basis of agreement.

In this philosophy Rousseau ignored the man whose factory brought wealth because of increased demand for the products it made, who gained his wealth by working harder than his neighbour or by showing greater ability. Yet it was to these men, the coming rulers of France, that Rousseau made most appeal:

> We are told that all power comes from God. I grant it does; but all diseases likewise come from the same hand, and yet who ever forbids us to call in a physician? If a robber ambushes me in the darkness of a wood, must I give him my purse not only by constraint, but also as a matter of conscience? Even though I should be in a situation to subdue or escape from him? We must grant, therefore, that force does not constitute right, and that obedience is due only to the legitimate powers.

The theories that Rousseau put forward attacked by implication government as it was established in France:

> Even the best Kings desire to possess the power of being tyrants if they please with impunity. There is one essential and certain evil attendant on monarchical governments, which must always render them inferior to Republics: it is that while in the latter, men of talents and information, whose abilities do honour to those that select them, are chosen by the people to fill the highest offices of state; those appointed by the single will of a monarch are too frequently a disgrace to their station.

Rousseau included within the term 'republic' all governments, even monarchies, in which the administration was guided by the public will. But his theories which are imaginary contrasts between the Government and the governed travel much further:

> We will suppose that men in a state of nature are arrived at that crisis, when the strength of each individual is insufficient to

defend him from the attacks he is subject to. The primitive state
can therefore subsist no longer; and the human race must perish,
unless they change their manner of life.

As men cannot create for themselves new forces, but merely
unite and direct those which already exist, the only means they
can employ for their preservation is to form by aggregation an
assemblage of forces that may be able to resist all assaults,
but put in motion as one body and acting in concert upon all
occasions.

This assemblage of forces must be produced by the concur-
rence of many: and as strength and liberty of man are the chief
instruments of preservation, how can he engage them (in the
public interest) without danger, and without neglecting the care
which is due to himself? This doubt, which leads directly to my
subject, may be expressed in these words: 'Where shall we find a
form of association which will defend and protect with the whole
aggregate force the person and the property of each individual;
under which every person while united with *all*, shall obey only
himself, and remain as free as before the union?' Such is the
fundamental problem, to which the social contract gives the
solution.

The articles of this contract are so unalterably fixed by the
nature of the act, that the least modification renders them vain
and of no effect. They are the same everywhere, and are everywhere understood and admitted, even though they may never
have been formally announced: so that, when once the social
pact is violated in any instance, all the obligations it created
cease; and each individual is restored to his original rights, and
resumes his native liberty as the consequence of losing that con-
tractual liberty for which he exchanged them.

All the articles of the social contract will, when clearly understood, be found reducible to this single point—*The total alienation of each association and all rights to the whole community.* . . .

If therefore we exclude from the social compact all that is not
essentially necessary, we shall find it reduced to the following
terms: 'We each of us place, in common, his person, and all his
power, under the supreme direction of the general will; and we
receive into the body each member as an indivisible part of the
whole.'

The sovereign power being formed only of the individuals

which compose it, neither has nor can have any interest contrary to theirs. . . .

In order to prevent the social compact from becoming a vain form, it tacitly comprehends this engagement, which alone can give effect to the others—that whoever refuses to obey the general will, shall he be compelled to it by the whole body, which is in fact only forcing him to be free. . . .

If you unite many men, and consider them as one body, they will have but one will; and that will must be to promote the common safety and general well being of all.

These were the political theories that sustained the aristocrats in their early struggles against the monarchy, the bourgeois in their struggles against the aristocrats and the populace in their struggle against the bourgeois. But it is an astonishing fact that few of the contemporaries who read the writings of Rousseau, or for that matter the Abbé Mably who considered that all property should be nationalized, appeared to think that they had any practical application to the circumstances of the time. Still less did they perceive until too late that the 'alienation' by an individual of his original right of freedom could lead to a tyranny more onerous than any yet suffered by France, or that once 'man' is treated no longer as a person but as an abstract unit, he is ripe for incorporation in a totalitarian state. No one appeared to recognize that if there is only one general will there can be no justifiable opposition, no balance of power nor two opinions about any matter because one of them must inevitably be contrary to this general will. Indeed the general will pushed to its logical conclusion can be determined by one man only. Yet the aristocrats of the eighteenth century were glad to feed and house philosophers who would question in the nicest possible way the absolutism of the French monarchs.

Perhaps of all the philosophers, François-Marie Arouet, who wrote under the name Voltaire, was the most corrosive. Spiteful, sparkling, witty and malevolent he assaulted whatever he dared at a period in French history when all books, even those on surgery and mathematics were censored.

This was no conventional revolutionary. His parents belonged to the Noblesse de la Robe and as a young and successful playwright he was welcomed by the aristocrats. He never left their circle. Four years before he launched his first attack on privilege in *Lettres*

Philosophiques he had made a fortune for himself by speculating in municipal bonds. He attacked the clergy as rich and useless parasites who consumed without producing and commanded without obeying. He attacked the Church as an institution to which the State had given everything and which responded with prayers. He insisted that there was no need to replace an institution such as the Church. He attacked fanaticism because it led to wars of religion. He demanded tolerance, 'for it is clear that anyone who persecutes a man, his brother, for not sharing the same opinion is a monster'. Men, he said, must bear with each other because all are infirm, inconstant and in many cases mistaken.

He insisted that holidays should be fixed by magistrates, not priests, and that the magistrates, too, should conduct marriages and the priest only bless them. He declared that the priest should not judge the sinner but rather pray for him. He defended suicide arguing that those who denied Christian rites to a suicide were more mentally unbalanced than the victim himself. The confiscation of a suicide's property by the State he maintained was robbery of the innocent. He threw doubt on the State's right to take life adding that a dead man was worth less to the state than a live prisoner. He disputed the right of judges to condemn a man by majority vote:

> How could men who are not flesh-eating beasts ever have thought that a small majority of votes could give them the right to tear a human being to pieces in terrible agony?
> Should it not need at least a three-quarters majority? In England all jurors must agree. And rightly. What a ridiculous outrage it is to play with the life and death of a citizen in a game of six to four, or five to three, or four to two, or three to one!

What Voltaire and Rousseau left untouched other French writers demolished so that among the bourgeoisie and poorer nobility there were few who did not look towards a new form of government— better administered than the one they knew in which they at least (if not the common people who did not read in any case) would be as well off as the privileged courtiers.

But the existence of privileges and of the philosophers who attacked them would not by itself have accounted for the onset of the Revolution. Another catalyst was needed—the same that touched off the Russian Revolution—war.

In Russia, during the First World War, a poorly equipped army, a disastrous failure of military communications, hideous casualties and total lack of sympathy between the officers and the men they led, were to combine to bring about a military defeat and to deprive the Tsar of his only real protection against the mob.

In the case of France there was no military defeat. But there were other consequences both economic and political. The American Revolution was fought to maintain amongst other things the principle of 'No taxation without representation' and for this the Americans withdrew their allegiance from Britain's King George III. It was not difficult for these political ideas to skip across the twenty or so miles of the Straits of Dover to France.

Furthermore the American war was very costly for France. Soon after the American Declaration of Independence, France had begun to help the former American colonies with money and arms, partly in order to keep her own West Indian colonies out of British hands and partly to revenge herself for her defeat in the Seven Years War, during which she lost her Canadian and American territories to Britain.

After General Burgoyne's surrender to the Americans at Saratoga in 1777, the French Foreign Minister Vergennes thought it was safe to conclude an alliance with the infant transatlantic Republic.

France's Admiral, François-Joseph-Paul de Grasse succeeded in dominating the waters of the Caribbean; he captured Tobago and, in October 1781, succeeded in landing a force of soldiers at Chesapeake Bay strong enough to contribute to the final surrender of the British troops at Yorktown.

And at the end of the war under the Treaty of Versailles, England gave up St Lucia, Tobago, Senegal and Goree to France and restored the French settlements in India. Thus French self-esteem was fully re-established. But at heavy cost.

Indeed Louis XVI's Finance Minister, the gout-stricken Anne-Robert-Jacques Turgot, warned the monarch that this campaign would bankrupt the country. He did not exaggerate. The American War of Independence is believed to have cost the French Exchequer something like the equivalent of two and a half years of ordinary revenue.

The French national debt, impalpable because there was no proper budget, because the accounts were at times twelve years behind and because the auditors were paid by officials whose accounts they audited, grew from year to year. New loans had to be raised at ever-increasing rates of interest until half the Government expenditure went on interest payable on previous borrowings.

Economies at a high level were not to be thought of. At Court it was bad form to take things too seriously. A good table, a splendid wardrobe, a fine carriage at the door and well-trained servants. these were matters of real importance. And what did it matter if these servants looked after themselves and feathered their own nests? After all they had to live and a man liked to have contented and respectful faces around him. So perhaps it was not so surprising that the Queen's bill for lighting came to 157,109 livres (£63,000) in a single year, that the King's lemonade and other soft drinks cost him 2,190 livres (£880) and broth for the two-year-old Princess 520 livres (£208).

As Dauphine, the Queen used up four pairs of slippers a week and two yards of taffeta a day for covering the basket in which her fan and gloves were carried. Coffee and a roll worked out at 2,000 livres (£800) a year per head and some people were credited with drinking a dozen cups of coffee or chocolate a day. A single fête held in September 1777 cost the Queen 400,000 livres (£160,000).

Bills got so behind hand that by the time Louis XVI came to the throne the royal treasury was paying five per cent interest on the tradesmen's bills that it could not meet, and in 1778 the King owed his wine merchant the sum of 800,000 livres (£320,000).

The extravagance of the royal Court was copied elsewhere. The Comte d'Artois had La Bagatelle pulled down, rebuilt and redecorated from top to bottom by nine hundred workmen employed day and night for a celebration which he was giving in honour of the Queen. Because there was a shortage of lime, plaster and stones, he sent out patrols of the Swiss Guard to seize and pay for what they could find on the highways of the land.

When the Maréchal de Belle-Isle ran up debts totalling 1,200,000 livres (£480,000), a quarter due to his own extravagance and the rest on account of the King, he was allowed compensation in the form of an income of 400,000 livres (£160,000) from the revenue from evaporated salt and an income of 80,000 livres (£32,000) from the company which had the privilege of refining precious metals. The mistress of one minister received 12,000 livres (£4,800) a year from the contract for bread for galley slaves; and Ducrest a barber, collected a pension of 1,700 livres (£680) as having once been hairdresser to a daughter of the Comte d'Artois who died as an infant before she had hair to dress.

Any attempt to cut down on expenses at Court produced loud outcries that economies of this kind were an attack on the prerogative of the King himself. Instead money was saved, in Paris at any rate, by doing without the street lamps on moonlit nights.

As each new loan was raised, professional men, merchants, financiers and bankers grew more and more concerned over their chances of repayment. Soon they were among the chief critics of the Government and of the uncontrolled spending of the Court.

The desperate state of finances was apparent when Jacques Necker, who was neither French nor even a Catholic, was called in 1776 to restore the kingdom's finances. Necker, whose family was of German origin began his career as an employee in a bank in Geneva. He quickly rose to be a director of it and was sent to manage the firm's interest in Paris. At forty-three he was already a multimillionaire. He married, comparatively late in life, Suzanne Curchod daughter of a Swiss pastor and, through her influence, began to cultivate the society of politicians and artists. The Neckers like many aristocrats and some bourgeois of the day, held a weekly salon and Pigalle, the sculptor, was a regular guest at their Friday receptions.

Necker was also representative in France of the interests of his native city Geneva and it was in this connection that he first came to the notice of the French Court. His appearance was highly suitable for the role he had to play in restoring faith in the livre. He was solid, ponderous and unemotional. His face was smooth and plump, and bore an expression of self-confidence—or possibly as his enemies said, of self-satisfaction.

As a banker his first thought was to introduce order into the chaos of French finances. His *Comte-Rendu au Roi*, published in 1781, was the first attempt in the history of France to penetrate the mysteries of what had hitherto been a State secret—the truth about the country's finances—and thus strike a balance between income and expenditure. The *Comte-Rendu* though by no means in accordance with modern accounting principles, disclosed for the first time the vast amounts of money spent on the Court and its pensioners and thereby earned its author abundant unpopularity among the courtiers and friends of the Queen. Necker, however, was apparently unworried, and never a man to underrate himself, eventually asked for promotion from the post he held of Controller General to Cabinet rank. This presumption led to his dismissal.

But this was no help to the Government finances. In 1787 the national deficit had risen to 125 million livres (£50 million). In addition 280 million livres (£112 million) of future revenue had already been spent in advance and additional loans to a total of 650 million livres (£260 million) raised.

Early in that year Louis called an Assembly of Notables to consider the appalling problems of the kingdom. But many felt that this was just a way of getting sanction for further taxes. The Notables were sent home in May without any new burdens having been agreed to.

The Paris Parliament, too, refused to allow the deficit to be reduced by means of a land tax. Instead they called for a detailed return of public income and expenditure. Abbé Sabatier of Castres went further. 'It is not the Etats de Finance (Statements of Account) that we need, but Etats Généraux (Estates General),' he said, reviving a suggestion made earlier by the King himself.

The Estates General, consisting of representatives of the three estates (clergy, nobility and commoners) throughout the kingdom, were assembled only on occasions of great national emergency and none had been held for a hundred and seventy-five years.

Meanwhile, to discipline the Paris Parliament, the King held a Lit de Justice at which the taxes they had refused to sanction were imposed. For their impertinence in opposing the royal will, the Parliament was exiled from Paris to Troyes. But the other twelve Parliaments of France also refused to sanction the land tax. So the plan had to be withdrawn and in September the members of the Paris Parliament returned in triumph to the capital. From then on they refused to sanction any further loan unless the Estates General were summoned. They also publicly denounced the whole system of Lits de Justice and other arbitrary measures used by the King.

At Vizille, near Grenoble, a local assembly of the three estates encouraged by the events of 7 June 1788 (known as the Day of Tiles), when the citizens defied from the rooftops the soldiers sent to subdue them, went further and declared themselves to be in permanent session until their grievances were met.

By this time there was less than enough to pay the Government stockholders, let alone the numerous pensions already awarded by grateful monarchs of the past and present. There was only one way out. In August 1788 the King sent for Necker again and signed a decree setting a meeting of the Estates General for 1 May 1789. It was to be a day of reckoning for the whole of France.

Chapter 2

THE KINDLING

W HAT hopes were raised throughout France by the news that the Estates General were to meet! The royal summons issued early in 1789 asked voters to send delegates with authority to make proposals for reform and to agree on any steps necessary for the national well-being. The King in return promised to use his good offices to carry out any agreements made between him and the Estates. Votes were generously bestowed. Every taxpaying head of family of twenty-five years of age was allowed to play a part in electing the delegates who were to advise the King. In towns, trade guilds from the bakers upwards were encouraged to state their preferences in a body.

In addition, each community, from the small country villages upwards, and in towns guilds such as lace-workers and cider-makers, were invited to prepare *cahiers des plaintes et doléances* or complaints-books setting out grievances. The simpler peasants may well have pictured the King sitting up late at night reading pleas for the seigneur's pigeons to be shut up during the sowing season or for the petitioners to be excused from the burden of cleaning out the castle moat behind which their ancestors might have taken refuge in bygone centuries.

But reforms were not to be carried out so easily. No Estates General had met since the year 1614 and no one living could remember how such a meeting should be organized. Some antiquarians who were asked to say what procedures had been followed in their district when the last Estates met were obliged to say that they had failed to trace any records. Others wrote voluminous treatises of no practical value. One thing was certain. The Estates General was nothing like the modern Parliament, and the methods used in the election were equally archaic. There were no political parties (indeed they were forbidden); the candidates offered no programme and made no election addresses. There were no established constituencies and voting was organized in ancient districts known as royal bailiwicks in the north of the country and royal seneschalsies in the south. No maps existed of these districts which varied in size from the Great Bailiwick of Vermandois (774,000 inhabitants) to the smaller district of Dourdan, about twenty miles from Versailles, which included fewer than 8,000 people. The local polling officials knew nothing of their duties and we find the eighty-five-year-old Comte de Mesgrigny-Villebertin being sworn in as Grand Bailli d'Epée of the Bailiwick of Troyes for the first time although he had held the office for forty years. In other provinces no baillis had been appointed. A great deal of time had to be spent in putting these anomalies to rights and in fact some deputies had not received their summons by the date appointed for the opening of the Estates General.

Costumes at least were prescribed—the same as had been worn in the days of Henry IV, a century and three-quarters earlier. This etiquette provided nobles with black coats and waistcoats with facings of cloth of gold, lace cravats and hats with plumes and a turned-up brim. The clergy were equally resplendent in their robes. The Third Estate however were to wear short coats, muslin cravats, knee breeches, white stockings and hats without plumes or other decorations.

The preparation of the *cahiers* of grievances presented some difficulties, for the peasants of the Third Estate who suffered most, knew least how to write of their troubles. In practice the village *cahiers* were often prepared by the local curé or schoolmaster and were forwarded to the nearest bailiwick where they were edited by a committee of relatively educated men—lawyers, local officials and others who struck out those complaints that failed to interest or convince them. Other *cahiers* were written for the Third Estate by propagandists or were based on model *cahiers* prepared by them and circulated widely throughout the country, and they dealt rather with the political theory of government than with practical abuses.

At first nobody knew how many deputies were to be sent by each of the three estates. But Necker no doubt remembering that the Third Estate provided most of the money he was hoping to collect, announced that the Third Estate should have the same number of deputies as the other two estates combined.

The system of election, like the system for representing grievances, tended to ignore the small man—even those of the Third Estate—for the peasants did not directly elect deputies of the Third Estate but merely chose people to elect them on their behalf. The result was that out of six hundred and twenty-one representatives of the Third Estate, only about forty had anything to do with the land and fewer still were peasants. More than fifty per cent were barristers, solicitors or officials of the complicated French legal machine making up what might be called the liberal academic bourgeoisie.

Among their number was Jean-Sylvain Bailly, afterwards President of the National Assembly. He was the son of the Keeper of the King's Pictures in the Louvre. He had already made a name for himself as a practical astronomer and had carried out an investigation with Benjamin Franklin into the 'cures' of Friedrich Mesmer. He had been elected to the Académie Française as had Target the President of the Paris electors of the Third Estate. Brillat-Savarin, the author and gastronome, was another deputy. Others including Robespierre were well-known public figures in their own home provinces. Another twenty per cent were merchants, bankers, landlords; the remainder included fifteen doctors, about the same number of nobles (who, like the clergy, were permitted to represent the Third Estate if they wished) and even three or four churchmen, one of whom the Abbé Sieyès was one of the ablest of propagandists.

The King had decided to hold the Estates General in Versailles for his own personal convenience and to save the expense of moving the Court. Despite the great interest and the flood of pamphlets circulating throughout the country, it never occurred to him that

these twelve hundred or so delegates assembled within a few miles
of Paris could be anything more formidable than a large group of
petitioners dependent for favours on the royal goodwill.

Thus when the deputies of the Third Estate or Tiers began to
arrive in Versailles from about April onwards they found a far
from warm welcome awaiting them. To begin with, the date of the
opening of the Estates General had been put off four days—because
of delays in the Paris elections—and the deputies found themselves
with nothing to do except to plan great speeches. And of course
being provincials they knew nothing of Court etiquette. They were
astonished when the Marquis de Dreux-Brezé, the Grand Master,
refused to entertain the idea of arranging several hundred private
interviews with His Majesty. They had come to Versailles only too
anxious to help the King with the advice that he had asked for and
as the chosen ones of the nation they felt they had the right to give
it to him in person. How could they write to their fellow provincials that they had been in Versailles for a week or two without
even having been to see the King?

Eventually they were told to appear on Saturday, 2 May, in their
lowly uniforms to meet the King *en masse* as had been the practice
in 1614. And whereas the other two orders had been received in the
royal Cabinet room with double doors full open for the clergy and
half open for the nobility in the morning, the Third Estate was
kept waiting till the afternoon and then herded down the palace
corridors between wooden barriers like sheep on shearing day and
were received in the Hall of Mirrors opposite the King's bedroom.
As they hustled past, the King stood looking at them with apathy,
which was hardly to be wondered at since the reception ceremonies
lasted for nine hours in all. As usual, he could scarcely find a word
to say in response to the greetings he received. Only once, when an
ancient farmer from Brittany passed wearing countryman's garb,
did the King brighten sufficiently to say, 'Good day to you, my good
man.' The Queen, who suspected that she was already a target for
criticism, appeared disdainful when they called to pay their
respects on her.

For the time being they were scattered in their various lodgings,
but the treatment they had received served to unite them in a
common attitude of resentment to the other more privileged orders.

On Monday, 4 May, a fine spring day, they reassembled, still
dressed in their uniforms, to attend a solemn Mass at which their

efforts were to be blessed. The procession gathered on the steps of
Notre Dame de Versailles to escort the Host in a solemn cavalcade
to the Church of St Louis. Nothing that splendour could provide
was wanting. The royal carriage was drawn by eight horses decked
with magnificent plumes. The nobles made a fine picture in black
and gold costume and the bishops wore equally splendid sacra-
mental robes. Ministers and courtiers sat on velvet seats em-
broidered with fleurs-de-lis. The church was hung with cloth of
gold and the King himself, who had kept the congregation waiting
for three hours, entered to the music of trumpets, fifes and drums
wearing the Golden Mantle of the Order of the Knights of the
Holy Spirit with a blue sash.

The King took his place on the right of the choir screen and the
Queen, loaded with jewels (as at least one deputy reported to his
constituents), sat opposite with the Princesses and ladies of the
Court. But whereas the nobles and clergy had been encouraged to
occupy the nave of the church, the Tiers were ushered, much to
their annoyance, into the aisles. This did not, however, prevent
them from applauding loudly when the Bishop of Nancy, during
his two-hour sermon, referred to the crushing taxation exacted
'in the name of the best of Kings'.

Consequently when Tuesday, the day for the opening of the
Estates General finally came, all the deputies and particularly
those of the Tiers waited with rising hopes for the speech which the
King himself was to make.

The Hôtel des Menus Plaisirs on the Avenue de Paris at Versailles
which was normally used as a storehouse, had been set aside for the
meetings of the clergy and the nobility and behind it in the rue des
Chantiers was a larger hall which, it had been decided, was to be
used for the sessions at which the King himself presided, when all
three orders would be present together. There was room there too
for foreign ambassadors, the courtiers and ladies of the Court and
even for sightseers who were interested.

It was here that the Estates General assembled at eight o'clock
on 5 May to begin their deliberations. The whole morning was
monopolized by the official busybodies who kept the delegates
waiting for three hours while their names were called over and their
place assigned according to the procedure followed a century
and three-quarters earlier. Once again the nobles on the left-
hand side of the throne, and the clergy in square caps and violet

robes with white linen sleeves on the right, added splendour to the scene.

The King duly arrived about one o'clock and when he opened the meeting many hoped that he would deal first with the question of how the Estates General should vote in their deliberations. This was what most worried the Tiers for in the past it had been usual to vote by orders which meant that they were outnumbered two to one by the other two privileged orders. The Parliaments who had for so long posed as champions of liberty on this point resolved to desert the Third Estate and support the views of the nobility to which in fact they belonged. But the Tiers could comfort themselves with the thought that on this occasion they had been given as many representatives as the other two orders combined and this arrangement made no sense unless they were to be allowed to vote by numbers together in a common assembly. In addition they hoped that the King would outline the reforms he hoped to introduce and the order in which they could be discussed.

But the King in his speech dealt with none of these points. His declaration was short and unsatisfactory. He made it plain that he was to be the judge of what they should discuss, and that the chief duty of the Estates General at Versailles was to bring order to the national finances. The King also spoke of 'an exaggerated desire for change' and warned the deputies against disregarding 'prudent advice'. Then having concluded his remarks he retrieved his hat and put it on his head. The royal speech was over. Barentin, the Keeper of the Seals, who followed the King, was no more helpful and not so easily heard. He did, however, go so far as to say that the three orders could vote together if they all agreed to do so—which of course was not to be expected of the clergy and nobility.

So the Tiers waited with all the more eagerness for some clear pronouncements from Necker. But the financier proved an even greater disappointment. He gave a long and detailed report on the state of the country's finances, but implied that there need be no crisis and that the Estates General had been assembled as an act of goodwill rather than to stave off national bankruptcy. On the question of voting he said no more than Barentin had done. His speech was so boring that he did not bother to read it himself but entrusted parts of it to a stand-in. He suggested no practical remedies for the abuses which had led to the crisis. And he did not even put forward an order of business along which the deliberations of the Estates General might develop. It became apparent that Necker, like many other successful bankers, was something of an opportunist, brilliant at profiting from circumstances but incapable of radically influencing them. It was clear, too, that the delegates, having received no lead from the King or his ministers, were going to have to make up their own programme.

But each deputy, before taking action, had to satisfy his colleagues that he had been properly elected and sent to Versailles. The nobles were willing to be verified only by members of their own order. The clergy took the same line. But the Tiers maintained that as each of the three orders had the right to determine whether the other two were legally constituted, the verification must take place in common assembly. And through accident—because they had not been allotted a separate hall of their own—the Tiers were able to instal themselves in the only hall capable of holding the one thousand two hundred members of the Estates General. And it was logical for them to insist that the other two orders should come and join them before any business could be transacted.

Thus the Third Estate were not politically exclusive. They could hardly be that since they were bitterly opposed to the barriers which debarred them from promotion in the Civil Service and the Army. Neither were they united in their political thinking. One reason was that they had not been moulded together in the fire of hidden conspiracies in the way that the Communists afterwards were. Having come to Paris from different regions of France, some of which were politically more advanced than others, they found it difficult at first to settle to a common rate of progress.

They were anxious to remould the constitution. And though they may have been convinced by the philosophers that the right kind of government could be discovered by a process of reasoning, they had prepared no practical blue print of such a government or of the methods by which it was to be achieved. They had no thought of getting rid of the monarchy, still less of rejecting the principle of private property on which they were as dependent as the sovereign himself. Certainly they favoured a redistribution of the nation's wealth, the abolition of feudal burdens and restrictions on trade which were quite unsuited to a country just beginning to manufacture steam engines and industrial machinery.

When the other two orders refused to join them, the Third Estate carried out what might be called a sit-down strike. They refused to verify their fellow deputies' credentials. They took no minutes of what was said and had no order of business. At first there seemed little chance of their getting their way. The nobles seemed impervious to arguments, and the clergy were notoriously conservative. However, they were not completely united since a fair proportion of their representatives had been elected by hard-worked curates who were out of sympathy with the wealthier prelates. The Tiers were helped too by the fact that the public could listen to and take part in their debates. The bolder spirits were encouraged to go forward and the faint hearts whistled or shouted down.

For weeks the stalemate continued. Necker tried to mediate and the King said that if no decision were reached he himself would arbitrate between the three estates. But the Tiers continued to summon the other orders to coalesce with them and to form what they afterwards called a National Assembly. At last on 13 June the Tiers were joined by three curés from Poitou and on 14 June by another six clergymen. It was the crack in the dam. On 19 June a majority of the clergy declared in favour of joining the National Assembly. Thus at a stroke, as Arthur Young perceived, a kind of Long Parliament had been formed of the type which had led to the execution in Britain of Charles I.

Meanwhile on 17 June the Assembly had declared that since the present taxes, not having been voted by the people, were unlawful, they would be authorized only so long as the Assembly continued to sit. At the same time the Assembly promised to guarantee the Government debts, and to put an end to the shortages of food and other necessities. Their programme was thus calculated to appeal to all tastes.

It is perhaps true to say that the French Revolution had not yet begun in theory because Bailly, who had been appointed Dean of the Third Estate, still maintained that the establishment of the National Assembly and the measures it took required the royal assent. But it is equally clear that the royal assent would not be forthcoming, for Louis had refused to answer a petition delivered by Bailly on behalf of the Third Estate.

On 20 June the Tiers found that the hall in which they were accustomed to meet was shut. It was said that the King had decided to hold another royal session (at which the deputies would be seated according to their orders) and that the hall had been closed to allow preparations to be made.

But the deputies could see that soldiers, not carpenters, filled the building. The rain was falling. So they moved to the nearest suitable covered building, the royal Tennis Court in the rue St François opposite the Petites Ecuries. They felt certain that their exclusion from the hall was the King's first move to close them down for good. It was hard to decide what to do. Some proposed that they should go in a deputation to Marly where the King had withdrawn for a few days rest after the death of the young Dauphin. Others, including the Abbé Sieyès, favoured breaking away altogether from the Estates General and setting up a headquarters in Paris. But this would have come close to open rebellion and the deputies decided instead to follow a suggestion put forward by Jean-Joseph Mounier, a deputy from the Dauphiné, who proposed that here and now in the Tennis Court they should swear and sign an oath to continue meeting until a new Constitution had been set up and firmly established.

At this point the French Revolution led by the bourgeoisie, as distinct from the nobility, formally began. Only one deputy, Martin Dauch, of Castelnaudary near Carcassonne, dissented. He put the word *Opposant* opposite his signature on the oath paper on the ground that the measure had not been sanctioned by the King. His protest was allowed to stand as a sign of the liberty of conscience recognized by the new rulers of France.

From then on the Comte d'Artois, the King's younger brother, took care to book the Tennis Court every day. But the church of St Louis at Versailles was then put at the disposal of the Assembly by its vicar, for it had by now become clear that the poorer clergy had as much to gain from reform within the church as the laymen of the Third Estate could gain from overthrowing the barriers of official privilege. Even the bishops, fearful for what they might lose if they became absentees from the National Assembly, began to take their places in it and on 22 June the Archbishops of Vienne and Bordeaux as well as the Bishops of Rodez, Chartres and Coutances, took their seats with the others. The nobles too began to follow suit.

Nevertheless when the royal session opened on 23 June one more attempt was to be made to put the Tiers in its place. And at the outset a mark of disrespect, if not contempt, was shown to the Third Estate. Its deputies were kept waiting outside the conference hall until the other two orders had taken their places. Then the King explained why he had been obliged to call the meeting and ordered an official to read out the decisions which he had reached. The atmosphere in which he spoke was, however, quite different from that of six weeks earlier. Then the King had been welcomed with acclamation. Now there was silence. Then M. Necker, the advocate of fairer taxation, had been present. But on this occasion he stayed away and was induced only with difficulty to withdraw his resignation.

The King's wish, the official spokesman declared, was that the distinctions between the three estates should be maintained as an essential part of the Constitution. Therefore they could not debate together except by mutual consent and with the express permission of His Majesty. The royal proclamation also cancelled the resolutions taken by the Third Estate a week earlier and told its members to disregard any instructions they might have received from their electors about organizing a joint Assembly. It forbade the Estates General to consider such matters as the abolition of feudal privileges or the position of the Church, and stressed that any decision involving the Church would have to be agreed by the churchmen themselves.

Having made clear in fourteen articles what he was *not* going to do, the King ordered another official to read out a declaration, thirty-five articles in length, setting out concessions which he was prepared to make. He promised that no new tax would be imposed without the consent of the Estates General, that accounts of expenditure and revenue would continue to be published, that each Department of State should have a fixed budget, that there should in future be no immunities from taxation and that the most unpopular taxes would be altered or abolished. He also announced that unpaid labour performed by the peasant for his lord should cease and that service in the militia would be made less onerous. The King also hinted that he would be prepared to consider the abolition of *lettres de cachet*, and a general reform of the law and legal procedure.

After this declaration had been made on his behalf, the King himself spoke for the last time. He declared that he would carry out these reforms with or without the help of the Estates General, which was a refined way of threatening the Estates General with dissolution if they did not fall in with his proposals.

Then, before they had had time to consider what had been said, the announcement ended and the King declared his wish that the

meeting should now break up and that the delegates should repair
on the following morning to their separate meeting places. The
King and his retinue then left the hall; most of the nobles followed
him and some of the clergy. The Third Estate hesitated, talking
among themselves. So many choices were open to them. They had
to decide first whether the reforms that had been offered went far
enough. If so, had they still a part to play in the future of their
country? Could they play this role if they were allowed to talk only
about subjects chosen for them by the King? What would their
constituents think if they decided, after hearing the King's offer, to
disobey him? What would they think of a deputy who returned to
his constituency without having brought about a change in the
Constitution? And would disobedience achieve anything in the
face of the troops which the King commanded? Then Honoré-
Gabriel Riqueti, Comte de Mirabeau, spoke up.

'I admit,' he said, 'that the speech we have just heard might have
been for the welfare of the nation if it had not been the product of a
despotism that will always remain a danger to us. . . . You are commanded to be happy. Who gives you this command? Your own
representative . . . he who should rather receive commands from
you . . . to whom alone twenty-five million people are looking for
their happiness. Therefore remember your dignity, your responsibilities and your oath. It does not allow you to separate until you
have formed a constitution.'

Then their ancient enemy, the Marquis de Dreux-Brezé, re-
entered the hall. As the sovereign's representative, he remained
covered with his plumed hat on his head. But the Tiers treated this
as a mark of disrespect to their own sovereignty. Some deputies
called on the Marquis to take off his hat. He refused heatedly and,
in a voice accustomed to authority, reminded the gathering,
'Gentlemen you have heard the King's orders.' Mirabeau, however,
was ready for this moment and was on his feet.

'Yes, sir,' he said, 'we have heard the wishes which have been
put into the mind of the King. But it is not for you who have no
standing in the National Assembly to remind us of them. However,
if you have been given orders to move us from here you will need
authority to do so by force, for we shall not leave our places except
at the point of the bayonet.'

A roar of agreement from the body of the hall greeted his words.
The Marquis then turned to Bailly, the President of the Assembly.

'I recognize M. de Mirabeau as the delegate for Aix but not as spokesman for the Assembly. I therefore ask you to confirm that you have received the King's orders.'

Bailly replied that since the Assembly wished to discuss the royal declaration he had no power to adjourn it without its freely given consent in the form of a vote.

'Is that the reply that I am to take to his Majesty?' pursued the Marquis.

'Yes, sir,' answered Bailly, 'for I assume that the representatives of the entire nation cannot be treated as subordinates.'

Soon after, again at Mirabeau's suggestion, the deputies voted that the members of the Assembly were inviolable and decreed the death penalty for anyone who prosecuted or arrested a deputy for any words spoken in the Assembly. And needless to say the Tiers were allowed to remain undisturbed in their hall.

And so the first of the great leaders of the Revolution emerged. Mirabeau, aged forty-one, came from Provence and became a deputy for the Third Estate after having been rejected by his own order because he did not possess a fief of land. He was thick-set, bull-necked and ungraceful with a shock of black hair and a face deeply pock-marked. Yet he had immense charm, for men as well as for women, and those who were prepared to despise him found themselves fascinated by his immense knowledge, good sense and the flattery concealed in his rough and ready turn of speech. Up to this time he had led a thoroughly discreditable existence.

He had deserted his regiment and at the age of twenty-six he had served a sentence as a State prisoner in order to avoid law suits brought by his creditors. Then, having quarrelled with his wife, he persuaded a young French Marquise to leave her husband and live with him abroad. For this he was sentenced to be beheaded in effigy (which meant that he lost all the rights as a citizen unless he surrendered himself to the court for trial within five years). On returning to France, he again sought safety in a royal prison. Set free from this, he abandoned the Marquise to her husband and ran away to England with a new mistress. Back again in France, he changed her for the wife of his publisher, and wrote a book on the basis of information received while he was working for the French Government called *Secrets of the Prussian Court*; it was burnt by the Government executioner.

Mirabeau's great triumphs came to him as an orator and

pamphleteer. After his rejection by his own order, he was elected in two places to represent the Tiers, in Marseilles and in his native Aix which he preferred. With his big craggy features and ungainly walk—he had been born with a slightly twisted foot—he soon became an easily recognized figure and, because he was an outcast from the nobility, a popular one. He had always found it easy to write and had already attacked from prison the system of *lettres de cachet* and the whole principle of despotic rule. And now he started a publication called the *Journal des Etats Généraux* which had as its motto a Latin inscription announcing 'the birth of a new order of things'. In its first number he complained of the slights offered to the Third Estate and in the second he made a violent attack on Necker's speech. Thereupon his journal was suppressed by an Order in Council. Mirabeau's answer was to bring out a new paper entitled *The Letters of the Comte de Mirabeau to his Constituents*. He was then told that he must report only what had happened in the Estates General without commenting on it, but he ignored this restriction from the first and soon other writers and pamphleteers did likewise.

Despite all provocations Mirabeau remained in favour of constitutional monarchy. Once when speaking in the National Assembly he said, 'I believe, Gentlemen, that the King's veto is so essential that I would prefer to live in Constantinople rather than in France if he were without it. Indeed I declare that I can think of nothing more terrible than the privileged sovereignty of six hundred individuals, who could make themselves irremovable tomorrow, hereditary the day after and who would end, like the aristocrats of every other country, in usurping all power.'

Here was no doctrinaire socialist. Indeed these words of Mirabeau's showed to what extent the French Revolution was an affair of improvisation in which the leaders foresaw neither that violence would be needed to accomplish their aims nor that this violence would sweep away moderates such as themselves.

On 27 June, only four days after the Assembly's defiance of Dreux-Brezé, the King wrote to the Cardinal de la Rochefoucauld, President of the First Estate, and to the Duc de Luxembourg, President of the Order of Nobility, inviting them to join the National Assembly. When they hesitated the King entreated them in personal interviews to fall in with his wishes. He had made other plans for preserving his power. While the Assembly began to debate

the formation of a new Constitution, as they had seen the Americans
do on the other side of the Atlantic, the King began to assemble
troops as if for a new Civil War.

Marshal de Broglie set up his headquarters in the palace at Versailles and encamped his men in the royal gardens. A trusty unit
was billeted in the Orangerie, and the King prepared to get rid of
Necker and other ministers who had supported efforts to equalize
taxation. They included Montmorin, the Secretary for Foreign
Affairs, Puysegur, the Secretary for War, La Luzerne, Secretary
for the Navy and St-Priest, Minister of the King's Household. The
Assembly, despite assurances from the King that they could move
to Noyon or Soissons if they liked, became thoroughly alarmed at
being ringed by troops.

They were saved by the Paris mob which outnumbered any loyal
troops which the King could bring to bear. 'Mob' is perhaps an over-
simplification and perhaps an undeserved slight on those who
stormed the Bastille. For although, to French historians like Taine,
the crowd was composed of the scum that rose to the surface,
criminals, tramps and paid agitators, to Michelet and Aulard the
mob represented the people of France, uneducated maybe, but
with the true instinct for the national interest of which they were
the sovereign guardians.

The truth lay somewhere between these two extremes, for at this
time conditions in Paris, as in many parts of France, were favourable to pressure by large crowds assembled for many different
reasons. Both agricultural and industrial unrest was concentrated
in Paris which, with nearly seven hundred thousand inhabitants,
was already an impressive capital. From the time that the National
Assembly met, a kind of national consciousness began to grow.
Other writers, apart from Mirabeau, wrote to their constituents.
Pamphlets galore found their way to the *salons de lecture* or read-
ing-rooms of the provinces, to the cafés, private study circles and
were discussed at public meetings.

The Paris from which they wrote was indeed a very different
place from Paris today. A wall ten feet high, broken only by fifty-
four customs posts, encircled the whole city and included the
Faubourg St Antoine to the east, St Martin and St Denis to the north,
Passy and Chaillot to the west and St Victor, St Marcel, St Jacques
and St Germain to the south. Some quarters of the city consisted of
chains of narrow passages, stairways and courtyards, the gates of

which were shut by night. In many streets it was impossible for two coaches to pass one another. Almost all the important buildings and institutions occupied a small area of about five square miles on the north side of the river. The Champs-Elysées, the Elysian fields, the playground for heroes, which Frenchmen had tried to establish on earth in the form of some extensive plantations of trees, marked the extreme western boundary. The prison fortress of the Bastille was in the north-east corner.

Laborde, the banker, was opening up the rue de Provence which ran almost parallel to the modern Boulevard Haussmann. The rue Royale was also being developed with buildings on a uniform plan. The Théâtre Français, later the Odéon, had just been built on the site of the Hotel Condé. A few of the new type of Argand lamps with glass chimneys had been installed and a few pavements had been provided, but those who were brave enough to walk risked being splashed, if not run down, by supercilious coachmen or soaked in torrents of water which poured from open gutter spouts overhead. After each downpour of rain the streets became a morass and it was not unusual to see planks and even small bridges on wheels in use. As Arthur Young put it, walking through the city was a toil for men and an impossibility for women.

There was no public cleansing service and sanitation was poor. The stench in certain parts of Paris during the summer was hardly to be borne. A newly formed corporation, the Compagnie des Eaux de Paris of which Beaumarchais, author of *The Marriage of Figaro*, was a director, had begun to offer a piped supply of water for those who could afford it, but most of the liquid was brought to the consumer in buckets from wells of doubtful quality. Streets were dark and narrow. Inside the buildings the lower floors were in perpetual twilight and the upper floors were to be reached only by walking up many flights of stairs. In some buildings the Paris concierge had already established his tyranny and controlled a rope by which alone the door of the house could be opened.

Amusements for the poor were simple . . . they included bull fights between steers and dogs, and visits to watch the fountains at St Cloud where wine, being sold outside the Paris wall, was cheaper.

Some areas of the city had been partly industrialized. There were breweries, glassworks and furniture warehouses in the Faubourg St Antoine and tanneries and dye works in the south of the city.

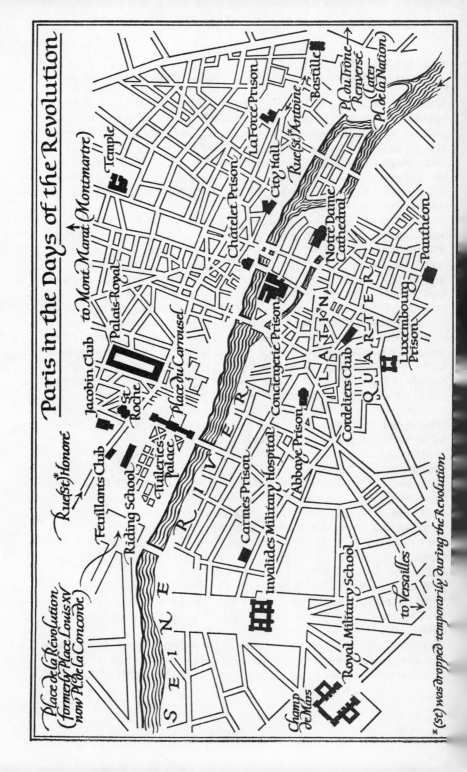

Paris in the Days of the Revolution

Place de la Revolution
(formerly Place Louis XV
now Pl. de la Concorde)

Rue (St) Honoré*

to Mont Marat (Montmartre)

Temple

Jacobin Club

Palais-Royal

Feuillants Club

St Roche

Place du Carrousel

Riding School

Tuileries Palace

Châtelet Prison

La Force Prison

City Hall

Rue (St) Antoine

Bastille

Pl. du Trône
Renversé
(later
Pl. de la Nation)

Carmes Prison

Invalides Military Hospital

Concièrgerie Prison

Abbaye Prison

Notre Dame
Cathedral

L A T I N

Q U A R T E R

Cordeliers Club

Luxembourg
Prison

Panthéon

S E I N E   R I V E R

Royal Military School

to Versailles

Champ
de Mars

* (St) was dropped temporarily during the Revolution

There the men were linked together to some extent by illicit trade unions which controlled sickness benefit funds, and to some extent also by the trade guilds to which they belonged. But there were also hundreds of small workshops where the masters, journeymen and apprentices ate and sometimes slept under one roof, or at least lived near at hand.

This helps to explain why we find masters as well as men among the 'mob'. Masters and men also suffered together from the concealed unemployment of Paris which expressed itself in the form of numerous public holidays. Sunday, naturally, was a day off. But so also was Monday. In addition there were a number of important Saint Days each month including the saint of the local diocese, of the parish and even of the guild. In fact nearly one day in three was a day off and therefore a day when the worker and his master were prepared to listen to revolutionary oratory and perhaps take action.

The artisans, clerks and other wage earners were on the whole not so interested in raising their wages as they were in making sure that the price of bread remained steady. For a steep increase in bread prices could mean that a labourer, instead of spending say thirty per cent of his income on bread, would have to lay out double. Small shopkeepers and the families working at home with hired machinery felt the same way and it was therefore generally at times when the price of bread was at its highest that the Paris mob was at its most dangerous. Many had flocked to Paris to benefit from the public relief works being carried out at Montmartre. And as Gouverneur Morris wrote at this time, though with some exaggeration, 'There are now in and about this city above a million of human creatures whose only resource for bread is the vigilance and attention of Government, whose utmost exertion however can but just keep pace with the necessity.'

Crowd work however might not alone have been enough to make a revolution if the crowd had not been encouraged and shown not only what they must do and why, but also how. This guidance was provided for them during the early days of the Revolution, when the Assembly was still at Versailles, by the orators and pamphleteers of the Palais-Royal, the grounds of which had been thrown open to the public by the Duc d'Orléans six years before and which was more or less exempt from the restrictions on public speaking. The ground floor of the buildings had been leased out to restaurateurs, confectioners, hairdressers, florists, milliners and cutlers.

Well-known meeting places included the Café du Caveau, the
Taverne Anglaise, the Café Corraza, the Café de Chartres, the Café
des Variétés and most famous of all, in the garden itself the Café
de Foy, where signed petitions canvassed by the orators were displayed for all to see. Here the crowds gathered for news. Here the
most inflammatory speeches were made to an assembled audience of
Frenchmen and foreigners drawn by the attractions which included
private gambling clubs and an abundance of trollops. Here
pamphlets on the latest Court scandals were sold. Arthur Young
wrote:

June 9th. The business going forward in the pamphlet shops
of Paris is incredible. I went to the Palais-Royal to see what new
things were published, and to procure a catalogue of all. Every
hour produces something new. Thirteen came out today, sixteen
yesterday and ninety-two last week. We think sometimes that
Debrett's or Stockdale's shops at London are crowded, but they
are mere deserts compared to Desennes, and some others here, in
which one can scarcely squeeze from the door to the counter. The
price of printing two years ago was from twenty-seven livres to
thirty livres per sheet, but now it is from sixty livres to eighty
livres. This spirit of reading political tracts, they say, spreads into
the provinces, so that all the presses of France are equally employed. Nineteen-twentieths of these productions are in favour
of liberty, and commonly violent against the clergy and nobility.
I have today bespoken many of this description that have reputation; but inquiring for such as had appeared on the other side
of the question, to my astonishment, I find that there are but
two or three that have merit enough to be known. Is it not wonderful, that while the press teems with the most levelling and
even seditious principles, that if put in execution would overturn
the monarchy, nothing in reply appears, and not the least step is
taken by the Court to restrain this extreme licentiousness of publication? It is easy to conceive the spirit that must thus be raised
among the people. But the coffee-houses in the Palais-Royal
present yet more singular and astonishing spectacles; they are
not only crowded within, but other expectant crowds are at the
doors and windows, listening *à gorge deployée* to certain orators,
who from the chairs or table harangue each his little audience.
The eagerness with which they are heard, and the thunder of

applause they receive for every sentiment of more than common hardiness or violence against the present government, cannot easily be imagined. I am all amazement at the ministry permitting such nests and hotbeds of sedition and revolt, which disseminate among the people, every hour, principles that by and by must be opposed with vigour, and therefore it seems little short of madness to allow the propagation at present.

In letters to his father Camille Desmoulins, the orator with the glittering eyes and dark sarcastic smile, who was to play a leading part in the events of 14 July, gathered the same impression:

They beat up a Countess the other day in the Palais-Royal where she had been speaking against M. Necker. All those with voices powerful enough to make themselves heard gather there every evening. They get up on a table; a gathering is formed to listen to what is to be read. The speakers pick on the most outspoken piece that has been written on current affairs. The silence is broken only by applause from the more lively sections of the audience. Patriots demand an encore. Three days ago, a child of four, full of intelligence and well trained, made a trip round the garden, in broad daylight, at least twenty times, carried on the shoulders of a porter. The child cried, 'Decision of the French people: Madame de Polignac to be banished a hundred leagues from Paris. Condé the same. Conti, the same. D'Artois the same. The Queen . . . I don't dare repeat it to you.'

Desmoulins also reported, apparently with complacency, that the crowd, having discovered a police spy in the Palais-Royal tore his clothes off him, ducked him in the fountain, and then hunted him as if he'd been a stag, stoning him and forcing one of his eyes out of its socket in a spectacle lasting five and a half hours. He wrote:

As soon as they see a Hussar, the crowd shouts 'There goes Punch!' and the stonecutters fling stones at him. Last night two Hussars officers, Monsieur de Sombreuil and Monsieur de Polignac, came to the Palais-Royal . . . chairs were flung at them and they would have been knocked down if they had not run away.

Desmoulins, who came from Guise about a hundred miles north of Paris, had tried without success to be elected as deputy for the Third Estate:

It's simpler to go to the Palais-Royal [than to the Assembly] because you don't need to ask the President's permission to speak or to wait your turn for a couple of hours. One proposes one's own motion. If it is supported, the audience gets the speaker to climb onto a chair; if he is applauded he calls the crowd to order; if they whistle in disapproval he leaves; the Romans ran their Forum this way. . . . The Palais-Royal has flooded France with pamphlets for six months, and has made philosophers out of soldiers; at the Palais-Royal the patriots form a grand chain with cavalrymen, dragoons, chasseurs, Swiss guards, artillerymen, put their arms round them, making them drunk, and pouring out money to make them drink the health of the Nation [in preference to that of the King].

The Duc d'Orléans himself played a leading part in fomenting agitation which he hoped would lead to his replacing Louis XVI on the throne of France. He had been elected to the Estates General as one of the nobility and had taken his place with the other members of the order instead of with the royal party at the opening ceremony. He was among the first of the nobles to break away to join the Third Estate in the National Assembly at Versailles. It was he who secretly financed some of the more venomous attacks on the régime, and he also helped to make the Palais-Royal the headquarters of the most advanced revolutionary groups. Camille Desmoulins was one of his supporters. So was Choderlos de Laclos, author of *Les Liaisons Dangereuses*, the book of the film the export of which was banned by General de Gaulle a few years ago. Adrien Duport who would have liked to be Prime Minister in an Orleanist Government was another Orleans man and so was the bull-necked, loud-mouthed Marquis de St Hurugue.

The immediate object of the Orleanists in the early days of July was to subvert the army units in Paris, in particular the five to six thousand French and Swiss Guards which were then the chief means of asserting the royal authority in the capital. Both men and non-commissioned officers were encouraged to come to the Palais-Royal and to fraternize with the crowds there.

But it could hardly have been a surprise to the authorities that the troops were not to be relied on. Necker, on the eve of the meeting of the Estates General, had said as much. And so also had Marshal de Vaux who, when putting down risings in 1788 in the

Dauphiné, warned the King that the soldiers seemed ready to fraternize with the crowds.

The gap between officers and men in the French Guards had always been wide but at least they had previously been led by a Marshal of France. The Duc de Châtelet, their new colonel, however, was not only of inferior rank. He was also a disciplinarian and therefore particularly unpopular.

On 30 June large crowds, with encouragement from orators in the Palais-Royal, broke into the Abbaye prison (off St Germain) and freed eleven guardsmen who, they were told, had refused to fire on the crowds at Versailles a few days earlier. At the request of the Assembly the soldiers returned voluntarily to the Abbaye Prison but were promptly released again at the request of the King. About this time Desmoulins wrote:

> Yesterday the artillery regiment followed the example of the French Guards, overpowered the sentinels and came over to mingle with the patriots in the Palais-Royal. The crowd surrounds any soldier they chance to see and takes them off to the nearest wine shop to drink the health of the Third Estate.

From 10 July onwards the crowd was encouraged to attack and burn down the customs posts surrounding the city. This was a highly popular move both with the shopkeepers and the consumers who objected to paying customs duties. It also made it much more difficult for the authorities to control who came in and went out of the city.

By 11 July the King was ready to strike. At dinner that night (Saturday), Necker received a note dismissing him. The note told him to leave the country immediately. The banker finished his dinner without telling anyone what he had learned. He got into his carriage with his wife and set off as if for St Omer. Then he took the road for Brussels.

The news of his departure did not become public until midday of Sunday, 12 July and it was not until Monday that the Assembly sent the Archbishop of Vienne to tell the King that their members did not cease to regret the departure of the former minister and would have no confidence in any other.

The citizens of Paris were not however prevented from acting on a Sunday. Camille Desmoulins, one of many unknown orators, began to stir the passions of the crowd that afternoon. He told them that the dismissal of Necker was the signal for a massacre such as had once taken place on St Bartholomew's Eve and that their only resource was to take to arms. He urged patriots to wear distinctive cockades so that they could recognize and protect one another, and, for the moment, they chose green, the colour of hope, and made their cockades from the leaves from the horse chestnut trees. They found plenty of ammunition in the form of stone quarried for the construction of a new bridge.

That very afternoon the crowd made their way to the house of the sculptor Curtius in the Boulevard du Temple. Curtius (like his niece the famous Madame Tussaud), kept a display of wax works and from him the crowd borrowed busts of Necker and the Duc d'Orléans to carry in their procession. They also carried black and white standards as a token of mourning for Necker. Passing along the rue St Martin and the rue St Denis, they reached the rue St Honoré compelling all they met to join them. In the Place Vendôme they carried the two busts twice round the statue of Louis XIV. A detachment of the German Guard tried to disperse them and were themselves put to flight by a shower of stones. The crowd continued on its way to the Place Louis XV, now the Place de la Concorde.

Here they were attacked by dragoons commanded by the Prince de Lambesc and thrown into confusion. A man carrying one of the busts was killed and so was a soldier of the French Guard. The crowd began to break up, some running towards the river, others towards the boulevards and a third section towards the Tuileries gardens, where they were pursued by the dragoons and lost among sightseers. Meanwhile a detachment of French Guards who had been confined to their barracks in the Chausée d'Antin broke out and drew up in battle array at the barrack gates. Seeing a detachment of dragoons in their path they cried out *'Qui Vive?'* 'Royal Allemand,' came the answer. 'Are you for the Third Estate?' 'We are for those who command us.' Then the French Guards opened fire on the Germans, killing two, wounding three and putting the remainder to flight. They then occupied the Place Louis XV and held it despite a counter-attack from loyal troops from the Champ de Mars. The Paris authorities, fearing to start a civil war, withdrew their troops from the centre of the city.

By this time the work of the royal officials who formerly ran the city of Paris had been taken over by the four hundred Electors of the Third Estate who, although they had finished their work on 18 May, had remained in session ever since. They consisted mainly of prosperous bourgeois who were alarmed both by the violence of the mob and by the fact that there now existed no troops who could be relied on to keep order and prevent looting. They were beset by threatening crowds demanding immediate supplies of bread and arms with which to protect the city. It was useless for M. de Flesselles, the Provost of the Merchants who had been appointed Chief Armourer, to assure the crowds that more arms were arriving in Paris at any moment or to send them off on wild-goose chases to non-existent depots. The crowd would not be put off.

Cutlers' shops were broken into. Gunsmiths were pillaged and even hunting knives were taken for the public service. Those who could find nothing better made do with stones and bottles. The mob demanded all the arms stored in the Hôtel de Ville, together with ninety-six barrels of powder, which they threatened to touch off if it was not handed out.

On the morning of the 14th, while the Ambassador of Saxony watched aghast, between seven and eight thousand citizens raided the Hôtel des Invalides. The defenders within the barracks had all but encouraged the crowd to help themselves, taking six hours to make twenty guns unserviceable. Thirty thousand muskets were taken. The Marquis de Sombreuil had to surrender and narrowly escaped being hung to his own railings. Any show of force or the appearance of troops in the streets merely made new recruits for the mob. The soldiers, many of whom had relatives in Paris, told their officers that they would disobey orders if told to open fire on their fellow citizens.

All was now ready for the storming of the Bastille. This fortress, with its walls ninety feet high and its moat seventy-five feet across, could be compared in some ways to Britain's Tower of London. Built originally for the defence of Paris, it had afterwards become a gaol for State prisoners and so a reminder of the injustices of absolute monarchy. In 1789 it held only seven captives. But it possessed one other special attraction. Two days earlier a large consignment of gunpowder had been moved from the main Paris Arsenal to the Bastille and another originally intended for Rouen to the Town Hall. The supplies at the Town Hall had already been doled out to the impatient citizens; there remained those at the Bastille.

The Electors of the Third Estate who were growing more and
more anxious at the turn of events, wanted this second consignment of the powder under their own control for the safety of the
city. They hoped that they could negotiate with the Governor of
the fortress for the powder to be transferred, or, if that was not
possible, for their own trustees to be admitted to the fortress.

The Governor, the Marquis de Launay, knew his duty. His
permanent garrison, consisting mainly of pensioners and others
exempted from normal military service, had been reinforced by
thirty-two Swiss Guards from the Salis Samade Regiment, one of
the smartest units in the whole French Army. He had mounted and
loaded the guns of the fortress and brought them forward to the
firing position, their barrels pointing out from between the ancient
battlements.

The first deputation from the Town Hall arrived at the Bastille
about ten in the morning. They were well received by the Governor
who, perhaps to gain time, invited them to his table and entertained them so well that the waiting crowds feared that they were
under lock and key. A second deputation was therefore sent in. It
represented the inhabitants of the district of St Louis de la Culture
(who feared that their own houses, within range of the fortress
cannon, would be the first to suffer), and was led by Thuriot de la
Rosière a local advocate with a gift for persuasion. De Launay had
withdrawn his guards to the inner fortress and a large crowd was
able to accompany Thuriot through the outer court as far as the
first of the two drawbridges protecting the fortress. After Thuriot
had been admitted, the Governor took him round and showed him
that, as a token of good faith, the guns had been withdrawn from
their positions. Thuriot was assured that the guns would not be
fired unless the fortress was attacked. But de Launay maintained
that he could not surrender the fortress unless the Electors at the
Town Hall could establish that they were authorized to order him
to do so. The crowd outside the walls began to get the impression—
rightly as it turned out—that de Launay had no intention of giving
in, but was playing for time until reinforcements and provisions of
which he was short should arrive. It was decided to waste no further
time. An officer, Lieutenant Elie, and a former non-commissioned
officer named Hulin, took command; the attackers climbed on top
of the guardhouse and hacked through the chains of the first drawbridge. When it fell, the mob, believing that the garrison had

surrendered, pressed on into the next courtyard known as the
Governor's Court. They were met by a hail of fire. The cries of
the wounded could be heard by those in the rear and from then on
there was no turning back. Several hundred including at least sixty
foot soldiers besides troopers and naval officers were ready for the
assault. At this point yet another deputation arrived from the
Town Hall, waving a flag of truce. They wanted the Governor to
agree to admit a contingent of municipal guards to help mount
guard over the Bastille. De Launay was ready to talk things over
but the deputies were unable to force their way through the crowd
and the second drawbridge remained raised.

The attackers then brought up three wagons filled with straw
and set them alight to provide a smoke-screen for their movements.
Under heavy fire, Elie and Hulin brought cannon to bear on the
great gate behind the second drawbridge. After two hours' bom-
bardment a white handkerchief was thrown from one of the towers
and, almost at the same time, a piece of paper was pushed through
a loophole near the main gate. Men could be seen standing on the
walls of the fortress with arms reversed, waving their hats to show
that they had stopped firing. A narrow plank was brought up and
laid across the parapet of the moat between the first and second
drawbridges. A volunteer walked the plank to fetch the paper.
He fell off and was killed. A second man, Stanislas Maillard, was
luckier. He brought back the paper, which was read aloud. It
declared that the Governor would blow up the fortress unless he
was given guarantees that the lives of the garrison would be spared.
The attackers, realizing that the precious powder was in danger
and scenting victory, redoubled their fire. The Governor was prevented by his own men from blowing up the magazine and at last
the footbridge over the moat was lowered and finally the main
bridge. The Bastille had fallen.

It was difficult to keep the victory an orderly one. Nearly one
hundred men had been killed in the assault and half as many again
wounded. Also some loyal soldiers had continued firing after the
second drawbridge had been lowered. This inflamed the crowd still
more. While a section of them tore the place to pieces, the garrison
with de Launay were formed up and marched under guard to the
Hôtel de Ville. But even the assurances by Elie that the prisoners
would be made to swear allegiance to the nation and not to the
King in future failed to pacify the avengers. The convoy had almost

reached the Town Hall when Denot, a cook living in the rue Campalon, claiming that de Launay had kicked him, struck the Governor down and cut off his head with a carving knife. His trophy was soon on display on the point of a pike, together with the head of M. de Flesselles who had been reluctant to hand out arms to the people and who was shot dead on the steps of the Town Hall. Three other officers and four soldiers were murdered.

It is easy to agree with Chateaubriand who, when the heads were paraded past his window, exclaimed, 'Brigands! Is this your idea of liberty?' Yet these brigands had been brought up as beasts by the ancient régime and even treated by the authorities to spectacles of public torture and execution.

On this occasion it was eventually resolved to offer further satisfaction to the citizens. The Bastille should be demolished. The contract was awarded to a builder named Palloy—one of those on the officially recognized list of 'the Conquerors of the Bastille'. He received no payment except possession of the site itself. But by using volunteer labour to pull down the building and by turning it into souvenirs he made a fortune. He carved miniature prisons out of the stones, turned the bolts into snuff-boxes and inkpots, and the chains into medals for the politicians. The marble mantlepiece of the Governor's house became a domino set with which the little Dauphin afterwards played in prison. Individual stones were bought by householders who fancied the idea of treading beneath their feet a relic of the bad old past. And Palloy's Museum of Liberty with its special curiosities continued to draw customers for many a year.

The night of 14 July was a testing time for the city of Paris. The so-called Civil Guard, formed to replace troops loyal to the King, to protect Paris against reprisals and to prevent looting by the mob, was only one day old. To begin with it was composed of two hundred volunteers from each of the sixty electoral districts of Paris, to provide a force of twelve thousand men, but there were plans to expand it later to something like four times the size. At first it had no officers, no headquarters, and no legal authority. But a primitive system of defence was worked out and street barricades were set up to prevent the city from being overrun. No arms or food were allowed to leave the city. Passwords and countersigns were allocated to prevent unauthorized movements from one part of the city to another. Householders were commanded to remain on the alert with lights showing in their houses to provide extra street illumination. They were warned to be ready to repel invaders or at least delay them with whatever weapons they could find. Axes, wood choppers, sickles and even roasting spits were mobilized. And those who had nothing better to strike with tore up the streets and prepared heaps of stones ready to be cast from the roof-tops.

But the plight of the National Assembly at Versailles seemed even more perilous. For they were without military protection and the more timid saw themselves as hostages for the good behaviour of those in the capital. They had been given reports that the Comte d'Artois and the Duchesse de Polignac had been entertaining the officers of the German Regiment with refreshments and were convinced that this was the prelude to their own arrest and imprisonment. After protesting against the dismissal of Necker, the Assembly sat all through the night of 13–14 July. They met again at nine in the morning on 14 July and again at five and listened with sinking hearts to the news from the capital. Again and again they asked the King to withdraw his troops from around Paris. His counter-proposal was that he should send his own officers to take command of the new Guards. Mirabeau wrote to his constituents:

We decided to continue our session through the night partly in order to show ourselves to our enemies, as the Roman Senate showed itself to the Gauls, in the midst of our sacred duties, and partly to be ready at any moment to make a final effort to influence the King and to lend aid to the Capital. No words can express the anxiety we felt. Never shall I forget the mournful spectacle of the nation's representatives, whom the King had called together, suffering as victims of a devouring dread; old men snatching an hour's rest on tables or on the floor; the weaker brethren sleeping on the benches; all conscious of the sword that threatened them and their country, and all fearing a tomorrow yet more terrible.

Nevertheless the Assembly decided to make one more effort to warn the King of the dangers of relying on foreign troops for his own security. But as the deputation left the Assembly Hall early the following morning, they were met by the Master of the Wardrobe, the Duc de Liancourt. He had used the privilege of his office to awake the King and to tell him that he was faced not with a revolt but with a revolution, and the King had decided to visit the Assembly in person. The Comte de Provence and the Comte d'Artois, who were with him heard Louis tell the Assembly that he had decided to recall the troops from Paris and Versailles. He returned to his palace on foot accompanied by the deputies and by shouts of '*Vive le Roi*'.

That night the first wave of émigrés headed by the Polignacs and the Comte d'Artois himself prepared to leave the country. The King was advised to follow their example. Instead he sent once more for Necker, and came to believe like many other observers of the day that the crisis was now over.

The Assembly's next care now that their immediate anxieties had been relieved, was to establish closer relations with Paris. For developments in the capital appeared to have got far beyond the capacity of the Assembly to control them. Accordingly a delegation of fifty deputies was sent with orders to bring back a first-hand report of conditions in the capital. They were shocked to see the changes which a few days had brought. Already the city had become a fortress. The streets were criss-crossed not only with barricades of spiked fencing but in many places with trenches too. Shops had been closed for three days. No one was allowed to leave in case they might give away the dispositions of the defenders and those moving through the streets were called on repeatedly to prove their identity and their business. The Electors of Paris were themselves besieged by crowds clamouring for bread and had not left the Town Hall since 13 July. They maintained that it was impossible for them to restore order until the people of Paris received an assurance from the King in person that he was not going to take reprisals for the events of the last few days. With this disturbing news the deputies returned to Versailles and the Assembly decided to urge the King to re-visit his capital and claim its goodwill as his ancestor Henry IV had done many years before. A hundred deputies offered to go with him to underline their public support.

After a day's pause during which the arrangements for the visit were prepared, the King was ready to face his people. He attended Mass, left instructions that the Comte de Provence was to rule in his place if he did not return, and set off, flanked by two double lines of deputies in unmatched pairs—a duke next to a parish priest and a bishop next to a worker. He dispensed with his State coach and took the carriage he used for hunting. He took officials rather than courtiers with him and employed the Town Guard of

Versailles as escort, in place of the Royal Guards. Lord Dorset, the British Ambassador, said in his report that Louis now looked more like a captive than a King and was actually led in triumph 'like a tame bear'. It was indeed a monumental humiliation both for the King himself and for the monarchy.

At the boundary he was met by Bailly, acting as Mayor of the city (an illegal appointment replacing the Governor appointed by the King). Bailly did not feel it necessary to kneel and remarked as he handed over the keys of the capital, 'These are the same that were presented to Henry IV. He had reconquered his people; whereas today the people has reconquered its King.' It was such a contemptuous welcome that Louis, turning towards the Prince de Bauveau murmured, 'I'm not sure that I ought to listen.'

On his way through the city before an audience of perhaps a quarter of a million people, he could not have failed to see the unfamiliar un-uniformed troops lining the route, or the fact that they did not 'present arms' but kept their swords in their scabbards and bayonets likewise.

At the Town Hall he could not have helped noticing the royal standard which once had flown from above the Bastille and now was covered with grime and blood. He had to listen to one of his own nobility, Trophime Gérard, Comte de Lally-Tollendal, who in an address which amounted to the obituary of the monarchy, praised the choice of Bailly as Mayor and of the Marquis de la Fayette as Commander of the armed forces of Paris, soon to be named the National Guard. And the King had to accept and wear in his hat the new tricolour cockade in which his own colour, white, was sandwiched in between the red and blue of the municipality. All this he endured with a vacant smile as an uncle might who had been invited to watch a children's party. His was a penance rather than a pilgrimage. But the crowd, believing that now at last they would have bread, cheered in response. They knew, now, that they could always summon the King.

Chapter 3

THE FIRE SPREADS

As the dust began to settle in Paris—and sometimes before—
new revolutions were afoot elsewhere. News of what happened
in Paris was reported in letters written by deputies in the Assembly
to their constituents. In Clermont Ferrand, the daily letter was
rushed to the town theatre and read there again and again to
different audiences who listened, it was noted, with far more interest
than they had ever shown towards the masterpieces of French
drama. 'Indeed,' wrote a correspondent, 'the public would rather
fast for forty-eight hours than miss their daily news-letter from
Paris. No one thinks of dining before he has heard the latest news.'

And so the provinces followed the lead of the capital. In sleepy
cities all over the country the bourgeois Electors of the Third
Estate elbowed the royal officials out of the way and claimed the
right in future to choose their own city mayors. Sometimes they
were helped by the mobs. In Marseilles, armed citizens threw out
the royal garrison and joined with the merchants of the chamber of
commerce to defy the Crown officials, the nobility and clergy or
anyone else who interfered with the independence of their city. In

Bordeaux, shipowners and wine-merchants combined with labourers and dockers to defy the Crown.

Sometimes, as in Paris, the soldiers were not to be relied on to put down riots. Mobs could not be controlled. At Rennes, where for months nobles had feared to appear in the streets unarmed and where a theatre audience had rioted because a nobleman appeared with his hat on, the citizens persuaded the garrison to desert and then seized power.

At Dijon, the Governor was arrested and the nobles and clergy confined to their houses. Townsmen attacked the fortress at Sedan, to which Marshal de Broglie had retired, and put him to flight. At Verdun the same kind of drama; and at Brest, the crowd aided by sailors and ropemakers stormed their Bastilles—the Fort de l' Amiral, the Fort de la Recouvrance and the Fort Gonète.

In parts of France there were the makings of a civil war between the loyal regiments and the new town guards. At Caen, Normandy, the Bourbon Regiment led by Comte Henri de Belzunce attacked men of the Artois Regiment who were so unmilitary as to wear medals struck in honour of M. Necker, and tore off these decorations. But the mob fell on de Belzunce, shot him in the main square of the city and tore his body to pieces.

At Besançon, the Intendant had to flee for his life and the local magistrates were compelled to burn in public the papers which the prosecution intended to use to bring the rioters to justice. Local judges hid themselves to avoid being compelled to commit illegal acts.

In Strasbourg a mob of five hundred stormed the City Hall while the magistrates fled through a back door. Windows were dashed to pieces, the doors forced with crowbars, and furniture, books and records thrown out of the windows. At Maubeuge, the customs offices were sacked from roof to cellar and the scales and weights thrown into the river. Naturally some of the good burgesses were disturbed by this turbulence but the alternative—suppression of them by the royal troops—was too frightful to contemplate.

A few cities set an example to Paris in their efforts to keep order. In Lyons where there had been troubles in the silk industry, a City Guard of eight hundred was set up ten days before the Fall of the Bastille, and this same force shot eighty rioters and took sixty prisoners in their efforts to control the mobs.

At Rouen, too, the Town Guard supported the authority of the

King's official, the Intendant, and helped to put down a formidable people's rising which took place at the beginning of August. In spite of pleas made by Bailly and La Fayette, the two ringleaders were hanged. Often the Town Guard, formed in many cases by the new aldermen to protect their own property, took little account of what went on outside the city walls. For a time, at any rate what happened between the peasantry and the nobility was of little concern to them.

But in the countryside too, the wind of change continued to blow. Every man who could get a gun or even a club went after game. Stag, boar, hares and rabbits were killed by the thousand, cooked over wood cut from the landowner's coverts, and eaten on the spot. Foresters and gamekeepers were careful not to show themselves. Crowds burst into the courtyards of manor houses, shot the pigeons there and offered those they did not want to the proprietor. Carp and pike disappeared for good from manor and monastery fishponds. Four châteaux near Vesoul were burnt within a week of the fall of the Bastille; soon afterwards three abbeys and eleven near-by châteaux were gutted. In the Dauphiné, twenty-seven châteaux were burned or destroyed and nearly forty in the Franche Comté. Deserted mansions were looted down to the very door hinges. Wherever possible, the parchment records of feudal rights and the findings of the manorial courts were burnt as well. At Luxeuil, the abbot who had lived in the district for forty-six years, was compelled with an axe held above his head to sign away his seignorial rights over twenty-three estates. Many another owner followed his example with a pitchfork or scythe held close to his neck. The victims were afraid to write letters for fear of being suspected by the peasants of asking for help.

The peasants knew that the King's system of justice had been replaced in the cities, and concluded with the greatest willingness that the feudal rights, which also depended on the King's authority, no longer held good either. Peasants not only refused to pay their taxes but demanded refunds on what they had paid in previous years. In the north where farming conditions were better they turned on the tax collectors and customs posts and, in Normandy, where there was unemployment both because of the commercial treaty with Britain and because of the introduction of new machinery, they burnt the factories.

Elsewhere, food shortages added to the tension. Peasants, fearing that they might be compelled to sell at below the market price, stopped bringing their food to market despite the high prices which it might have expected to fetch there. They knew too that the authorities in the large cities, in order to keep down prices, were refusing to allow grain to be sold to customers coming from other near-by markets which they had hitherto supplied.

At Troyes, the peasants arriving at the city gates four days after the fall of the Bastille refused to pay the *octroi* or local duty on their produce, claiming that the Assembly had declared these dues to be illegal. Rather than pay they went away. A near-famine resulted. The bakers sent a special agent to Britain to procure rice, but the citizens, believing reports that the rice was poisoned, dragged the Mayor Claude Huez out on to the steps of the Town Hall and beat him to death.

Rumours that sacks of grain were being flung into the Seine and that cavalry horses were being trained to eat growing wheat in the fields infuriated the starving population of Paris. It was said that having failed to subdue the people of France by force 'they' were trying to do so by starvation.

About this time, the countryside experienced a new convulsion quite distinct from the revolts of the aldermen, the riots for bread and the attacks on the châteaux. This was the phenomenon known as La Grande Peur or Big Panic which spread from one side of the country to the other for no obvious reason and added considerably to the general unrest. It took the form of a rumour that large numbers of 'brigands' were passing through the countryside burning everything in their path. In a countryside which had seen so much unrest and so little authority to put a stop to it, these rumours bore the ring of truth. Who could tell? Perhaps the brigands had been let out of prison by the King as an act of revenge? It would be logical to suppose that La Grande Peur had been launched by the same agitators who frequented the Palais-Royal or even by counter-revolutionaries, but no conclusive evidence has been produced to support this line of thought.

When the Grande Peur struck, householders buried their money and cattle were driven in from the fields for protection. In remote villages men fled to the woods treading down their own crops in their eagerness to escape; women took refuge in the church belfries; in towns the tocsin was sounded and the walls manned. Priests pronounced General Absolution.

In Gueret, a town in the Department of La Creuse, panic struck
at about five o'clock in the afternoon of 29 July. The tocsin was
sounded. Women ran out of the town and hid themselves in ditches
and copses, the men volunteered as auxiliaries to the Town
Guard. Couriers were sent to neighbouring towns and villages asking for help and bakers were told to bake enough extra bread for
the expected reinforcements. Eight to ten thousand men turned up
and had to be fed at the town's expense before it became clear that
there were not and never had been any brigands.

Château-Thierry had had the same panic in the same week.
News arrived there that two thousand five hundred brigands were
advancing towards the town along the road from Soissons. The
tocsin was sounded and the men of the Town Guard were sent out
to drive away the invaders. On their way, the Guard learnt from a
miller that the brigands had just sacked Bouresches and set it
aflame. But when the Town Guard neared Bouresches they could
see only the reflection of the setting sun on the roofs of the houses.
Next the brigands were said to be crossing the River Marne at
Essommes. But when the Guard reached Essommes, they learnt
that what they had seen was the women of the town in flight. The
women had been convinced that the Town Guard from Château-
Thierry were brigands.

The appearance of a single stranger on the road was liable to set
off a shock wave. At Chaumont a man covered with dust appeared
and declared that the brigands were not far away though he could
not be sure where and had not seen them himself. Even so the
tocsin was rung and all preparations made to repel the invaders. Of
course the brigands never came. At Brive, it was said that the English were invading the country from Bordeaux and at Tulle it was
said that the Austrians were advancing from Lyons. In Poitou it
was said that the Poles had landed by sea.

On the same day the tocsin sounded at Angoulême about three
in the afternoon. Fifteen thousand bandits were said to be advancing towards the city. The Town Guard was called to arms by drum-
beat. Cannon were mounted on the town walls. The suspense became almost unbearable as a cloud of dust was seen rising from the
road. It proved to be the mail coach on its way to Bordeaux. After
some reflection it was decided that the brigand forces probably
numbered fifteen hundred and not fifteen thousand.

But they were bound to be dangerous, and twenty thousand men spent the night on watch, listening to everything but hearing nothing. Three o'clock in the morning saw a fresh alarm with rumours that the brigands had burned Ruffec, Verneuil and other near-by places. Once again the Town Guard paraded in battle array. The next day reinforcements poured in from the countryside around from volunteers anxious to fight the shadowy foe. By nine o'clock there were forty thousand extra men to feed. Then the rumour got round that the bandits had not shown themselves because they were lying in concealment waiting to attack. A force of a hundred cavalry and foot soldiers then set out to comb the most likely piece of cover, the forest of Braconne. To their amazement they found nothing there. The bandits, they concluded, must have moved. But for days the vigil was kept up and the fears of the townsmen, when conveyed to Bordeaux, were so convincing that the city of Bordeaux offered to send them up to thirty thousand reinforcements. Curiously enough a parish only a short distance away from Angoulême had an almost exactly similar experience at almost the same time.

The credulity of the peasants was inexhaustible. Arthur Young, who was travelling at this time, was told at Dijon in great seriousness that the Queen had been convicted of a plot to poison the King, to give the Regency to the Comte d'Artois, to set fire to Paris and to blow up the Palais-Royal with a mine. At Colmar, he learnt that the Queen's plot was to blow up the National Assembly with a mine and order the Army instantly to massacre the people of Paris:

> A French officer present presumed but to doubt the truth of it, and was immediately overpowered with numbers of tongues. A deputy had written it, they had seen the letter, and not a hesitation could be admitted. I strenuously contended that it was folly and nonsense at the first blush, a mere invention to render persons odious who, for what I knew, might deserve to be so, but certainly not by such means; if the Angel Gabriel had descended and taken a chair at table to convince them it would not have shaken their faith. Thus it is in revolutions, one rascal writes and a hundred thousand fools believe.

But could a people with little education, who had been allowed neither discretion in decisions affecting themselves nor opportunity to use their judgement on the affairs of others, be expected to reject rumours so directly affecting their own welfare and safety,

when there was no means of disproving them? As countrymen they
must have known that sheep survive not through their own
superior intelligence but by following unquestioningly and blindly
the unforeseen unpredictable impulses of the rest of the flock.

Meanwhile as the châteaux burned on summer nights the
National Assembly at Versailles had been at work . . . talking. The
going was hard. The Assembly was twice as big as the House of
Commons, yet it had no effective rules of procedure.

Arthur Young, who attended some of the debates, noted, 'More
than once today there were a hundred members on their legs
at a time and Monsieur Bailly absolutely without power to keep
order.'

No wonder progress was slow. The speeches were delivered from
a kind of pulpit known as the Tribune reached by means of a spiral
staircase. Invariably there was a queue of orators waiting to speak,
each struggling to maintain his own position and anxious to dis-
place whoever else was already speaking. The acoustics of the hall
were such that only the finest orators could make themselves
heard. And the deputies who were more accustomed to the clois-
tered courtroom than to public debate were at a disadvantage and
found it exasperating to have to conduct business at the top of
their voices. Their tempers suffered.

There was no such thing as unparliamentary language at the
Assembly and its members insulted and abused each other in un-
measured terms.

Mirabeau, on the advice of English M.P.s who attended some of
the sessions, provided the Assembly with a translation of the rules of
procedure of the House of Commons, but the Assembly would have
none of this 'anglomania'.

As there were no rules of debate, the proceedings often took the
form of a series of academic speeches most of which, having been
prepared in advance, had little relevance to what had passed
earlier in the session. Under the old régime political speakers had
not been encouraged. Such speeches as were made were given
from the pulpit or in the lecture-room of some academy and they
had about the same equally remote relationship with practical
everyday affairs. Inevitably the Assembly was also completely
out of touch with the day-to-day business of government. Not a
single member of the Cabinet was represented in it or answerable
to it. Thus there was little contact between those who were planning

to devise a Constitution and those who would have to make it work on a national basis.

The Assembly worked long enough hours and sat seven days a week but this served only to inflame tempers and to delay agreement. Frequently the work of the Assembly was interrupted by such distractions as a group of citizens who wanted to present the oldest man in France to the National Assembly or by a deputation of worshipful hairdressers who were concerned about the growing unemployment which followed the departure abroad of France's most liberal spenders—the aristocrats.

Many of the sittings were occupied in reading over petitions on almost every conceivable subject and many of the motions proposed involved so many different issues that it was difficult to settle any single one. The nobles who had been induced only by royal bidding to join with the Tiers in debate, felt justified in delaying and obstructing the work of the National Assembly to the greatest possible degree in order to discredit its reputation.

There was voting, of course, but not of an orderly nature. In the early days of the Assembly its deputies were little known by sight and strangers wandering about the hall were often able to vote on measures about which they felt strongly. Deputies usually voted by standing up if they were in favour of a motion and by remaining seated if they were not. So it was not too difficult to influence a few votes one way or another by pulling at a man's coat tails if you wanted him to oppose the motion on hand and prodding him with your shoe if you thought he should be standing up. There were at the outset no political parties or even groupings so that it was impossible for one man to represent the views of anyone but himself.

It was not long before the orators at the Palais-Royal saw that they could easily lead the Assembly by the nose. All they needed to do was to send enough people with penetrating voices into the galleries of the Assembly hall. These orators could show by interrupting speeches of which they did not approve how the business of government should be conducted. Those who resisted the will of the people could be dealt with and intimidated after they left the Assembly and told that their houses would be burnt down.

Malouet wrote about this time, 'For every impartial man, the Terror began on July 14,' and he made sure to take a pair of pistols with him to the debates.

The deputies should have understood clearly that they must

prepare a Constitution at the earliest possible moment if there was
not to be complete anarchy throughout the country. This Constitution would have to safeguard their liberties and provide the
authority under which they could be governed. But, instead, they
preferred to give priority to the Declaration of the Rights of Man, a
manifesto setting out the principles on which, without having discussed them at all, they thought the Constitution should be based.

On 4 August, when they were still in the opening stages of discussing the Declaration, they received a sharp reminder of where
their duties lay in the form of a report tabled the previous day by
the Assembly's Research Committee of the breakdown of law and
order in the provinces. It was all in the report—the châteaux
aflame, tax collectors on the run, the records destroyed, customs
offices wrecked. And all this was happening in the home towns that
the deputies themselves were representing. It was clear that there
was no longer much hope of protecting the ancient privileges of the
nobility and clergy and that attempts to do so would not only fail
but would destroy whatever forces still retained their loyalty to the
central Government. The news helped wonderfully to clear the
deputies' minds.

After the report had been discussed, the Vicomte de Noailles,
thirty-three-year-old cousin of La Fayette under whom he had
served in America, was the first to reach the Tribune. He declared
that the riots had occurred largely because the people had no assurance that the Assembly was prepared to abolish the feudal burdens
under which they suffered. Calm would return at once, he said, if
this uncertainty were removed—by abolishing all the remaining
feudal privileges. He was backed by other nobles including the
Baron de Menou and the Duc de Lévis, as well as by deputies of the
original Third Estate. And so the landslide started. The Duc
d'Aiguillon proposed that all should be equally taxed. The Bishop
of Chartres suggested the abolition of game laws. The Archbishop
of Aix called for the salt tax to go (it was removed seven months
later), and the Bishop of Uzes recognized that the nation had rights
over the possessions of the Church.

Serfdom was wiped out without compensation. And it was agreed
that other feudal rights should be cancelled by purchase. The protected dovecots and rabbit warrens were banned as well as the
special hunting rights of the nobility. All tax exemptions, whether
for individuals, cities or even provinces, were abolished, back to the

previous 1 January. Tithes were wiped out. The clergy were forbidden to hold more than one appointment. Legal appointments
were no longer to be sold and promotion in the Army and Navy
was to be open to noblemen and commoner alike.

No wonder Lally-Tallendal passed up a note to the President
reading, 'Everyone has lost their self-control; break up the sitting.'
But already it was too late. The proposals which the Assembly had
passed as a series of resolutions were accepted throughout the
country as having the force of law. For that, however, they needed
to be officially published, and over this there was considerable
delay since they amounted to part of a new Constitution for France.

Furthermore, although feudal privileges were to be bought out
no one had made arrangements to provide the money for this
operation. Thus the Assembly had told the people of France what
taxes they need not pay before they had any plans to raise the
money in other ways. All that the people understood was that taxes
were illegal and should therefore not be paid.

Moreover this 'night of orgy' as Mirabeau called it did nothing
towards relieving the famine prevailing in many parts of the
country. Far from restoring order, it introduced chaos into those
areas where it was not already the rule. And the landlords made
every effort to collect the money formerly paid in tithes.

The resolutions had another unfortunate consequence because
they brought to a head again the struggle between the King and his
people. The King did not want to publish the Resolutions of 4
August. Neither did he approve of the Declaration of the Rights of
Man which was finally agreed by the Assembly on 27 August. It is
true that the Declaration said nothing controversial about the right
of association between subjects (i.e. political parties) or about freedom of speech. Freedom of the Press was permitted only in so far
as it did not disturb public order. And the ownership of property
was one of the sacred rights of man, who could not be deprived of it
save through public necessity under legal procedure and with due
compensation. Much of the Declaration was based on the *cahiers*
for which the King himself had called and parts of it reflected thinking which had influenced the American Declaration of Independence for which French troops had fought. But in other respects it
was not so reassuring to the King. For amongst other things it laid
down that in the face of oppression resistance was a most sacred
duty.

There were negotiations of course between the King and the Assembly both on the Resolutions of 4 August and the Declaration and, on 11 September, the King agreed to publish the Resolutions provided that, in the Constitution which was by then being hammered out, he was granted a veto valid for two sessions of the Assembly. This would have permitted him to hold up urgent legislation for years at a time, but the Assembly with great reluctance agreed.

A week went by and still the Resolutions of 4 August remained unpublished. The King told the Assembly in explanation that while he approved of the general sense of the Resolutions, he had some reservations about some of them and proposed to consider these and this would take some time. Meanwhile he had a number of criticisms which he wished the Assembly to consider.

Next day the President of the Assembly was sent to the palace to call on the King to order immediate official publication of the 4 August decisions. The King hesitated for a further three days and then allowed them to be printed but not on the royal presses. Later he refused to publish any articles of the Constitution, other than those proposed on 4 August, until the whole had been agreed and only then would he consider the Declaration of Rights. And he would agree to this much only provided that he retained an absolute veto without a time limit on it. He was still in this frame of mind on 5 October when once again the Paris mob took command of the situation.

Ever since the Fall of the Bastille, Paris had a new 'people' to deal with. They were armed, and efforts of the city authorities to buy back the people's weapons had largely failed. They were easily led. Hatred of the privileged classes provided the fuel for crowd action and, to the mob on the move, every kind of imposture was to be expected from the authorities.

As Arthur Young had realized there was no simple way of discrediting rumours. For example, a report is brought that the authorities have kept the windmills near the Ecole Militaire turning to calm the populace but no grain has been milled. Who can contradict such a story without undertaking a lengthy expedition to the Ecole Militaire? Or suppose a man is arrested on suspicion of being a spy. He tries to clear himself by showing identity papers which naturally are unsupported by photographs and his captors are unable to read the documents he carries. A textile worker at the head of a band of brigands in Alsace was able, by decking himself out in blue ribands, to pass himself off for some months as the King's brother.

Newspaper reports even in the dailies often were out of date before they were read. Ministers did not attend the meetings of the National Assembly, and so there was no means of telling what was in their minds on even the most urgent questions of public concern.

Fear was another powerful spur to crowd action. The populace—and not always the poorest section—feared lest the authorities launch a counter-revolution to starve them into submission. This helps to explain why the crowd insisted so often that officials should implicate themselves and show openly by wearing a cockade whose side they were on. Even the popular 'leaders' were equally in a state of terror. They knew their own lives would be forfeit if once their own brand of revolution failed.

Consequently the orators did their best to fan the flames not only during the demonstrations themselves but also from day to day. They spoke in the wine shops and in the food markets as well as at the Palais-Royal. They encouraged people to threaten the nobility with having their houses burnt about their ears. Frequently the houses of the victims were marked with chalk as an indication that they were 'on the list'. The Assembly itself added fuel to the fire by offering rewards to those prepared to denounce enemies of the State or of the Public Welfare.

Once a riot had begun every man shed his own responsibilities. His neighbours on either side carried them for him. And as the moderate section of the crowd tired, the extremists took over.

A typical incident took place three days after the Fall of the Bastille which led to the murder of Jean-François Foullon a seventy-five-year-old Army contractor who had been appointed Minister of Finance after Necker's dismissal. After Necker's return Foullon spread rumours of his own death and, to make his story more easily believed, he dressed his family in mourning. He was followed, however, and seized at Vitry in the country house of M. de Sartines, the ex-Minister of Police. Then he was brought back to Paris to the Hôtel de Ville, in the early hours of the morning of 17 July.

The Electors decided that as the crowd already knew that he was at the City Hall and were in an ugly mood, in his own interests Foullon had better be moved the following night under cover of

darkness to a more secure place. His new destination was the
Abbaye Prison.

But by midday the crowd were already massing in front of the
City Hall demanding the death penalty for Foullon. La Fayette,
who was out on his rounds of inspection, was urgently summoned.
The crowds grew larger and more menacing. It was decided to send
out a group of influential Electors, mainly churchmen, together
with Mayor Bailly himself to pacify them. Bailly told them of the
decision to bring to justice all those accused of crimes against the
people's liberty. But the crowds grew still larger and still more
ominous. Again the Electors came out onto the steps of the City
Hall and tried to convince the multitude that it would be necessary
to judge M. Foullon before punishing him if he were found guilty.
But this move merely gave the crowd the idea that the Electors
were helping the prisoner to escape. They threatened to burn down
the City Hall and the Electors with it if their demands were not
complied with.

Panic struck the Electors. Foullon could not be found. He had
arrived at the City Hall between five and six in the morning and
the night staff who had booked him in had since gone off duty. No
one knew where to look for the prisoner. It was even possible that,
unknown to the Electors, he had already made good his escape.
Obviously, as soon as M. Foullon could be found, he must show
himself at a window of the City Hall so that the people could be re-
assured that he was still in custody.

His appearance was greeted with cheers, but a moment later the
crowd broke through the barriers and the guard and poured up the
staircase, across the courtyard and into the main hall of the building. Some of the Electors rushed forward and persuaded the leaders
of the mob to sit down. Soon the hall was packed and there were
continual cries for M. Foullon to be produced. The Electors insisted
again that no one could be punished without first being brought to
justice, tried and found guilty. They believed that every moment's
delay counted because La Fayette was expected back at any
minute. It was proposed that the prisoner should await trial by a
tribunal to be set up by the National Assembly to deal with such
cases. But the crowd shouted, 'No, no. He should be judged at once
and hanged.' The Electors then argued that since the people did
not want the matter to be handled in the ordinary way, special
judges would have to be nominated. At first the crowd insisted that

the Electors should choose the judges but when it was pointed out that the Electors had no such powers, the crowd agreed to do so.

Three judges were nominated. But M. Osselin, one of the Electors who was standing on top of a desk acting as spokesman for the city authorities, said that three judges were not enough and that there must be seven and a clerk.

These, too, were found. Then a prosecutor. But as yet no crime had been alleged against M. Foullon. Several were quickly suggested. He was said to have wished to vex the people, that he had said that he would make them eat grass, that he had tried to bankrupt the country, and that he had hoarded grain. At this point the Curé of St-Etienne-du-Mont and the Curé of St-André-les-Arcs, both of whom had been nominated as judges, said that they could not try the case as the laws of the Church forbade them to pass a death sentence. Some of the crowd accepted this objection. But others took it badly. They ran their hands across their throats and made signs that the prisoner's head ought to be cut off. A few pushed forward brandishing clenched fists under the noses of the Electors and accusing them of trifling with them while the prisoner ran away. They insisted on seeing him again. Two judges were named in place of the curés and M. Foullon, guarded by four of the mob, was brought out and made to sit in a chair in front of the main office. At last La Fayette arrived and succeeded in convincing those who were best placed to hear him, that Foullon should be taken to prison. But men at the other end of the hall shouted down the proposal. Foullon himself tried to talk and declared that 'here in the midst of the people so just and generous and among his fellow citizens he feared nothing'. The words seemed to rouse the mob to even greater fury and one individual comparatively well dressed asked, 'Why bother to judge a man who has already been judged for thirty years.'

La Fayette spoke again but his words were lost and new cries arose from the back of the hall asserting that rescue parties were on the point of taking away the prisoner. A new multitude pressed forward into the hall pushing everyone onward towards the prisoner. His chair was overturned. From then on he was in the hands of the crowd. 'A few moments later,' records the Electors' official report of the proceedings, 'it was learnt that the people had hung him on the lamp post opposite the City Hall.' The same treatment was accorded that evening to M. Foullon's son-in-law, M.

Berthier de Sauvigny, former Intendant of Paris. It was a warning
of the days to come, and Bailly records in his memoires that he
prayed for downpours of rain that would keep the crowds off the
streets.

The main hope of avoiding anarchy lay with Marie-Joseph Paul
Yves Roch Gilbert de Motier, Marquis de la Fayette. As a young
man of nineteen he had left his wife and young child and his post in
the French Army to fight in the American War of Independence.
There he had shown himself to be a loyal and courageous leader
with sufficient tact to live down the fact that he was a foreigner.
He became a personal friend of Washington and rose to the rank of
Major General. Having left France an outlaw he returned a hero.
Even in 1787 he had pressed for the Estates General to be summoned. He had also played a prominent part in framing the
Declaration of the Rights of Man. To this extent he would be re-
spected by the people.

But he was also viewed as a reliable man by the bourgeois and to
some extent by the more liberal peers. For he had stood for the
Assembly as representative for the nobility of Auvergne and had
made no effort to join the Third Estate until formally asked to do
so by the King.

Not only was La Fayette acceptable to both sides, he had also
had experience of commanding republican troops for whom normal
disciplinary methods did not answer. On the very day after the
Fall of the Bastille he was nominated by the Electors of Paris to
command the force which was later to become the National Guard.
To La Fayette the appointment was a call to a crusade to liberate,
under the sign of the tricolour cockade not only France but all
Europe from tyranny. Still only thirty-two, tall, long-faced and
serious to the point of priggishness, he believed that, just as he had
been prepared to forsake everything for the cause of liberty, so the
King too should divorce himself from the past and put himself at
the head of the revolution which was bound to come.

Certainly the royal family, and the Queen in particular, had need
of a patron, for the popularity which she had earned among the
common people when the Dauphin was born in 1781 had long ago
vanished. The pamphleteers paid by the Duc d'Orléans were seldom
short of material for their attacks on Marie Antoinette but they
were presented with an unusually good opportunity over the affair
of the diamond necklace and Cardinal de Rohan.

This famous piece of jewellery, valued at more than one and a half million livres had been ordered in 1774 from the Paris jewellers Boehmer and Bassange for Madame du Barry, mistress of King Louis XV, but the King had died while the piece was still being made up and it had been left on the jewellers' hands. Six years later, at a time when France was at war, it was offered to the Queen who rejected it, saying that she could buy a new frigate for that price.

Still five years later, a lady called at the jewellers', saying that she had been sent by the Queen. Her Majesty had changed her mind and would like to buy the necklace but without any publicity, using Cardinal de Rohan, the Grand Almoner, as intermediary. It was an ideal choice. De Rohan, a comparatively young and worldly prelate, had been attracted to Marie Antoinette when she was still unmarried and he was French Ambassador in Vienna. He had planned an ambitious political career for himself. It was therefore a double disappointment for him when both in Vienna and Paris, Marie Antoinette showed not only disinterest but positive distaste for his advances. And it was doubly welcome news when he learnt one day from a lady with the name of the Countess de la Mothe-Valois that the Queen had lately changed her mind. She was ready to meet him privately by night in a glade at Versailles. Naturally the Cardinal fell for the bait and naturally the Countess sent a young girl veiled and closely resembling the Queen as stand-in. Cardinal de Rohan was told that the past had been forgotten. Delighted, he wrote the Queen a series of devotional letters and gave them to the Countess to pass on. Naturally he was encouraged to continue. Then he was asked to give a proof of his devotion. He was told that the Queen greatly desired a certain necklace but not daring to ask her husband to buy it for her, had decided to buy it herself. Would the Cardinal be kind enough to negotiate the deal? It was proposed that a quarter of the price of the necklace should be paid five months after delivery and the remaining three-quarters in six monthly instalments. The Cardinal accepted the task. The jewellers accepted the terms and handed over the necklace to the Countess who quickly broke it up, sold some of the diamonds and sent the rest with her husband to be disposed of in London.

In due course the jewellers, not having received a single sou, complained through officials to the Queen who indignantly denied having received any necklace. The Cardinal, about to celebrate

High Mass of the Feast of the Assumption, was arrested and taken to prison in his full ceremonial robes. He denied nothing. But when the trial took place fifty-three members of the de Rohan family presented themselves at the court to protest against it. Popular feeling turned against the Queen as an Austrian who had brought one of the oldest names in France into disrepute, and after five days' deliberation the Cardinal was found not guilty by the magistrates by a vote of twenty-six to twenty-three. The Countess was condemned to be branded but soon escaped to London where she produced a new series of corrosive attacks on the Queen.

At the same time rumours were circulated that the Queen was getting her money out of the country and that the émigrés who had already left France were conspiring with the foreign Governments of Prussia, Austria, Spain and Sardinia to launch a counter-revolution in France.

And Marie Antoinette, feeling herself hated by all as 'L'Autrichienne' and as 'Madame Déficite', regarded all around her as enemies who were determined to drag the crown of France in the mud together with herself and her helpless husband. And Louis too was earning further unpopularity for himself, not only with the Assembly but also with the Electors of Paris.

The more moderate section felt that the Revolution could be contained only if the King were ready to come to Paris and make a bargain with them. And the more extreme section felt that the Assembly was becoming influenced by the Court into betraying the people, and that both the Assembly and the King should be brought to Paris where the people could better watch over their activities. Supporters of the Duc d'Orléans in the Palais-Royal started a movement to bring the King to Paris as far back as the end of August. It was not supported by the Assembly who were still hoping to come to terms with the King. But Louis's conduct over the veto had undermined all confidence in his reliability.

The Assembly's worst suspicions were confirmed when it became known that on 14 September the King had given orders for the Flanders Regiment to be recalled from Douai and that at a banquet given to them by the bodyguard at Versailles, royalist songs had been sung and the tricolour flag dishonoured. Desmoulins called on the people to go and fetch the monarch.

But only one motive could give the people the necessary energy to march twelve miles to Versailles *en masse* and force the King to

leave the palace—hunger. For some days the people's leaders had
been telling them that the veto about which the Assembly was
arguing with the King was a veto on flour going to Paris . . . but a
veto-riot organized by the Marquis de St Hurugue had been suppressed with severity by La Fayette's guard.

The leaders decided therefore that they would have a better
chance of success if they organized a demonstration led by women.
This was easier to arrange than might have been thought. For
bread was getting so short that the men were elbowing women out
of their places in the queue. This was no time for coyness. The
female horde which brought the King a captive to Paris began to
assemble on 5 October almost at dawn in the central markets and
the Faubourg St Antoine. The crowds who clamoured to march to
Versailles included fishwives, stall holders and some comparatively
well-dressed women wearing hats. They all demanded cheaper
bread. One section was led by a small girl who was beating a drum.
The crowds, swelling with each step they took, forced the bell-
ringer of the church of Ste-Marguerite in the Faubourg St Antoine
to sound the tocsin. Then they proceeded to the Hôtel de Ville, invaded it and had the tocsin sounded again. They then proceeded
to the Place de Grève, which they reached about eleven o'clock.

In the early afternoon a crowd of between seven and eight
thousand women with men behind—there were many unemployed
at the time—left for the twelve-mile march to Versailles, led by
Stanislas Maillard who had distinguished himself in the assault on
the Bastille. When they arrived in Versailles about six in the evening, the Assembly was already in an uproar over the King's delay
in approving the Resolutions of 4 August. The women of Paris
descended upon the Assembly Hall and more than two hundred of
them pressed to be allowed to come in. They broke up the debate
with cries of 'Du pain, du pain, parlez-nous du pain'. While
Mounier, the President, went off to the palace with a deputation,
the others paralysed the Assembly with new calls for request
speakers.

The King returned from hunting (for life at Versailles, though
overshadowed by the importunate Assembly, followed its traditional pattern) and was warned that a vast crowd of women was
moving in the direction of the palace demanding bread. 'They can
be sure that if I had any at my disposal I would attend to their
request,' he said complacently. Eventually the story circulated that

Marie Antoinette, viewing the crowd from her window, had suggested that those who couldn't get bread should eat cake. But Rousseau, without apparent foundation, had quoted a similar story in 1740 and so had John Peckham, Archbishop of Canterbury (1225–92), in his *Latin Letters*.

The Queen fled in panic from the Trianon never imagining that she would never see it again. The main body of the crowd approached the palace and surrounded it. But the King was still unmoved. 'An order of battle against an army of women . . . you must be joking,' he replied to someone who suggested that measures of defence should be taken.

He had scarcely got inside the building when a body of women began advancing down the avenue leading directly to the château. A member of the King's bodyguard arrived at full gallop to report that the approach was filled with harpies full of evil intent. 'Tell them up at the château that we will be there soon to cut off the Queen's head,' one woman shouted at him as he passed.

The King thought once more of seeking safety in flight but could not make up his mind. The Queen urged him to take a decision one way or the other. But he merely smiled and said to the Queen, 'Gently, gently, Madame.' He would wait until the crowds had left. But at four o'clock, as the autumn day came to a close, they were still there clamouring for bread.

A call to arms was sounded throughout the palace. The Flanders Regiment, showing their loyalty, filled the Place d'Armes in front of the main entrance. The women attacked them demanding to be let past, as they said, to tell the King to resign and 'to bring back something from Marie Antoinette'. The Cabinet favoured putting the crowd to flight but the Minister of War did not dare to give the order to fire and the colonel of the regiment refused to issue cartridges.

Meanwhile the King allowed one of the more presentable of his petitioners, a sixteen-year-old herring-girl, to enter the palace, clasped her in his arms and promised that supplies of grain would be delivered. Mounier, with his deputation from the Assembly, was also allowed an audience.

At one point someone fired a shot and the Marquis de Savonnières was thrown from his horse, but by a miracle a general engagement was avoided and eventually the troops were withdrawn to their barracks.

By now La Fayette had entered the picture. At first he seemed unsure of what to do about the march to Versailles. Obviously he could not head it, for it was a march of insurgents aimed at coercing the King. Yet what did the National Guard count for if it could not protect the King? At length he received orders from the Commune of Paris to request the King to take up residence in the capital and when he left for Versailles he had with him some of their representatives. He set out with three companies of Grenadiers, one company of Fusiliers, three cannon and twenty thousand officers and men of the National Guard.

By this time the King, surrounded as he was, would have had to fly secretly, if he had wanted to do so. He decided against taking such a risk. Instead he visited the Assembly and gave his approval to the decrees of 4 August and those parts of the Constitution that had already been passed, thus awarding a victory to the women of Paris that the men of the Assembly had been unable to achieve. Then, thinking that trouble was over for good, he sent a message to La Fayette telling him that his services were not now needed. Apparently the King knew nothing of the orders which La Fayette carried.

Meanwhile the regiment of women continued to occupy the Assembly and to drown all debate with cries for bread. The President of the Assembly, at his wit's end, sent out not only for bread but for wine. An orgy was soon in progress.

When La Fayette reached Versailles about eleven o'clock, he too made for the Assembly. He told his audience that he planned to see the King, to secure from the King the withdrawal of the Flanders Regiment and support from him for the tricolour. The French Guard, which had betrayed its allegiance in Paris in July, were stationed round the palace. The National Guard would see to order in the town and on the following day the Flanders Regiment would resume the tricolour cockade. The royal family went to bed, so did La Fayette. The crowd slept in what shelter they could find, amid falling rain.

At five in the morning they were on the move again and one prowler found that the palace gate leading to the Court of the Princes, which had been handed over to the French Guards, was unwatched. At once the crowd broke in and attacked the bodyguards on the staircase leading to the royal apartments. The Queen in a shift and petticoat, her stockings in her hand, fled up the secret staircase leading from her bedroom to that of King. Two guards, who were unable to withdraw into the royal apartments quickly enough, were cut to pieces. La Fayette, awake now, urged the King to promise to return to Paris. Already the crowd who had lost a day's work by their journey to Versailles, were hinting that if they did not take back the King with them to Paris they would have La Fayette's head instead. And so in an act of courage the King, Queen and the children appeared on the balcony to assure the crowd that indeed they would return to the capital.

A moment or two later, as if threatening to shoot her, the crowd demanded that the Queen should reappear without her children. But they cheered as she faced them again composedly and in company with La Fayette. It took the National Guard wearing tricolour cockades to clear the crowds from the palace.

The Assembly, hearing what was afoot, declared that it was inseparable from the King and decided to send a strong delegation with him to the capital. A few hours later the convoy was ready to leave. An advance guard went ahead carrying with them on pikes the heads of the two royal guards as evidence that their mission had been satisfactorily accomplished. Two hours later the main procession of nearly thirty thousand set out. The National Guard first with bread stuck like trophies on bayonets, then came the bodyguard now disarmed, the Swiss Guards and the Flanders Regiment, all fraternizing together. La Fayette rode beside the royal carriages. Carriages carrying one hundred Assemblymen followed, then some National Guards and finally the straggling crowds.

Women carried pikes or, when they could not get these, branches of poplar trees to wave. Some sat astride gun barrels or on wagons of grain decorated with leaves, as if to prove the truth of what the crowd was saying—that they had brought with them the head baker, the baker's wife and the baker's errand boy back to Paris so that the people should have enough bread.

They did not reach Paris until after dark when the rain which had held off during a fine and sunny autumn day began to fall again. The King was taken first to the Hôtel de Ville and then to the Tuileries. At Versailles they began to pull down the blinds. There would be no more hunting for the King.

Chapter 4

THE ESCAPE FAILS

AND now came failure by the bourgeois lawyers of France, the main leaders of the Revolution, to form a constitutional monarchy. Having prompted the Revolution they wanted to put an end to it. Earlier they had watched unmoved while the philosophers, encouraged by the nobility, attacked the absolute monarchy and while the nobility attacked the royal Government by withholding revenue from it. Throughout France they had profited from mob attacks on royal officials whose appointments they then took over. They had watched the feudal uprisings of the peasantry crush the Nobility of the Sword.

And now it was time to call a halt . . . to draw breath and to prepare a Constitution with a King as its figure-head, a form of rule which would do honour to France and to the bourgeoisie who now ruled the land. But it was already too late, for one very simple reason; they distrusted the *menu peuple*—the minor people—who had helped to free them.

The Assembly did not leave Versailles for Paris until a fortnight after the King arrived there. Having seen what the Paris mob could do, the deputies faced the change with some misgivings. It was one thing for the *King* to be taken prisoner. But the members of the National Assembly had not left their homes in order to suffer the same fate. In fact about three hundred of them, including some of the ablest, decided that it was time for them to hurry home since from all accounts there was plenty that needed putting right there.

The eight hundred bold spirits that remained, reassembled first in the residence of the Archbishop of Paris, in a room so long and narrow that they could hardly circulate. Moreover, their constant admirers, the people, flocked to see them in such large numbers that the supports of the gallery eventually gave way, depositing the public on the heads of the deputies and severely injuring Deputy Viard from Lorraine.

Next, on 9 November, the deputies moved to the Royal Riding School, or Manège, north of the Tuileries gardens and reached through a narrow passage from the rue St Honoré or through a walled courtyard from the rue Dauphin. In modern terms it lay between the rue St Honoré and the rue de Rivoli near the rue de Castiglione.

The Manège had been built by Louis XV to encourage horseman-ship but was seldom used since it possessed no resident instructors. It too was a long and narrow hall and far from ideal for the pur-poses of the Assembly. However, six rows of benches were placed on each side of the hall with a kind of elipse between them. The President sat in the middle of the south side of the hall nearest to the Tuileries gardens and faced the orator who spoke from a tribune or platform opposite. As before, the Assembly's meeting place was overcrowded. The ventilation was poor and vinegar had periodi-cally to be sprinkled to freshen the air. Public demand for seats in the gallery was so brisk that those prepared to arrive early could make a steady living by selling their places to the late-comers. But at least there were boxes for the Press, a bar and café on the ground floor, a restaurant upstairs and plenty of other eating places, such as the Café du Perron, the Glacier des Feuillants and Chez Pascale, for the deputies who were not afraid to stroll abroad.

These improvements were not enough, however, to secure the dignity of the Assembly. Members who failed to please their masters sitting in the public galleries were pelted with rotten fruit and, in times of crisis, the gallery audience was artificially inspired by agents hired by the political leaders to guide the Assembly in its deliberations.

It was still impossible to prevent deputations from calling and wasting the Assembly's time on trivialities and anyone, without warning, could propose a motion on any subject. Discipline was lax and neither the President's bell nor the ushers' calls for silence produced any great effect. The orators continued to base their style on that used in the theatre, the pulpit or the Academy and rational discussion seldom took place outside the thirty-one standing committees set up to deal with various aspects of Government business. These committees resembled to some degree the Government Ministries of today—except for two serious deficiencies. They had, in the first place, to deal with a Civil Service that was reactionary in character and therefore obstructive; and secondly they were not chosen by the King nor were they in his confidence. (It would have been as much as their lives were worth to have been palace favourites.)

Neither the Assembly nor its committees succeeded in winning the full confidence of the future political leaders of France. Indeed its business was rehearsed in advance in political clubs which acted as 'shadow Parliaments'. Nothing shows more clearly the improvised hand-to-mouth character of the French Revolution.

It was in these clubs that speeches to be made the following day in the Assembly were tried out. There were debates, self-criticism, denunciation and expulsion for those showing signs of deviation from the people's will. Petitions were read. Counter-arguments brought forward—until an agreed position was reached. The most famous of the political clubs was the Jacobin Club. This grew out of a merger between the association of Breton deputies and the Society of Friends of the Constitution which included other deputies from Anjou and the Franche Comté. Meetings were held at first in the library of the Dominican Convent in the rue St Honoré but later in the church of St Jacques (belonging to the same Foundation) which gave the club its nickname. Meetings were not restricted to members of the Assembly and Dominican friars attended some of the earlier gatherings. The general public and even foreigners were allowed to attend the debates if suitably vouched for. Thus the Jacobins became a kind of National Research Committee and a centre for the rectification of abuses. It was not long before the Jacobins founded branch clubs in the provinces to

whom they circulated letters explaining Jacobin policy and sug-
gesting ways of carrying it out.

The Cordeliers Club on the left bank in the Faubourg St Marceau
area was next in importance after the Jacobins. Founded in April
1790 as the Amis des Droits de l'Homme et du Citoyen, the club
got its name from the fact that it had occupied the church and later
the refectory of the Franciscan Friary in the rue des Cordeliers. The
Cordeliers was a more popular club and at times more extreme than
the Jacobins. It was the Cordeliers who, after the King's flight, invaded the Jacobins and demanded that the King should be replaced. Danton made his name in the Cordeliers and so did Ana-
charcis Clootz, a Prussian Baron who called himself the First
Citizen of the world. The club met about three times a week to discuss new motions, forthcoming decrees and the work of Government Committees. Its badge was an Eye of Vigilance. Those attending needed a card signed by the local district office confirming that
they were 'good citizens'.

There were many other political clubs ranging from the Societé
des Ennemis du Despotisme, through the Club des Halles to the
Club des Indigents, the Fraternal Society of the Two Sexes, and the
feminist Societé des Citoyennes Républicaines Révolutionaires.

Newspapers grew to be influential at this period of the Revolution, and deputies found that they could get better publicity for
themselves and their causes by running their own daily or weekly.
Many of the newspapers were one-man affairs containing perhaps
a single article written by the editor himself in a spare half-hour in
some café.

Here for example is an article written by Jean-Paul Marat
in *L'Ami du Peuple*. The piece attacked the Assembly bitterly,
and La Fayette, after reading it, issued an order for Marat's
arrest.

> Frenchmen! Free and frivolous people! Will you never dis-
> cern the evils that threaten you? Will you always fall asleep on
> the very edge of the abyss?
>
> Thanks to the blindness of your former rulers, to the laxity of
> the enemies of the State, and to a conjunction of unexpected
> events, you have broken your chains and have arms in your
> hands. But instead of seeking unwearyingly to punish the public
> enemies, you have handed yourselves over to the rule of feeble or

corrupt men who are striving to save those enemies from your just vengeance and to bring them back among you. . . .

Light-hearted people, abandon yourselves to rejoicing, run to the Temples, preserve the music of your songs of triumph, and weary the Heavens with your dancing, for benefits that you do not enjoy. You have no more tyrants, but you still suffer the results of tyranny. You have no more masters but don't you still feel the evils of oppression? You have only a mirage of happiness and are further away than ever from the real thing. And why the self congratulation?

From end to end of the kingdom the country is in travail and convulsions, you are in a state of misfortune, your workshops are empty, your production abandoned, your commerce stagnant, your finances ruined, your troops disbanded. . . .

Reflect carefully. The political machine never rights itself without violent shake-ups just as the air is never cleared except by a storm. So let us gather in the public squares and agree on the means of saving the State: but alas would we still succeed in recognizing them? The source of our present troubles is that the committees who rule us are too numerous and too devoid of wise men: then the cohorts serve only to spread disorder everywhere. . . . The sole means of eradicating our evils is to purge the committees of men whose principles are suspect or dangerous, of men who hold some post or pension from the Government. Let us ask the National Senate, too, to purge itself, and let the Senate's first decree declare that anyone who receives any benefit from the Court or who converts the glory of serving his country into an exercise in speculation is declared incapable of sitting. Let every member who has a post or a pension from the Court, be invited to return them: let every member make it a point of honour not to receive any favour from the Court until ten years after the end of the session in which he sat. If the Senate refuses to purge itself, let the powers of the deputies in whom one can no longer place confidence (they are known, the voice of the public openly declares their names) be revoked by the constituents and let men of true merit be called in their place.

The present Estates General have been formed on the basis of the bad principles of feudalism; now that there is but one class of citizens in the kingdom—now that the sacred hierarchy of the nobility no longer sits there as a privileged class, let there be

admitted only those who have shown evidence of their patriotic
zeal and let the National Assembly, reduced to a quarter of its
size be made up uniquely of enlightened and virtuous men.

Government by character-assassination had already begun. But
Marat, who had helped to popularize it, had to go into hiding and
work underground for three years afterwards.

The Palace of the Tuileries where the King now found himself
was outwardly imposing. It had formerly been the château of
Catherine de Médici, mother of three French Kings, and consisted
of two pavilions flanking a massive central block seven storeys
high. But despite its magnificence galore and three private theatres,
it had been neglected by Louis XVI, and had been turned into
grace and favour apartments for pensioners, needy artists and
deserving widows. Passages had been blocked off, extra walls built
and staircases cut; vast assembly-rooms were divided to make
separate flats. And unfortunately, as with most conversions, there
were disadvantages. For although there were now many more
rooms than when the palace had been built, the number of chimneys remained the same, with the result that the palace was badly
heated and also badly ventilated. It was freezing in winter and
baking in the summer. Despite its size (and the fact that many of
its tenants had moved out) the Tuileries Palace was not big enough
to hold the newcomers. Some courtiers had to live and sleep in a
single room and the billiard-room became a dormitory. The lack of
comfort soon communicated itself from the servants and courtiers,
who had to suffer from it, to the King himself.

His own way of life too had suffered a change. He had had to
give up his only real interest—hunting. For the Assembly could not
take the responsibility of letting him take to the woods without a
strong posse of guards, who would have disturbed the game. Besides there were peasants who still thought that the good King had
gone to Paris to escape from the seigneurs, and who would have
been disappointed to know that he was a prisoner of the burghers.
It was all very unfortunate, because while Bailly spent most of his
day making arrangements to see that Paris did not starve, the
King, for want of exercise, grew fatter and fatter.

At first Mirabeau thought that he could turn the King into a
monarch of the type seen in England. Through a King's man, the
Comte de la Marck, Mirabeau, in return for his debts being paid,

sent the King a series of carefully thought out 'State Papers'—
policy suggestions full of good sense. The King, he thought, should
refuse to accept foreign help to restore his position. He should call
on patriotic Frenchmen to do the job. But he did not dare to act
openly as adviser to the Crown for fear of losing his influence in
the Assembly. And neither the King nor the Queen really trusted
him.

La Fayette too saw himself as the saviour of the monarchy, but
the National Guard which he commanded became less and less
popular with the crowds and the Assembly turned to him only as a
policeman who could protect them from the tyranny of the mob.

The King himself made some efforts of his own to keep in step
with the march of time. In February 1790 he declared himself to
be the leader of the Revolution without however providing an atom
of leadership. The Assembly found it useful to have the royal support for their decrees and in June 1790 were happy to approve
annual grants of twenty-five million livres to the King for the upkeep of his palaces and of four million livres for the Queen if she
should survive him.

However, much of the goodwill which Louis earned was thrown
away in August when the sale of the crown property for the benefit
of the nation was being considered and the King asked that all his
palaces, including those which he never used, should be exempted.

That summer saw the first anniversary of the Fall of the Bastille
and an enormous festival in Paris to celebrate it. Delegations from
every corner of the country were invited to Paris to pledge before
the altar of the nation, set up on the Champ de Mars, that at
last France, instead of being a conglomeration of provinces held
together by the Kings who had conquered them, was a single
federated nation unified by the loyalty of Frenchmen towards each
other. Fifteen hundred enthusiasts came from Brittany alone.

The people of Paris, who acted as hosts to the visitors or *fédérés*
as they were called, were busy for weeks beforehand on preparations for the great day. Their houses were decorated with green
branches and flowers. La Fayette himself helped in the construction
of the vast amphitheatre nine hundred yards long and of the turf
seats that surrounded it. David, the brilliant artist and pageant
master of the Revolution, had devised the spectacle and posters
announcing the detailed arrangements were to be seen in all parts
of the capital.

At seven in the morning the vast procession including representatives of the Assembly, the city of Paris, of the National Guard,
the Army and the Departments set out in disciplined ranks from
the site of the Bastille. A giant balloon decorated with the symbols
of patriotism was released. The procession made its way across the
capital, crossed the Seine over a bridge of boats specially built for
the purpose, and proceeded to the Champ de Mars. When all the
units had taken up their correct position there, Mass was sung by the
choir of Notre-Dame accompanied by one thousand two hundred
musicians and celebrated by the Bishop of Autun, better known
as Talleyrand, while four hundred priests wearing white robes decorated with the tricolour sash stood by. The banners of the eighty-
three Departments into which France had been divided were blessed.

A deep silence followed while La Fayette as Commander of the
National Guard was carried shoulder high to the altar to take the
oath on behalf of himself and the troops and the *fédérés*: 'We
swear eternal fidelity to the nation, the law and the King; to maintain to the utmost of our power the Constitution decreed by the
National Assembly, and accepted by the King; and to remain
united with every Frenchman by the indissoluble ties of fraternity.'
This was followed by a ceremonial salute of forty guns and cries of
'*Vive la Nation!*' and '*Vive le Roi!*' The President of the Assembly
took the same oath which was repeated by all the deputies.

Here would have been a chance for Louis to show himself as
King of the French. He should surely have been the first of his
countrymen to swear on the altar of the nation to preserve its
liberties. Instead the King contented himself by taking the oath
from where he sat, in a voice that carried only for a few yards. It
was said that he had deputed La Fayette to go first to the altar
because it was raining, though, as some pointed out, he had not
been known to forego hunting because of a shower. And he did not
even make a speech. The omission did not pass unnoticed.

Meanwhile in the nine months that had passed since the Assembly
had moved to Paris a great deal of work had been done towards
making a Constitution. It was put together piecemeal in the form of
a series of enactments which came into force as soon as they had
been approved by the Assembly, which was now called the Constituent Assembly, or simply the Constituent, because of its con-
stitution-making activities.

Sovereignty, the Constituent decided, resided in the nation

and the general will of the nation was expressed in laws passed by the Assembly. The responsibility for carrying out the general will was allotted to the King as the Chief Executive. His office was hereditary. He retained the right to appoint all ambassadors, and some ministers who must, however, not be chosen from the Assembly. He could withhold his approval from some laws for a limited period although this did not apply to financial bills, impeachments or proclamations by the Assembly to the Nation which could override the veto. The King kept the right to declare war and direct foreign policy but such decisions had to be approved in advance by the Assembly. His own person was declared to be inviolable.

The Assembly kept control of the armed forces and the money needed to maintain them. Moreover, in any case of dispute it retained the right to declare how the Constitution should be interpreted. The Assembly was to consist of a single Chamber (no House of Lords for the French) which would sit for two years at a time. It could not be dissolved by the King. It was to contain 745 members for France proper and a number of additional delegates for the French Colonies.

The Departments into which France had been split were named after local rivers, mountains and other natural features which fostered local pride and helped the countrymen of France to forget that they were once Normans, Bretons or Bearnais of different racial stocks. The Departments were sub-divided into communes (districts) and still smaller cantons. Paris too was reorganized and the sixty districts with their bodies of Electors were replaced by forty-eight Sections.

The customs barriers no longer followed the boundaries of internal provinces but were moved up to the frontiers. Indirect taxes were abolished and salt no longer had to be transported only along certain scheduled roads of the country at certain fixed times.

Tax farms were closed and thus all the revenue collected went directly to the State (though for the time being things were tighter because the Treasury had to make do without the advances on receipts that had formerly been paid by the farms).

One other score remained to be settled in the battle of the bourgeois for power. It will be remembered that in the days before the Revolution, the Parliaments in various parts of France (composed of Nobles of the Robe who had bought their positions as

hereditary magistrates) had posed as guardians of the public welfare against the tyranny of the Crown, but that later, in common
with the other nobles, they had resisted the merger of the Three
Estates in the National Assembly at Versailles. So, in retaliation
for this betrayal of the bourgeois cause, in November 1789 the
Assembly sent the Parliaments off on permanent vacation. They
were never heard of again.

In other ways too justice was streamlined. Judges were hence-
forward elected. Open debate in court was permitted. A jury system
was introduced. Protestants were allowed the same civil rights as
Catholics. No arrest could be made without a judge's order unless
the culprit had been caught in the act of committing the crime. And
within twenty-four hours of the arrest the judge must make
arrangements for the accused to be provided with a Counsel. But
the ghastly punishment of being broken on the wheel was still retained.

In other respects the Constitution fell short of being a people's
charter. It gave political rights—including the right to vote only to
those 'active citizens' who paid taxes equivalent to three days'
work. And even these voters could not themselves choose deputies
to the Assembly. They could vote only for Electors who paid the
equivalent of ten days' work and who chose the deputies. The
deputies needed a tax qualification equivalent to fifty-two days'
work. So it was still a long way short of a People's Democracy.
Soldiers could not vote—until they had completed sixteen years'
service—and members of the National Guard only if serving at
their own expense. About one-third of the electorate was thus dis-
qualified.

Later, other not-so-democratic decrees threatened to suppress
the political clubs altogether if they exercised influence on elections
or interfered in public affairs. Other conservative tendencies remained unchecked.

La Fayette virtually excluded the Parisian man in the street
from his National Guard by compelling all volunteers to pay for
a none-too-cheap uniform. Passive citizens—those not paying
taxes to the value of three days' work—were excluded from the
National Guard after May 1791. The Government did not dare to
purge the Army of its royalist officers. Nor did it trust the people.
A law was passed outlawing strikes. Group petitions were banned.
Trade guilds were considered to be a barrier interposed between

the Government and its subjects and were therefore banned as well. Furthermore, as will later appear, the new Constitution was never submitted to the people for ratification. When they had come to the end of their labours in September 1791, the Constituent Assembly merely dissolved itself in preparations for new elections (under the new Constitution) of a Legislative Assembly.

These contrasting elements in the Constitution—radical on the one side and conservative on the other—reflected the emergence of conflicting parties within the Constituent. For example, Jacques de Cazalès, an ex-cavalry officer and one of the ablest speakers on the right wing of the Assembly, was not afraid to say, 'Let us attack the tyranny of the people as well as the tyranny of Kings.' and Adrien Duport, Antoine Barnave and Charles de Lameth, three of the ablest members of the Assembly, called for the King to be given more power than he was actually granted in the final Constitution. They planned to increase the amount of the property which citizens needed in order to qualify as Electors, to introduce an upper House and to allow members of the Assembly, i.e. their own friends, to become ministers. They also hoped to keep themselves in power by allowing deputies who had sat in the Constituent Assembly to be elected to the Legislative Assembly which was to replace it after the Constitution had been agreed. Royalist newspapers such as *L'Ami du Roi* and the *Petit Gauthier* were on sale and were not above attacking the Assembly on the ground that it had never been given a mandate to sit beyond a year from May 1789. The paper known as the *Logographe* was founded with money provided by the Court. And the *Feuille du Jour* was able in December 1790 to write a spirited attack on the Revolution: 'A King without a Crown, an Assembly without repute, troops without obedience, finances without credit, a monarchy without order, a thousand conflicting opinions without any public spirit, such is at this moment our position.'

But the early leaders of the Revolution, however distrustful of the mob, had no doubts whatever about the need for overthrowing the nobility. In June 1790 titles, liveries and armorial bearings were declared illegal; the preposition 'de' in surnames banned. No individual was to be addressed in future as 'Your Highness' or 'Your Eminence', and coats of arms on buildings could be forcibly removed in Paris after a period of one month and in the provinces after three months. No incense was to be burnt except in churches.

It was in 1790 that the famous revolutionary song *Ah! ça ira*
appeared. The melody was heard first about the time of the
federation celebrations on the first anniversary of the Fall of the
Bastille, under the title of *Le Carillon National*. It was simply a
tune written for the Contredanse or Square Dance and at first had
no words. They soon followed.

> Ah! ça ira, ça ira, ça ira
> Le peuple en ce jour sans cesse repète:
> Ah! ça ira, ça ira, ça ira,
> Malgré les mutins tout réussira!
>
> Nos ennemis confus en restent là
> Et nous allons chanter Alléluya!
> Ah! ça ira, ça ira, ça ira. . . .

Later came some even more characteristic sentiments:

> Celui qui s'élève, on l'abaissera,
> Celui qui s'abaisse, on l'élèvera.
> Ah! ça ira, ça ira, ça ira. . . .

Democracy spread to the theatre where Marie-Joseph Chénier's
play *Charles IX* recalled the King who had led France into the wars
of religion and had given the signal for the Massacre of St Bartholomew's Eve. The play was a thinly veiled attack on monarchy as an
institution.

Soon authors no longer bothered to put their words into the
mouths of classical or historical characters in order to beat the
censor. They started to write contemporary dramas on such subjects as the Storming of the Bastille. Talma, the French actor who
was afterwards to delight Napoleon, was the first of a new school of
'natural' players—and incidentally a supporter of the Revolution.

But all these straws in the wind would not have prevented
France from having had a constitutional monarchy—if the King
too had played his part. Instead of which he tried to run away
with his family.

Various arguments have been put forward to justify the royal
flight. Certainly the Tuileries had become little better than a prison
and the royal family dreaded the thought of spending another
winter there, amid the deadly monotony of ceremonial impotence.
But there was also the fact that the King was gradually losing

his influence abroad. The émigrés who had abandoned all their
possessions in order to preserve France from the tyranny of the
people were beginning to take over the leading parts in the counter-
revolutionary movement. Indeed the émigrés were threatening to
invade France and restore the old order of things, and were making
it impossible for the King to get on good terms with his subjects. In time he would undoubtedly have been in danger of his
life—especially if any attempt had been made to rescue him. And
the longer Louis continued to live in Paris and to acquiesce in the
new order, the less influence he would possess over the people of
France.

It has also been urged with some justice that the King's conscience was shocked by the treatment of the clergy in France and
by his weakness in having consented to it, and this perhaps is the
most charitable explanation for his decision to free himself.

At first there had been no differences on religious doctrine between the clergy and the Assembly. But the Church as an organization ran counter to the philosophy of the Revolution. There was
first of all a general prejudice against any kind of corporation—
even a religious one. Voltaire had attacked the fanaticism of any
faith that could lead to wars of religion. The Church was also vul-
nerable both because it denied the perfectability of man and because it claimed the right to teach.

Consequently the Assembly were not prepared to declare the
Catholic faith to be the State religion. It was generally admitted,
moreover, that the leaders of the Church were over-privileged and
had failed to provide adequately for the curés whose ministrations
were of most value to the people at large. And it was obvious that
since the State had deprived the clergy of the right to collect
tithes, it must now provide for the clergy from the national
treasury. Accordingly, in November 1789, the Assembly passed a
decree declaring that all Church possessions were at the disposal
of the nation, that no individual was to hold more than one appointment and that every curate was in future to be paid not less
than one thousand two hundred livres a year. With all this money
to be found from somewhere it was unthinkable for the State to
leave land reputed to be worth four hundred million livres in the
hands of a Church which was ultimately controlled from outside
the country.

Not long after this Necker, who was still Finance Minister,

announced the failure of the two latest attempts to raise money by loans, and the natural idea occurred to the financial wizards of the Assembly that the Church lands could be sold in order to raise the necessary funds. But of course the land could not be sold merely by passing laws and the Assembly hit on a splendid idea for anticipating the money that the nation would receive. Cash certificates known as assignats would be issued by the Government in payment of the debts that it owed, and the assignats could be bought and used by anyone for the purchase of the Church property.

The idea shocked Necker so much that he resigned his office and this time there was no move to prevent him from leaving the country.

The Assembly, having undertaken to pay for the upkeep of the Church, took care that those serving it should be good patriots. Formerly the King had chosen the bishops. From now on they were to be elected instead of being chosen by the King, by the Electors (including laymen) of the Department in which the see was situated and were to be confirmed by a senior bishop in the presence of two notaries. The Departmental authorities were made responsible for discipline and there would be only one bishop per Department. Monastic foundations were suppressed unless they ran schools or charities (and were closed down later even if they did). And these too were not to recruit new members. Those who gave up their calling to return to civil life were guaranteed a pension.

The curates were still allowed to keep the records of births, deaths and marriages and to perform the necessary ceremonies, but not to charge for them.

Louis was prepared to regard these changes as purely administrative measures taken for financial reasons and gave his consent to them in August 1790.

No difficulties were expected from Pope Pius VI. The Church had been reorganized both in Poland and in Russia without any protests from Rome. Most of the reformers were convinced that the Pope's rights were limited to matters of doctrine and they never supposed that he would want to interfere in the day-to-day administration of the French clergy.

Meanwhile the State had decided to call for reassurances that the clergy would be prepared to place their loyalty to the State above all other ties. A decree proposed by a deputy named Voidel

compelled bishops and curés to swear loyalty to the Constitution.
They were to swear the oath within ten days of November 1790 when
the decree became valid if they were in their home diocese, within
a month if they were elsewhere in France and within two months if
absent from the country.

The oath was to be sworn publicly by each cleric after Mass on
Sunday in the presence of the local Council. If no oath was taken
the Mayor, or other leading official, was held responsible for replacing the erring priest. Those attending services of unsworn
priests were to be treated as disturbers of the public peace.

The proposal was strongly supported by those deputies who suspected that the priests were counter-revolutionaries in disguise,
and who hoped that those who refused the oath would be exposed
as traitors. After all, why should priests if they are patriots object
to taking the same kind of oaths as were sworn by policemen or
soldiers?

But already in October the clergy had become worried at being
forced into a quarrel with the Pope. Mgr Boisgelin, Archbishop of
Aix in his *Exposé des Principes du Clergé sur la Constitution Civile*
warned that many of the clergy would have objections to taking
the oath, particularly since the Constitution had not yet been completed. This soon became apparent in the Assembly itself where a
number of bishops publicly refused to swear allegiance. Others
made reservations or retracted their oaths later, and in the church
of St Sulpice in Paris the organist had to play *Ça ira* on the organ
at full blast to quiet the congregation after the curé had preached
a sermon attacking the Assembly. One hundred and twenty-five
bishops supported the Archbishop of Aix's report. Only four
beneficed bishops took the oath—Sens, Orléans, Viviers and Autun
together with three others whose work lay *in partibus infidelium* at
Lydda, Babylon and Trajanopolis.

One of the most difficult problems was to find new clergy to
replace those who refused to take the oath. Talleyrand, the
Bishop of Autun, ordained new prelates for the sees of Soissons and
Quimper before he was personally excommunicated by the Pope
and so the apostolic succession was preserved. In the lower ranks
some of the new recruits came from the monasteries, others were
promoted deacons.

In the spring of 1791 the Pope, pressed perhaps by other Catholic
powers, declared publicly that these changes, which cancelled the

authority which he wielded over the bishops by Canon Law and which suppressed most of the monastic orders, were unacceptable.

The King found himself in as great a dilemma as any of the French clergy. He tried to satisfy his conscience by persuading himself that all priests would have been massacred if he had not agreed to the reorganization of the Church, but he was not prepared to receive the sacrament from a priest who had taken the oath and defied the Pope.

The final provocation that may have decided the royal family to fly came shortly before Easter in 1791 when the King wished to travel across Paris to his place at St Cloud, as he had done the previous year, in order to hear Mass there from a priest who had not taken the oath. The good people of Paris would not permit this and not even La Fayette could persuade them to let the King's coach leave the Tuileries. The royal family may have felt with reason that La Fayette's influence over the people of Paris was declining and that he could no longer be relied on to secure their safety.

However the flight was no impulsive action taken in the heat of the moment. It was a carefully and deliberately planned project kept on ice until the right moment came along. As far back as November 1789 Louis, in a letter to King Charles IV of Spain, had repudiated concessions extracted from him by force and the Spanish Ambassador, Count de Fernan Nuñez, was fully informed of the King's plans to regain his freedom.

The possiblity that the King might want to take leave of his good people had not been overlooked in Paris. Indeed a decree had been passed in March 1791 enjoining the King to reside within twenty leagues of the Assembly when sitting.

On 19 April, the day after he had been stopped from going to St Cloud, the King appeared before the Assembly and protested his loyalty to that body. He undertook to order French ambassadors at all missions to deny that he was unhappy in Paris or wanted to be rescued.

Louis had to choose between a number of possible ways of regaining his freedom. Certainly he could count on support abroad not only from those who feared that the Revolution would spread to their own domains but also from the family connections of Marie Antoinette. The Emperor Leopold was her brother, one sister governed the Netherlands and another ruled in Naples. Mirabeau on the other hand had advised the King to regain power by civil war if need be, rather than by seeking help abroad, since a foreign invasion of France would turn every Frenchman into an enemy of the monarchy.

Louis hoped to get the best of both worlds by putting himself at the head of loyal (to him) French troops near the eastern frontier of the country. And the Marquis de Bouillé who had earned praise from the Assembly for putting down the great mutiny of Nancy a year before, persuaded the Austrians to make a feint attack towards the frontier to give him an excuse for concentrating his own troops in the area near Sedan where the King would make his headquarters.

Marat who, with all the illogicality of the typical French revolutionary, wished to preserve a limited monarchy, wrote on 17 February 1791:

> The true and only way of saving yourselves from the terrible misfortunes which would follow the flight of the King is to have weapons of war delivered to you . . . seize the Post Offices for as long as they are not in your hands you have no way of letting your brothers in the provinces know of the dangers threatening the capital. Send couriers to warn the municipalities of neighbouring Departments for twenty leagues around; warn the National Guards of this terrible plan so that they are called to arms and halt without distinction all carriages drawing away from the capital.

A week later in another piece castigating the people for their stupidity he wrote:

> Deaf to my voice you have gone to sleep in the arms of your enemies and now that they are ready to eat you are alarmed at the dangers that threaten you and you do nothing to extricate yourselves from them. You have allowed the King's aunts to escape [this was true] and perhaps the Dauphin with them [this was untrue]; the King's brother is getting ready to fly in his turn . . . the King himself and his wife will escape in the end. . . . I tremble to think of the bad times that await you: the King will be hardly across the frontier before the enemy legions will advance towards our homes to make rivers of blood run . . . no one will be spared, men, women, children and your representatives themselves will be the first victims.

However, these things could not be arranged in the twinkling of an eye and in any case it was thought advisable not to start before 12 June when the King would have received his next quarterly allowance from the Assembly. And even then the flight had to be deferred for some days until a maid whose loyalty was suspect had been replaced.

The leading organizer in the conspiracy was handsome and romantic, a Swedish aristocrat, Count Axel Fersen, then thirty-five years old, who had first met the Queen at a masked ball at the Opera House when he was a young man of eighteen. It was said that he remained in love with her ever since, and his relatives considered that certain phrases used by the Queen in her letters to him were so compromising that they eventually burnt the correspondence. The curious have speculated for centuries the exact relations between Fersen and the Queen. Those with strong royalist sympathies have refused to believe ill of the Queen; others have been only too pleased to believe that she was unfaithful. Fersen was certainly a lady's man and during the five years that he fought in the American War of Independence he became engaged to a Miss Catherine Lyell who afterwards married the 4th Earl de la Warr. He was friendly, too, with Miss Sullivan who was also a good friend of the Prince Regent of England and, since returning from America, he appeared to have been on intimate terms with at least one other lady of the Court, to judge by a series of unsigned letters from her to him in which she warned him of the dangers of his association with the Queen.

Historians are often reluctant to admit that love affairs shrouded in the impalpable sentiments of two individuals, the potence of which can be assessed only by conjecture, might influence the true pattern of history or the logical cause of events. They distrust attempts to confer historical significance on the actions of individuals whose motives are so far removed from those of statesmen or generals.

All that we can say is that the Queen and Fersen wrote to one another as if they had been lovers and apparently behaved as lovers almost as if the world did not exist around them. We know too that Valentin Esterhazy, the Governor of Valenciennes, for instance, was privy to this relationship. La Fayette probably knew of it too.

At six o'clock on the evening of 20 June Fersen left the Tuileries where he had been discussing the final details of the escape and betook himself to the rue Clichy to the house of Quintin Crawfurd, an eccentric Scottish art collector who was also in the secret of the projected flight. A large travelling coach or Berline painted dark green and yellow designed to conceal the travellers as far as possible had been built for the job and had been left for the past day and a half in Crawfurd's stables. Fersen saw that the coach was loaded up with trunks, parcels and provisions including a dish of Boeuf à la Mode, five bottles of water and some still champagne. Then he sent the Berline off with his own coachman Balthazar Sapel and two trusty ex-bodyguards to wait outside the barrier of St Martin.

Fersen next disguised himself as a coachman and hired an ancient cab. He then waited with other cabbies in the Cour des Princes at the back of the south wing of the Tuileries. Soon after dinner, at about ten, the Queen slipped out of the drawing-room, woke the Dauphin and his sister and had them dressed. She brought the Dauphin (disguised as a girl), his sister, Madame Royale, and their governess, Madame de Tourzel, through the palace, avoiding the sentries by passing through the empty rooms of an émigré courtier. Then Marie Antoinette returned to rejoin her husband, Madame Elisabeth her sister-in-law, and Monsieur, the King's brother, and his wife, who as usual had been dining at the Tuileries, in the drawing-room. Soon afterwards the party broke up to go to bed.

At least that was what the National Guard thought who were watching the gates leading from the palace and the gardens and so did the six hundred picked men from the city Sections who padded up and down the courtyards, the corridors, the staircases, the rooms and even the kitchens of the Tuileries day and night. But meanwhile Fersen after making sure that he was not followed doubled back along the rue St Honoré to a back street near the former gate of the royal stables where he waited for the rest of the party. Two of the three prisoners, the Queen and Madame Elisabeth, who all their lives had been accustomed never to move without attendants, managed the journey on their own. The King made the most sensational getaway of all. La Fayette, who had been warned that the royal family might be thinking of escaping, himself attended the coucher and had reinforced the guards at the palace. At the end of the coucher after the public had retired, the bolts of the private apartments were shut home, and the King prepared to retire for the night with the help of two valets one of whom, Lemoine, actually slept in the same room. The King undressed and was seen to bed by Lemoine who drew the Chinese silk curtains before himself retiring into the next room to undress. This gave the King the chance he needed. Louis slipped noiselessly out of bed and into the Dauphin's empty room, threw on an inconspicuous suit and a hat with a rounded brim and made off.

Behind him the silk curtains slipped back into place. Lemoine returned to the royal bedroom in his night-shirt, suspecting nothing, and conscientiously attached to his wrist the emergency cord for the King to pull when he needed anything. The King walked across the courtyard cane in hand without being challenged. Madame Elisabeth, in a dark costume and veiled hat, had already reached the carriage. The Queen, in a grey silk dress, short black coat and a black hat with a trailing violet, came last.

Everything in Paris seems to have been organized down to the last detail . . . even to the extent of giving Madame de Tourzel a note in the King's own hand confirming that she was taking the royal children away by royal command so that if discovered during the first stage of the escape she would be blameless. The royal party were lucky too with their weather. It was a very dark night.

From Paris the route across France had been carefully planned in advance. But it involved risks. The King did not want to travel north-eastwards through Rheims to Sedan and Montmédy because he had been crowned in Rheims and he felt there was a greater chance of his being recognized there.

An alternative route led due east to Metz through Verdun but this was little better because the citizens of Verdun were notorious for their strongly revolutionary views. Therefore it was decided to branch off northwards from the main road to Metz after Clermont-en-Argonne and proceed across side roads to Thonnelle near Montmédy.

Châlons was the only city of any size on their route and shortly after it at Pont-de-Somme-Vesle they would be met by sixty Dragoons and forty Hussars under the command of the Duc de Choiseul-Stainville, Colonel of the Royal Dragoons. At the following two relay points Ste-Ménehould and Clermont there would be dragoons commanded by Captain d'Andoins and M. de Damas, and from there there would be escorts at each village to guide the party to the midst of Bouillé's army. One of the trusty bodyguards was

to ride permanently ahead to arrange for fresh horses to be ready
at each relay post, and extra horses had been sent to Varennes and
villages beyond where there were no post stations from which the
King could hire new horses.

The royal family travelled under a passport provided by the
French Foreign Office at the request of the Russian Minister in
Paris for a certain Baroness Korff, two children, a companion, a
valet and two other servants. Baroness Korff existed—indeed she
was a friend of Fersen's—and she had been persuaded to apply for a
duplicate passport on the grounds that while packing to leave Paris
she had burnt the original by mistake with some of her private
letters. The duplicate was duly granted.

Madame de Tourzel was cast in the role of Baroness Korff, the
Queen took the part of the governess—Madame Rochet, the King
posed as a servant with the name of Durand, Madame Elisabeth
was the Baronness's companion Rosalie, and the Dauphin and
Madame Royal his sister were the two small girls.

The party transferred themselves to the Berline as planned outside the walls of Paris and set off at top speed with Fersen himself
beside his coachman on the box. At three in the morning they made
their first change of horses at Bondy where Fersen left them to go
north to Belgium with a view to joining them later.

At six in the morning they reached Meaux, at eight they were at
Ferté-sous-Jouarre. At eleven they reached Montmirail and the
King no longer bothered to conceal himself. He got out of the
carriage not only when the horses were changed but on steep hills
where they had to be rested.

At two-thirty in the afternoon they reached Chaintrix where
for the first time the King was formally recognized by Gabriel
Vallet, the son-in-law of the postmaster. Vallet had seen the King
the previous year at the Festival of 14 July.

Vallet insisted on driving the coach on himself to Châlons where
there is little doubt that the royal party were again recognized at
the posting station. Neither the Mayor nor the postmaster of
Châlons were prepared to hold up the coach, but there was always
the risk that from now on the news of the King's progress eastwards would run ahead of him.

There was a set-back for the party at Pont-de-Somme-Vesle
where there were no Hussars to welcome them. Choiseul had expected the King to arrive at two-thirty in the afternoon. He waited

till four and then withdrew his troops and took it on himself in
addition to tell troops further to the east that the royal party
would not be coming through that day.

This seems at first sight to have been an almost incredible lack of
zeal on Choiseul's part, but we have to remember that troops loyal
to the King were operating in what amounted to enemy country.
They were not in a position to take station in one town or village
and stay there.

Bouillé, as we have already seen, had had to pretend that the
Austrians were about to attack in order to find an excuse to concentrate his troops where they could protect the King. And the
population was just as suspicious of smaller movements. In fact
when the Hussars, who were due to meet Louis at Pont-de-Somme-
Vesle, arrived at Ste-Ménehould, the Town Guard was called to
arms because the municipality had not been warned in advance of
their approach.

Thus Choiseul may well have concluded that in his position the
important thing to avoid was any advance publicity because once
the news of the King's approach became widely known it would be
impossible for his forty Hussars to afford any real protection. For
this reason he is said to have told Leonard, the Queen's hairdresser, who was riding ahead, to warn the other officers that the
expected operation had been postponed for a day.

The same reasoning may help to account for the fact that when
the royal party reached the next post at Ste-Ménehould they found
that another party of forty Dragoons who had been awaiting
them there had unsaddled their horses. They had been waiting all
day and the townspeople in the hope of finding out who they had
come to fight had been plying them with liquor. There might well
have been a commotion round the royal Berline if the call to saddle
horses had been given. It was decided that the best thing to do
would be for the royal party to change horses with as little fuss as
possible and then move on.

At Clermont they found almost the same state of affairs. Damas
was in the town but the townsfolk had protested so vigorously
at the unexpected arrival of his troops that he had had to billet
them outside the town. Even after the coach had left, Damas was
unable to rally his men or to follow the convoy. After Clermont the
Berline was off the beaten track.

But measures had already been taken to stop the King leaving patriot country. Soon after the Berline had left Ste-Ménehould Captain d'Andoins, in charge of the Dragoons there, was arrested and taken to the Town Hall. There he was asked to show the orders that had brought him to the town. He said that he had been told nothing more than that he was to expect a consignment of money which was due to arrive from Châlons.

Jean-Baptiste Drouet, the acting postmaster, was then summoned and asked if he had noticed anything unusual about the passage of the coach. He said that all that he had noticed was a short-sighted heavily built man with a long aquiline nose and asked whether this description would fit the King? Therefore at this stage, about an hour and a half after the coach had left Ste-Ménehould, Drouet had only the vaguest suspicion about the identity of the passengers since he did not know what the King really looked like. His suspicions were not aroused until rumours began to spread through the town, as they had done in every place through which the coach had passed since Chaintrix.

At the same time the town received news from the Mayor of Neuville-au-Pont near by, that cavalry coming from Pont-de-Somme-Vesle had passed by making for Varennes and that they had avoided Ste-Ménehould in order not to alarm the people. The Mayor of Neuville added that he did not know what to make of all this but that he felt apprehensive and had mounted a guard. This news so alarmed the townsmen of Ste-Ménehould that they thereupon insisted on disarming d'Andoins's men and throwing him and his lieutenant into the town jail.

But it is now almost certain that after the coach had left the good people of Ste-Ménehould had received from another source news that the vehicle did in fact contain the King. For not long after the royal party had left Châlons with the connivance of the postmaster M. Viet, another courier sent on from Chaintrix arrived with the news not only that Louis had been recognized at Chaintrix, but that the Assembly had officially confirmed his flight and had given orders that the coach was to be pursued and its occupants arrested.

Drouet and Guillaume le Hure, so called because he kept an inn with a sign outside it bearing the head of a wild boar, were chosen to follow the Berline. They knew the roads and were fortunate enough to meet one of the postillions returning with the horses that had taken the royal party to Clermont. The postillion told Drouet something that he might not otherwise have known, namely that the Berline had turned off the main road to Metz and was making for Varennes. Drouet who knew his way round the countryside was able to take a short cut to Varennes and arrived there ahead of the Berline.

The royal coach had stopped on the hill above the town because none of the party knew exactly where the fresh horses were to be found. And until the relay point had been found their present postillions were unwilling to move on, having received strict instructions not to take the horses beyond Varennes as they were needed next morning to get in the hay.

The new relay horses had in fact reached Varennes but they were the far side of the river and it was only after considerable delay that they were discovered and the postillion agreed to take the Berline down into the town itself.

Meanwhile Drouet and Guillaume, finding that the Berline had not yet arrived in Varennes, went up the hill to the top of the town and saw the lights of the Berline which had drawn up to one side of the road. There was not a moment to be lost. Drouet collected as many patriots as he could, told them why he had come to Varennes and called on them to stop the Berline. They debated whether to sound the tocsin. No. It was better to block the bridge over the river first. This they did with the furniture van belonging to a M. Wacquant which stood ready to leave in the morning fully loaded.

Drouet was now convinced that his quarry was the King and may have realized too that his own life might be forfeit for having failed to recognize the fugitives when he first saw them in his own village. His audience in turn realized that if they allowed the King to escape he could become the leader of a counter-revolution that would restore the ancient régime that they had got rid of with so much difficulty.

There is not much more to tell. The royal party were stopped as the coach came down the main street of the town. Jean-Baptiste Sauce, the grocer and law officer of the town, was pulled from his bed to carry out his official duty of inspecting the passports. Sauce had to confess that the documents were in perfect order but Drouet insisted that they could not be genuine. 'I'm certain that it is the King and his family,' he said, 'and if you let him pass into foreign country you are guilty of high treason.' Sauce temporized by saying that it was now late and that the passports would be stamped in the morning. To the royal protests that there was nowhere in Varennes where they could sleep Sauce replied that his own house was at their disposal and the fugitives were thus compelled to spend the night in a room on the first floor over the shop. The King did make one effort to move on but it was clear that the townsmen were not going to let the coach move off. The passengers were made to get out.

Every minute, however, that he remained in Varennes made it more difficult for him to leave in freedom for the townspeople, expecting an attack from Bouillé's Hussars, began putting up barricades and called out the Town Guard.

Officially the royal fugitives had not been recognized nor had they declared their identity. Since no one else in Varennes knew what the King looked like it was necessary to fetch Destez, a local judge, who had been married at Versailles, and had actually seen Louis. When he entered the grocer's first-floor room he fell on his knees, 'Your Majesty,' he cried. The King, deeply moved, declared himself, 'Yes . . . to be sure . . . I am your King,' he answered.

At last the sounds of approaching cavalry were heard and the fugitives felt that at last they were about to be saved. The horsemen were in fact those that should have met them at Pont-de-Somme-Vesle, and had lost their way in the forest on the way to Varennes.

Their commander, Choiseul, asked the King whether he would like to continue his journey at the cost of a skirmish but Louis, feeling sure that he would be rescued the following day by the troops that should already have been in Varennes, thought it wiser to stay where he was. And in fact it was clear that Choiseul's troops like so many others, were not prepared to engage in a battle against civilians.

Meanwhile the Town Council of Varennes had taken another decision. They sent a reliable messenger off to Paris to ask for instructions. The crowd felt too that Paris was where the King should go to. Every moment that he stayed in Varennes added to the danger that they themselves would be attacked by Bouillé's troops in the course of a rescue operation.

So despite all protests the King, Queen and royal family were bundled into their Berline early the next morning before Bouillé had time to mount a rescue operation against the five or six

thousand men, who by now had flocked into the town from the
surrounding countryside. The flight to Varennes had ended.

It has sometimes been argued that only the purest bad luck led
to the failure of the flight, and that all would have been well but
for a score of accidents and misunderstandings. Yet the greatest
misunderstandings were due to the obstinacy of the King himself
who determined to travel with his family in a single Berline. This
meant that despite eleven hours' start they were overtaken by
couriers bringing news from Paris. Recognition of the King might
not in itself have been dangerous. To be caught up by Assembly
messengers was fatal. It was a miscalculation to suppose that small
detachments of troops whose loyalty was not above suspicion
could operate safely in a hostile country. It was also clearly impossible for the officers who should have escorted the Berline to do
so in safety.

Perhaps Drouet had some luck in discovering from a postillion
that the royal party had branched off from the main road on the
secondary road to Varennes. But it is not inconceivable that he
would have found out from some other traveller that the Berline
was no longer on the main road.

The return to Paris was an anti-climax. It was a slow and
stifling journey along dusty roads during which the King was up-
braided for causing alarm to his subjects. When the Berline, still
under escort, arrived at Châlons on the night of 22 June, groups of
young men and women offered baskets of flowers to the King and
Queen but next morning the crowds outside were so menacing that
the royal party had to leave without the breakfast that had been
got ready for them. They spent the night at Dormans.

The next morning, 24 June they were in the Berline and under
way again at six in the morning in the company of three commissioners whom the Assembly had thoughtfully sent 'to receive'
the King. One of them, Pétion, crammed himself into the Berline
and sat down between the King and Queen.

The night of 24 June was spent at the palace of the Bishop of
Meaux who, having but recently sworn the Constitutional oath, had
neither furniture nor table appointments and had to borrow both
from the good people of the town.

The cavalcade was on the road again at six the next morning
on a day that promised to be another scorcher. At three o'clock
at Pantin they were met by La Fayette and his General Staff. He

was determined to keep order and the word had been passed round in Paris that the King was to be greeted with hats on and no shouting. Shortly before being driven down the Champs-Elysées, Louis asked for a glass of wine which he drank at a single draught. It may have been to keep up his courage. The road back to the Tuileries was flanked with two lines of Guards, their arms reversed as at a funeral. It was that of the French monarchy.

Chapter 5

THE ANGRY DAWN

THE flight to Varennes had discredited the royal family beyond redemption. For while the King and his family were bowling eastwards towards the frontier, the Constituent Assembly had continued unconcernedly to discuss the drafting of a new Penal Code. The formal note which the King left behind him to justify his absence barely interested them for it contained grievances about his lack of freedom rather than threats or appeals. The Assembly did not even bother to discuss it. Obviously the royal sanction was no longer necessary for laws, and the King was not permitted the use of the veto until nearly three months later when he formally recognized the Constitution.

La Fayette, in an attempt to placate the crowd, told them that since the royal budget amounted to twenty-five million livres, they had each inherited one livre. Sightseers thronged to the Tuileries and left notices reading: 'Lost: King and Queen. Ample reward for non-recovery.'

Mirabeau's fatal illness two months before the flight to Varennes deprived the King of the best advice he could have had. And any minister in whom the King had confidence could expect to be treated as a criminal by the Assembly and with obstruction by the French Civil Service, as conservative then as now.

Before the week was out, the King was suspended provisionally from his functions but, under the Constitution, he could not be deposed without question of a successor arising. And the only successor on hand in France was the Duc d' Orléans whose reputation was no better than Louis's.

The more advanced Revolutionary leaders claimed that Louis had deserted his post and had thereby forfeited his throne. They felt, however, that if power were really to be transferred to the people, it would probably be better to retain Louis as King until arrangements had been made for an orderly transfer. Otherwise they might find themselves in a republic under La Fayette.

Louis's supporters on the other hand argued that he had not committed any crime but had merely fled from danger; they said that his fall would only provoke the invasion of France. They claimed indeed that only the intercession of the King and Queen could prevent this calamity. Therefore it would be pointless to imprison the King since the crowned heads of Europe would undoubtedly reject any appeal coming from Louis if they thought it had been extorted from him by those who had violated his rights. No one, in short, was in favour of immediate action.

A kind of compromise ruling was reached, therefore, in mid-July which the Assembly declared that, in future, flight *from the country* would amount to abdication. (This absolved the Assembly from demanding immediate abdication while encouraging Louis to stay at home as King [and hostage].) It was also proclaimed that the King had been kidnapped and, in this way, the Assembly absolved itself from any blame in associating with Louis and incidentally cleared the King himself.

This, too, was advisable because, since war in those days was the sport of Kings, it was advisable to have a King to lead the nation, figuratively speaking, into any battle that might be forced upon it.

Meanwhile, outside France, the picture looked rather different. The eighteenth century had been the age of the enlightened monarchs and several of them, including Joseph II of Austria and Charles III of Spain had, earlier in the century, favoured the ideas of the Philosophers. But Europe's rulers were not prepared for the violence, vulgarity and cruelty of the Revolution that followed.

King Frederick William of Prussia had thought of intervening in France as early as July 1790 and Leopold of Austria (who had succeeded Joseph) had deferred action largely because he hoped that Louis and Marie Antoinette, his sister, would soon be outside France.

After the flight to Varennes excuses for inaction were harder to find. But neither sentiment nor family ties would by themselves inevitably had led to war if there had not been trouble on the French borders.

In past treaties, France had guaranteed feudal privileges in Alsace to certain German Princes who owned land there. But towards the end of 1790 the French Assembly passed a resolution claiming the right to abolish these privileges on the ground that the people of Alsace had participated in the Federation celebrations in Paris and therefore wanted to be at one with the rest of France. Thus for the first time during the Revolution, the French proclaimed the credo of all international revolutionaries—i.e. that it was permissible for agitators to appeal to the subjects of foreign allegiance over the heads of its own rulers. The French offered the German Princes compensation for the prospective loss of their rights. But the Princes not unnaturally complained to the Austrian Emperor to whom they, in turn, owed feudal allegiance. They were as anxious to keep their privileges as the feudal nobility of France had once been.

At the same time the new rulers of France quarrelled with a far more powerful adversary—the Pope—by declaring that the four-hundred-year-old agreement by which Avignon had been handed over to the Pope had not been made 'by the people of France' and therefore no longer held good.

Against this background the Emperor of Austria quickly made peace with the Turks in order to leave himself free to deal with the upstart French.

On 27 August 1791 at Pilnitz near Dresden he signed a declaration jointly with the King of Prussia and the Comte d'Artois appealing to other European monarchs to join with him in restoring order in France since this was a matter of European concern. The declaration called for freedom of movement for Louis, for dissolution of the mutinous Assembly and for the restoration of feudal rights of the Princes of Alsace.

War between France and Austria was deferred when Louis, after swearing allegiance to the completed Constitution, was restored to his throne. But on 12 November, the Emperor of Austria again circulated another appeal to his fellow rulers inviting them to form a coalition against the French.

In January the Assembly, now seriously alarmed, called on the Austrian Government to confirm by 1 March 1792 that the alliance of friendship between the two countries, signed more than thirty years before the Fall of the Bastille, still held good. The answer came in the following month, in the form of a new treaty between Austria and Prussia pledging that if either were attacked each would aid the other with twenty thousand troops. And Francis I who succeeded Leopold as Emperor on 1 March confirmed this arrangement.

Between France and her enemies stood the French émigrés, a permanent source of irritation to both. They had left France in several waves. The earliest movement was triggered off by the Fall of the Bastille and the violence which accompanied the King's return to Paris two months later. A second wave followed soon after the failure of the King's flight to Varennes and others were to leave from 1792 onwards as a matter of self-preservation or through the consequences of civil war.

It is usual to think of the émigrés as being aristocrats equipped with lorgnettes and dressed in long coats and short breeches. But this was not so. In fact a large proportion of the later emigrants were drawn from the Third Estate. About a quarter were churchmen who had refused to take the constitutional oath and more than one-third were officers in the Army and Navy who could neither abide the indiscipline of the new French Army nor sympathize with the objects for which it fought. Businessmen and property owners also formed a sizeable section of those who escaped from France especially during the civil war and one well-reasoned estimate puts the percentage of nobility at less than one-fifth of the total number of émigrés.

However, more noise was made about them than about all the others put together. The King's brother, the Comte de Provence, who was afterwards to rule in France as King Louis XVIII had escaped from Paris on the night of the flight to Varennes. Disguised as a servant and with a false passport, he had crossed undetected into Belgium.

The Comte d'Artois who had left earlier still, set himself up first in Turin at the Court of his uncle, the King of Sardinia, and later on the German border under the protection of the Elector of Trèves, while the Prince de Condé, one of the Bourbons, assembled an army at Worms. Lenoir, a former lieutenant of police in Paris formed an émigré spy ring based on the lakeside city of Constance.

The émigrés were not of one mind in their attitude towards the invasion of France. Some believed that they should liberate their country (and recover their estates) by any available means. Others, however, thought that it would be a mistake to rely on foreign aid in order to do so.

Louis and Marie Antoinette did not behave as the émigrés expected, for Louis hoped to act as the mediator between his people and the foreign powers which threatened to invade France, and did not need the help of the émigrés for this purpose. Indeed, he criticized them for planning rash and premature schemes.

The attitude of the foreign rulers was as puzzling to Louis as his attitude was to the émigrés. For while Empress Catherine the Great of Russia, King Gustavus of Sweden and King Victor Amadeus of Savoy supported the émigrés, Frederick William of Prussia and Leopold of Austria lent their support to Louis.

To the Assembly it was clear enough that, whatever support the émigrés might or might not have, they were not well disposed towards the new rulers of France and a series of measures was therefore prepared against them. A decree voted as far back as January 1790 declared that the goods of those who were then absent from the country and who had not returned within three months should be sequestrated. Another decree, passed three months after the Comte de Provence's flight, called on him to return to France. The following month, November 1791, the Assembly passed a decree providing that all Princes and officials who remained outside the country after 1 January 1792 should be condemned to death.

The King vetoed this decree but was compelled to call on both his brothers to return to France. (They refused on the grounds that the King had not addressed them by their proper titles.)

By the end of March the French had not received a satisfactory reply from Austria to the ultimatum which had expired at the beginning of the month. On 20 April they sent a formal declaration of war, and thereby began a conflict which was to last for more than twenty years. But the decision to fight had not been unanimous.

LOUIS XVI (1754–1793),
after the painting by Boze

COMTE DE MIRABEAU (1749–1791),
painted by Boze

CAMILLE DESMOULINS (1760–1794),
from the portrait in the Musée Carnavalet, Paris

MARQUIS DE LA FAYETTE (1757–1834),
as Commander of the National Guard in 1789.
From the engraving by Deboucourt

JEAN-PAUL MARAT
(1743–1793),
an idealized portrait
in the Musée Carnavalet,
Paris

A typical assignat of 1793, threatening forgers with death and
promising rewards for denunciation

The end of the flight to Varennes, June 1791, from a painting
by D. Pellegrini

MADAME MANON ROLAND (1754–1793),
from the painting in the Mansell Collection

CHARLOTTE CORDAY
(1768–1793),
from the portrait in the
Musée Carnavalet,
Paris

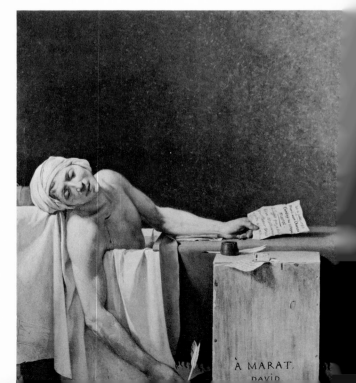

The Death of Marat
by Louis David,
from the painting
in the Musées
Royaux des Beaux-
Arts de Belgique,
Brussels

MAXIMILIEN ROBESPIERRE (1758–1794),
from a sketch by David at a meeting of the Convention

MAXIMILIEN ROBESPIERRE

A small-scale model
of the guillotine in
the Musée Carnavalet,
Paris

GEORGES-JACQUES DANTON (1759–1794), engraved by W. H. Mote

Four typical revolutionaries (1793–4): a member of the Commune; a jailer at the Temple Prison; an agent of the Committee of Public Safety and a Section leader summoning a general assembly

A Republican Belle—a British view of a French woman in 1794,
cartoon by I. Cruikshank

A street in Paris during the Reign of Terror, 1793. Drawn by
G. Durand for *Quatre-vingt-treize* by Victor Hugo

LOUIS (DE) SAINT-JUST
(1767–1794),
from the portrait in
the Musée Carnavalet, Paris

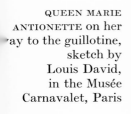

QUEEN MARIE
ANTIONETTE on her
ʾay to the guillotine,
sketch by
Louis David,
in the Musée
Carnavalet, Paris

QUEEN MARIE ANTOINETTE (1755–1793),
Sketch by F. L. Prieur, in the Musée Carnavalet, Paris

The King favoured a war and agreed willingly to three armies being called up because he believed that foreign monarchs would intervene to save him only after they had themselves been attacked by the French rebels. La Fayette likewise thought that war might strengthen the King's position as leader of his country, though not of course if the King accepted foreign support against his own countrymen. Brissot, who was one of a group of deputies later known as Girondists, because some of its leading members came from Bordeaux on the River Gironde, favoured war because he and his friends thought that their power would be bound to increase over both the high born and low born if they continued to govern the country in wartime. Contrary to La Fayette, they thought that a war would actually weaken the King's position since he would have to disavow either his own people or his best friends abroad. They believed that monarchies all over Europe were tottering. They also believed that foreign workers and peasants would welcome the French invaders and that therefore prolonged fighting might even not be necessary.

Other political leaders including Robespierre were against war on the grounds that it was necessary to deal first with the King. Before any battle could be won however, it was important to reorganize the French fighting forces. Under the old régime they had not even been all French. The cavalry, for example, included the Royal Allemand Cavalry (which had French officers but was recruited in Germany). The infantry included eleven Swiss regiments, eight German, three Irish and one Italian. There were also proprietary regiments run like the tax farms avowedly for profit. Conditions were deplorable for the rank and file who sometimes had to sleep three to a bed. Frequently the officers, instead of looking to the welfare of their men, embezzled their pay.

The nobility regarded the Army as a convenient receptacle for their own unwanted younger sons with the result that it was heavily over-officered. It has been calculated that in 1789 there was one general for every hundred and fifty-seven men and that more than half the total army budget was spent on maintaining the officers. In 1781 new restrictions had been introduced limiting commissions to those who could show sixteen quarters of nobility (i.e. four generations without a misalliance with a commoner), but even before this, the poorer nobility had rarely been able to rise above the rank of captain.

A new form of Austrian drill had been introduced in 1787 but
few of the regiments had troubled to master it and those who did so
were regarded as unpatriotic.

Great changes came with the Revolution, but they were not all
for the better. For as soon as the idea got around that even a common soldier had rights as a citizen, discipline began to break down.
Thirty thousand troops joined in mass desertions during the three
months following the Fall of the Bastille. The men of the Royal
Champagne Cavalry mutinied at Hesdin because the officers did
not invite them to join in a regimental banquet. Elsewhere the men
sent petitions to the War Office asking for the regimental plate and
other resources to be shared out between them, and on 9 August
1789 two men of the Régiment du Roi stepped out of the ranks on
parade and demanded that the accounts of the regiment should be
produced since the year 1767 when the Duc du Châtelet had
assumed command. The officers thereafter agreed to hand over a
hundred and seventy thousand livres. Swiss troops at Châteauvieux
staged a similar mutiny. The ringleaders were flogged but later
the tables were turned; officers were imprisoned and compelled to
hand over forty-seven thousand livres. A wild and drunken party
followed, and Bouillé who came to restore order lost forty officers
and four hundred men in the process. The leader of the revolt was
broken on the wheel, twenty-two others were hanged and forty-one
sent to the galleys for thirty years.

The Jacobins feared that a disciplined army would be a tool in
the hands of the monarchy. But discipline was equally lax in the
Navy and by July 1791 nearly three-quarters of its officers were
absent from their ships without leave.

This was not the stuff of which victories were made. And it
compelled the bourgeois leaders to rely permanently on allies they
had hitherto despised, namely the common people. By the autumn
of 1792 passive citizens were admitted to the National Guard.

The French did not wait to be invaded by a counter-revolutionary army that would take away their newly won privileges.
They calculated that a sudden attack on Belgium might be successful since they could count on the people there to rise against their
Austrian rulers, and accordingly French forces crossed the frontier
on 20 April. The invasion was mounted in two columns. One, led
by an Irishman, Théobald Dillon, advanced north-eastwards from
Lille and the other, under the Duc de Biron who had fought in the

American War of Independence, started from Quiévrain, still farther east. The attack was well timed. Prussia had not yet mobilized her troops. Austria was disorganized to some extent through the recent death of the Emperor Leopold. There were hopes that England might remain neutral. The King of Sweden had recently been assassinated and Russia was, as usual, occupied in partitioning Poland.

But it needed only a single confrontation with the enemy to defeat the flower of the French Army. It was said and believed in royalist circles that Biron's troops had insisted on taking a vote before they would advance on the enemy. The officers realized that they were fighting with undisciplined troops and the troops in turn distrusted the officers some of whom, be it said, absented themselves on the eve of the offensive. At any rate on 29 April at the first sight of the Austrian troops, Dillon and Biron decided to order a retreat. Biron's men disbanded, claiming that they had been betrayed. Dillon's men distinguished themselves by murdering their own general and some of their Austrian prisoners.

A large number of officers deserted their posts. Rochambeau, the Commander-in-Chief, and de Grave, the Minister of War, both resigned their positions. The generals still remaining in the field laid the whole blame for the defeat on the quality of their troops and made this the pretext for avoiding a further offensive which had no charms for them.

By the end of July, the Prussians, reinforced with some Austrian troops and even a few émigrés, were ready for their counter-offensive and the Duke of Brunswick, who was leading the armies, published, on 25 July, a manifesto which had been prepared for him by the émigré Marquis de Limon and approved by Fersen. It called on Frenchmen to disown their Government. It declared that those who defended themselves against the invaders would be subjected to all the rigours of the law of war and their houses burnt or pulled down if they shot at the invaders 'either in the open country or from the windows, doors and openings of their houses'. The declaration added, on the word of the Emperor and the King of Prussia, that if complete liberty were not immediately granted to the King and the royal family the invaders would exact 'an exemplary and ever memorable vengeance by delivering the city of Paris to military punishment and total destruction and the rebels who are guilty of outrages to the punishment they deserve'.

The result of this was to unite firmly round the Government all those who had taken part in the Revolution. On 19 August the Prussian troops crossed the French border. On 22 August the town of Longwy was bombarded and surrendered the following day. Verdun, besieged a week later, fell on 2 September after its commander Beaurepaire died, probably by his own hand.

The state of tension in Paris can easily be imagined. But at least France had a new battle hymn written in Strasbourg by Captain Claude Joseph Rouget de Lisle for the Rhine Army.

News that war had been declared reached Strasbourg, then the Headquarters of the Army of the Rhine on 25 April, and the Mayor of the city, Frédéric Dietrich, proclaimed the news. And the local branch of the Society of Friends of the Constitution posted an appeal for volunteers. The appeal read, *Aux armes, citoyens, l'étendard de la guerre est déployé, le signal est donné. Aux armes. Il faut combattre, vaincre ou mourir. Aux armes citoyens. . . . Qu'ils tremblent donc les despotes couronnés. Marchons. Soyons libres jusqu'au dernier soupir et que nos vœux soient constamment pour la félicité de la patrie et la bonheur du genre humain.*

Champagne and Rhine wine flowed at dinner that night at Army Headquarters, and the talk turned later on to songs and to the fact that *Ça Ira* and similar civilian dance-jingles were not the kind of tunes that would stir the pulses of a soldier on the march. So after dinner Rouget seized his violin and composed the melody which he called *Chant de Guerre pour l'Armée du Rhin*. After two hours he rushed round to play it to his friend Masclet and then to Dietrich. That evening arrangements were made to launch it in public on the following Sunday, 29 April, at a march past of volunteers of the Rhône-et-Loire battalion leaving for the frontier.

Hand-written copies were soon circulating in Strasbourg in advance of those run off by Dannbach the city printer and chords were added to the melody by Madame Dietrich the wife of the Mayor. The words—of which there were probably many impromptu versions at first—make use of several of the phrases from the Jacobin appeal for volunteers. They were not published in any Strasbourg paper until early July but leaflets may have been in circulation before then and appear to have reached Marseilles via Montpelier some time before 2 July, when the Marseillais volunteers started on their march to Paris. By singing it at every village the

Marseillais converted it into a national treasure, a single anthem, sung in French all over France.

But singing could not help France over her difficulties. An inflation of vast proportions was sweeping the country. So many assignats had been put into circulation that by the end of 1791 their total was greater than the value of the State land offered for sale. Large cities such as Lyons and Orléans issued their own paper money. At one time there were sixty-three different kinds of banknotes circulating in Paris.

The authorities had been hoping that the assignats would be gradually taken out of circulation as people used them to buy the land confiscated by the State. But the land did not sell as quickly as had been hoped. Perhaps the peasants feared that it might be taken away from them again if the counter-revolution (against which they were being constantly warned) ever came to pass. Few of them could afford large sums and the cities had to act as middlemen by buying large lots of property, splitting it up and selling it in smaller lots paid for in instalments spread over ten or twelve years. The instalments were not always paid promptly and, even if they were, they did not always reach the State because the municipality had in the meantime issued their own currency which had to be redeemed.

Once confidence in the assignats had been undermined no one wanted to hold on to them. Those with ample resources changed their assignats into gold and hid the metal away, confident that the longer they kept it the more assignats it would buy. For ready cash people preferred coins made from surplus church bells to official paper. By January 1792 the purchasing power of the assignat had fallen to about six-tenths of its original value. Sugar rose to three and a half times its normal price.

It was a time for scapegoats. Most of the émigrés were out of the country beyond the reach of the law but the priests were ready to hand and on them fell the full displeasure of the people of France. The Revolution had begun in a spirit of religious toleration in as much as the State was ready to allow its members to worship as their reason or their conscience dictated. But only about half the clergy had been willing to swear the oath pledging their loyalty exclusively to the State. Unsworn priests embarrassed the authorities by declaring that any children not baptized by them were illegitimate and that parents who had not been married by them

were committing mortal sin by living together. Counter revolutionary priests were becoming a danger to the State. A decree of
November 1791—vetoed by the King—demanded exile for all of
them.

In August 1792, all those who had not taken the oath were listed
for deportation. Only a short while later divorce was proclaimed
legal while at the same time the registers of births, deaths and
marriages were taken away from the clergy and handed over to the
civil authorities. Priests were forbidden to wear ecclesiastical dress
when not actually conducting a service. They were allowed to
marry and divorcees to remarry, a change which undermined the
position of those priests who had sworn the oath of loyalty to the
Constitution but who still retained their traditional religious
beliefs.

A newspaper of the time, *La Feuille Villageois*, in its issue
of 10 April 1792, clearly summed up the feelings of the time on this
question:

> This [priestly] costume nourishes religious discords. It is the
> standard, the rallying point of seditious hypocrites; it is what
> makes the so-called schism of the oaths. Abolish it and the
> schism would cease. The priests' robes, by sheltering trouble
> makers, compromises and exposes the well-doer. When trouble
> begins, when there is disorder caused by priests and an angry
> crowd looks for the authors—their dress marks them out for
> vengeance; and you will often see the anger deserved by some
> guilty priests fall on the head of some other virtuous and tolerant
> cleric.

> These are the results of this distinction of dress, and even if
> it possessed none of these dangers, I ask you, men of honour, to
> admit that a dress that grants honours to an individual that are
> not due to the task he performs when he appears in public away
> from his work, does this not set up civil inequality—a veritable
> aristocracy? Why should anyone who acts only as an ordinary
> citizen want to be thought superior to other citizens? Why
> should anyone wish to deceive the people?

> A free nation should venerate only two things, the Law and
> Virtue. If the particular garb of a magistrate commands respect
> it is because it represents the Law. . . . That is why he wears it
> only when he is speaking or taking action on a legal matter.

What would you think of a mayor who went out into the fields or the market place wearing his robes of office? What would you think of a judge who was so foolish as to get out of bed first thing in the morning wearing the plumed hat which the Law had provided for him on the Bench? We have known of one of the former Grands Seigneurs inflated by the winds of his own vanity to the point where he could not bear to part with his Blue Riband. His mania for it was so great that he wore it even in the bath. . . . Well, a priest's robes outside a church or apart from religious activities, though perhaps less ridiculous, is also out of place.

So it was not perhaps surprising that those priests who still wore robes were the first to suffer in the famous September Massacres which began on the second of that month and continued for nearly a week.

The Massacre was, of course, a carefully planned operation carried out because in no other way was it possible for the bourgeois to persuade the troops to leave Paris and go to the front. For who wanted to risk their lives in defence of their country while aristocrats were being maintained in comfort in prison? In order to get the troops on the move, the authorities had to convince them not only that there was no immediate danger of the aristocrats breaking out of prison and overturning the Revolution during their absence, but also that the menace would be averted once and for all.

There was only one logical way of doing this without long-drawn-out trials—a mass murder. The step was urged by Marat who provided his own list of suspected traitors, and organized by Danton and Billaud-Varenne.

At the beginning of August 1792 there were about one thousand six hundred people under lock and key in Paris. Before the end of the month another thousand suspects had been arrested, partly through house-to-house searches, and were ready for processing. Then, in less than a week between one thousand one hundred and one thousand four hundred were dispatched . . . some before even their names had been entered in the prison registers. But only two hundred and twenty-three—less than a quarter—were apparently priests or counter-revolutionaries. The rest were common-law offenders. The operation served therefore as a warning that even those in favour of the Revolution might be safer at the front than in Paris.

The massacres began on the afternoon of Sunday, 2 September outside the prison of the Abbaye of St Germain des Prés to which a party of twenty-three priests was being transferred in four carriages to the Abbaye. The carriages were held up in the narrow street leading to the prison and surrounded by a threatening mob armed with sabres and pikes. A prisoner in the first carriage, a young man in a white robe on whose head could be seen the marks of a clerical tonsure, was pulled from his carriage and surrounded. His cries for mercy seemed to break the spell. Suddenly he was struck down by a volley of blows. One by one the other priests, all save one who escaped into the Abbaye, were pulled from their seats and cut to pieces. Then the massacre was continued inside the prison by professional butchers recruited by Maillard, the agitator who had played a leading part in the Fall of the Bastille. His orders in turn appear to have come from the Vigilance Committee of the Commune which controlled the Paris police.

In order to preserve some semblance of legality, Maillard set up at the Abbaye a People's Court or Tribunal of twelve, which included an innkeeper, a hat-maker's assistant, a watchmaker, some disbarred lawyers, and a member of the Paris Commune wearing his scarf of office.

The Commissioners sat round a table covered with bottles, glasses, pipes and sabres and the 'judges' heard their cases, which rarely lasted a minute, standing, drunk, or asleep. They had an audience, some of them *fédérés* from Marseilles, who applauded verdicts they agreed with and booed those that they resented. In order to prevent prisoners from offering resistance and so wasting the court's time, those that were to be executed were told that they were being transferred to another prison. It helped them to die with tranquillity. About twenty executioners took part in the Massacre at the Abbaye de St Germain. The murderers were paid three to four francs subsistence money. They were obliged to hand over rings, jewellery and other valuables but were allowed to keep the clothes after they had made clear that they would slash each garment that they were not allowed to keep. The prisoners were hacked down as they stepped into the prison courtyard. Those who walked in with their hands behind their backs suffered least. There the killing went on all night by the light of bonfires and into the dawn. At least one prisoner escaped because his clothing was too worn for him to be worth putting to death. Others were spared after they had been obliged to swear an oath of loyalty standing on top of a pile of bodies. Some were compelled to enlist in the Army as the price of freedom. Abbé Sicard escaped death by posing as a member of the tribunal.

There were similar scenes at the other prisons. One hundred and fifty priests had been taken to the Carmelite convent. Some barricaded themselves in their cells. Others tried to hide in the garden of the convent and one or two succeeded even in escaping over the wall. There a People's Court arranged for the victims to meet their fate at a controlled rate of just under one a minute. The trial took place at the foot of the stairs. Those condemned were murdered at the bottom of some stairs leading up to the garden of the convent. They were told that they were being transferred to the Abbaye prison.

It was the same at the La Force prison where the second day's massacre was held. There the 'court' was set up in the concierge's room and the prisoners murdered at the door of the prison.

Women did not escape the slaughter. The Princesse de Lamballe, Superintendent of Marie Antoinette's Household, who had returned from safety in England to share the Queen's troubles, was killed with a pike-thrust at the door of the La Force prison because she refused to denounce her mistress in public. Her legs and arms were wrenched from her body, and her heart torn out and eaten.

Thirty-five women of the town were murdered at the La Salpetrière prison on the third day of the massacres and on the following day thirty-three boys and girls, aged between twelve and fourteen, were dispatched at the Bicêtre prison.

For five days and nights the slaughter continued and the Commune of Paris, once having implicated itself, felt that leaders in the provinces should be encouraged to do likewise. A note signed by Marat and dated 3 September read:

The Commune of Paris hastens to inform its brothers in the Departments that many ferocious conspirators detained in its prisons have been put to death by the people—acts of justice which seemed to be essential in order to cow hidden traitors at a time when it was about to march against the enemy. The whole nation will surely hasten to adopt this measure so vital to public safety, and all Frenchmen will proclaim, as Paris has done, 'We will march on the enemy, but we will not leave brigands behind us to murder our wives and children.'

Within a fortnight of the end of the September Massacres, France's armies had their first success and the country desperately in search of a hero had found one: Charles François du Mourier, a Frenchman from Cambrai (now in France) who had, however, also a dash of Provençale blood. Dumouriez, as he came to be called (since, to democratic Frenchmen, all names beginning with 'de' or 'du' suggested connections with landowning feudal aristocrats), was already past fifty when the Revolution began. As a child he had been weakly and had had at one time to wear irons and travel in a wheeled chair. But as he grew up he survived and overcame these disabilities. By the time he was of military age he was strong enough to fight. He was brave and able. He fought in the Seven Years War of 1756–63 and, when this ended, he became a mercenary and took part in campaigns in Italy, Flanders, Spain and Portugal. He also served in the campaign mounted by Louis XV for the reconquest of Corsica, the success of which made Napoleon a French subject. He took part in the fighting for the Fall of the Bastille and, as one of the few revolutionaries with fighting experience in the field, he was put in command of the 12th Division in June 1791. But Dumouriez had had other qualifications for advancement. His experience abroad led to his being sent by Choiseul on a diplomatic mission to Poland. What could be more suitable than that he should become Foreign Minister? The King, with whose approval he was appointed, hoped that he had found another La Fayette and Dumouriez himself fancied himself as a politician.

Dumouriez's appointment as Foreign Minister lasted only three months. This was not because of any failings on his part but because things were going so badly at the front. The Assembly needed victories and in June, 1792, he left Paris with the rank of Lieutenant-General in the army of Marshal Luckner. He took several sound ideas with him to the front. He realized that his troops were a mixture of volunteers, National Guards and old regulars and that he could not expect from them the same degree of discipline to be found in a regular army. The principle of blind obedience to orders was discarded and replaced by a system known as Intelligent Obedience. Dumouriez reasoned that if the men understood why they were being given a particular order, they would more readily obey it. Tactics had to be altered too, for there had been no opportunity to drill the men to advance or retire in line abreast. Instead, attacks were made in column formation with the emphasis on mobility and, if possible, surprise.

At the same time Lazare Carnot propounded the doctrine, originally put forward in 1789 by Dubois-Crancé, of a nation in arms, a revolutionary doctrine indeed in those days when the fighting was done entirely by professional armies. Carnot argued that 'From the first moment that danger threatens, every citizen becomes a soldier', and he carried this doctrine to its logical conclusion by arranging for the manufacture of weapons that any citizen soldier could use without requiring military training. He did in fact what Napoleon did when Paris was besieged—and indeed what Britain did at the most critical point of the Second World War when their Home Guard was organized. He called for the manufacture of pikes which could be issued to all Frenchmen who could be trusted to use them in defence of the country.

The fact that the men could not be relied on to keep regular station in line abreast called for new tactics. The age of pitched battles had to come to an end and, instead, the tactics of mobility used by Napoleon began to take shape. Since their first reverse, however, the French remained on the defensive, and the first French success came when the Prussians attacked French troops drawn up near a windmill on the heights of Valmy on the route between Paris and Verdun. The Frenchman's rapid fire caused the Prussian front line to waver and Brunswick, the commander, sounded the retreat.

Valmy won the French not only prestige but also valuable time to reorganize, for the Prussians, still virtually unsupported and without the prospect of a rapid victory, felt it wise to pull back still farther to the line of the Meuse. Other local victories followed at Chambery, Nice, Worms, Mainz and Frankfurt. Finally the Battle of Jemappes on 6 November conquered Belgium for the leaders of the Revolution. But as we shall see, neither the King nor Dumouriez profited from these successes.

The cry for a republic in France was nothing new. As far back as May 1790, Camille Desmoulins, in his *Révolutions de France et de Brabant,* deplored the lack of interest shown by Frenchmen towards the idea of republican institutions. Three months later the *Patriote Français* argued that though the Constitution provided a monarchy it did not forbid people to advocate a republic.

On 1 July 1791 the Assembly was somewhat disturbed to find fixed to its door the translation of a manifesto by Thomas Paine developing the principles of his famous work, *The Rights of Man*, which had recently been published in London. It ran:

Brethren and Fellow Citizens, the serene tranquillity, the mutual confidence which prevailed amongst us during the time of the late King's escape, the indifference with which we beheld him return, are unequivocal proofs that the absence of a King is more desirable than his presence, and that he is not only a political superfluity, but a grievous burden, pressing hard on the whole nation. . . . The nation can never give back its confidence to a man who, false to his trust, perjured to his oath, conspires a clandestine flight, obtains a fraudulent passport, conceals a King of France under the disguise of a valet, directs his course towards a frontier covered with traitors and deserters, and evidently meditates a return to our country with a force capable of imposing his own despotic laws. . . .

In every sense in which the question can be considered, the reciprocal obligation which subsisted between us is dissolved. He holds no longer any authority. We owe him no longer obedience. We see in him no more than in different person, we can regard him only as Louis Capet.

The history of France presents little else than a long series of public calamities, which takes its source from the vices of Kings; we have been the wretched victims that have never ceased to suffer either for them or by them. The catalogue of their oppressions was complete, but to complete the sum of their crimes, treason was yet wanting. Now the only vacancy is filled up, the dreadful list is full; the system is exhausted; there are no remaining errors for them to commit; their reign is consequently at an end.

What kind of office must that be in a government which requires for its execution neither experience nor ability, that may be abandoned to the desperate chance of birth, that may be filled by an idiot, a madman, a tyrant, with equal effect as by the good, the virtuous, and the wise? An office of this nature is a mere nothing; it is a place of show, not of use. Let France, then, having reached the age of reason, no longer be deluded by the sound of words, and let her deliberately examine, if a King,

however insignificant and contemptible in himself, may not at
the same time be extremely dangerous. . . .

Others, including Danton, saw that there could be no strong
Government under the Constitution as it stood and a motion at the
Cordeliers called for the King's fate to be decided by plebiscite.
The Assembly refused to consider a procedure so dangerous to their
own principles. A second petition met with an equally firm rejection. A third petition was prepared by the Cordeliers in alliance
with the Jacobins to be deposited on the Altar of the Nation on the
Champ de Mars. It called for the replacement of the King by any
means that the Constitution allowed. On Sunday, 17 July, the
Jacobins got cold feet and withdrew their support. The Cordeliers
then prepared their own petition calling for the replacement and
trial of the King, left it on the Altar and called for signatures.

In a short time six thousand signatures had been obtained, some
from well-educated people, some from crowd leaders and some
from the little men of Paris including the unemployed.

The authorities began to lose their heads. They made use of a
decree that had been passed in October 1789, allowed them to declare martial law by the simple expedient of hanging a red flag out
of the window of the Town Hall. The decree provided that after this
signal had been given, all those who assembled together in crowds
committed a criminal offence. The instigators of the mob were liable
for three years' imprisonment even if the mob were unarmed and
dispersed quietly. If the crowd were armed the penalty was death for
the instigators. If any violence was committed, members of the
crowd, even if unarmed, could receive one year's imprisonment. If
they were carrying arms a three-year sentence was earned and if
they themselves had committed violence the penalty was death.

It took the authorities the best part of the day to act and when
the forces of law and order appeared on the Champ de Mars with
cavalry preceded by the red flag and with artillery and infantry, it
was already half past seven in the evening. Many of the petitioners
had already gone home and others were preparing to do so but the
red flag brought their anger to the boil. Stones began to fly. The
soldiers fired first over the heads of the crowd and when the people
failed to disperse, into their midst. A dozen fell dead; thirty or
forty were wounded. But the incident became the Massacre of the
Champ de Mars.

The lesson of that evening was clear and unmistakable. It was that the people could expect no more understanding from the present Assembly or from the municipality than they could have had from the King himself. The Massacre of the Champ de Mars ended the first bourgeois revolution and foreshadowed the fate of its leaders. Indeed Bailly, then Mayor of Paris, was afterwards guillotined on the very spot on the Champ de Mars where he had read the proclamation of martial law.

It was clear now that not only the city authorities and the King would have to be replaced. The Constitution itself could not endure. It was already out of date. The two years that had been spent in drawing it up had proved a fatal delay. It was the natural defect of a revolution which unlike the Russian Revolution had been improvised almost from start to finish.

Yet what was to be done? The Constituent Assembly had already finished its work and had decreed its own dissolution at the end of September. Elections for a new Assembly, a Legislative Assembly with the power of making laws in accordance with the new Constitution, were to begin on 25 August and the new Assembly was to swing into action in October.

It had further been decreed that the new Constitution was not to be altered for ten years. In fact safeguards were so great that the Constitution could not be altered before the year 1801 and then only if three successive legislatures sitting for two years each had recommended this. Moreover those who knew most about it and had done most to establish it had precluded themselves by a self-denying motion from sitting in the new Legislative Assembly. Thus it was easier to defeat the King than to change the Constitution.

In fact the behaviour of Louis helped to make both possible. His attitude to the new Legislative Assembly was distant. On 12 November 1791 he vetoed its decree declaring all émigrés to be suspect and the property of émigré princes to be sequestrated. On 19 December 1791 he likewise vetoed the decree which deprived priests who refused to swear the constitutional oath of their stipend and declared them suspect. He failed to support La Fayette when the latter stood for election as Mayor of Paris. He equally failed to co-operate with the Girondists—Pierre-Victorin Vergniaud, Armand Gensonné, Marguerite-Elie Guadet, and Jacques-Pierre Brissot—who were prepared to accomplish the Revolution by constitutional means.

The final showdown came soon after the defeat of the French
Army and the murder of Dillon in the spring of 1792. On 30 May
the Assembly came to the conclusion that in the circumstances it
was dangerous to leave the King with a bodyguard of twelve
thousand infantry and six hundred cavalry who could not be
trusted to be loyal to the Revolution. Moreover, it was reported
that the King had recently increased the strength of his personal
army by calling on four hundred and fifty Swiss to serve at the
palace. The Assembly gave orders that the bodyguard should be
dismissed, in view of its unpatriotic spirit, and its duties performed
by the National Guard. The King in turn vetoed the proposal to
set up an armed camp of up to twenty-thousand men who could be
trained outside the walls of Paris for service at the front.

For this he received a strong letter of remonstrance signed by
Jean-Marie Roland, Minister of the Interior, but undoubtedly
dictated by his wife, Manon Roland, who completely dominated
him. Roland's note told the King, 'Public opinion already suspects
your Majesty's intention and further delay [in passing the proposed
measures] will lead the disillusioned people to think they see their
King as an accomplice of conspirators.'

Louis's reply was to dismiss his Government.

On 20 June the people made their reply. They asked the Paris
city authorities for permission to parade on the anniversary of the
signing of the Tennis Court Oath (20 June), wearing their uniforms
of 1789 and carrying arms in order to present a petition to the
King and to the Assembly. They also proposed to plant a 'tree of
liberty' on the terrace close to the palace. No one had the courage to
forbid the demonstration; they remembered the consequences of
the Massacre of the Champ de Mars. Accordingly, on the appointed
day, a mob numbering about twenty thousand drawn from the
most advanced Sections of the city converged on the Assembly
carrying their arms. The leaders of the demonstration claimed that
the procession was entirely peaceable in character. But when the
Assembly admitted a small group who wanted to 'pay their respects
to the Assembly', they had to listen to an ominous harangue from
an orator who, to applause from the gallery, demanded that either
the dismissed ministers should be recalled or the King deposed.
Soon the crowd broke into the Assembly Hall and trooped defiantly
through it. An hour's singing and dancing followed and the tree
was duly planted. Then at about four o'clock the mob broke into

Bertaux P. del. Dupleßi B

aguā forti.   Duprćel Sculp.

the palace gardens, smashed down the doors and stormed up the
stairs into the King's room. There, almost unguarded, Louis had to
listen to a reprimand and a string of orders. He was told to withdraw his veto . . . to recall the patriot ministers . . . to hunt down
the counter-revolutionary priests, to choose between his people in
Paris and the émigrés in Coblentz. But Louis stood his ground. He
maintained that the palace was not the place nor this the occasion
on which to make laws and added that, though he disagreed with
the ministers, he was nevertheless as good a patriot as any. And to
show this, he was ready to wear the red bonnet which had now become a symbol of the Revolution and to drink a toast to the new
France. But even this did not satisfy the crowd and they made a
thorough inspection of the royal suite pushing into the Queen's
room to see the Queen, Madame Elisabeth the King's sister, the
Dauphin and his sister. It was after six when Pétion the Mayor of
Paris arrived with the National Guard to usher the crowd out of
the Tuileries. By ten o'clock the palace was back to normal. But
Paris knew that they had seen a dress rehearsal for a still more
memorable drama.

The dethronement of the King took place on 10 August, a few
days after Paris had received the news of the Duke of Brunswick's
threatening manifesto, and soon after the arrival in Paris of the
fédérés from Marseilles. It was also ten days after the Assembly had
refused to impeach La Fayette for deserting his troops and making
an unauthorized trip to Paris to protect the King. It was well
organized. On 26 July a secret Directory of Insurrection was formed
from the Central Committee of *fédérés* together with members of
the original committee which had planned the 'tree-planting'
ceremony of 20 June.

On 8 August the Marseillais were transferred from their barracks in the rue Blanche to the Cordeliers with their colours, their
arms and their movable cannon.

That evening it was decided to replace the General Council of
the Municipality with a new insurrectional Commune composed of
three men drawn from each of the Sections. This illegal committee
at once began to sit in the Town Hall ready to take over from the
legislative officials. This they did before seven the following morning.

During the night attackers broke into the arsenal and armed
themselves. At midnight the tocsin sounded and the insurgents

assembled in their formations. They advanced in two columns
gathering supporters as they marched. Louis-Pierre Manuel, the
Town Clerk, had thoughtfully given orders for the artillerymen,
who had been stationed on the Pont Neuf to prevent the two
columns approaching from opposite sides of the river from joining,
to be withdrawn.

Respectable defences had been established at the palace to protect the King and his family but they were soon disorganized.
Pétion, the Mayor, who was supposed to be responsible for keeping
order in the capital, was called away from the palace to the Town
Hall, where, to his relief he was placed under armed guard. Galliot
de Mandat, who was in charge of the defence of the palace, was also
called to the Town Hall where he was accused of having given
orders to fire on the crowd. He was stripped of his command and
put to death on the steps of the Town Hall.

Before dawn, the Queen sent for Roederer the Recorder of the
Department of Paris and asked for his advice. Roederer suggested
that the safest protection for the King lay in the Assembly and
urged the King to go there. At five o'clock the King reviewed the
troops drawn up in front of the palace for his defence. Some
shouted, 'Vive le Roi' but others shouted, 'Vive la Nation' and took
up positions showing that they were ready to attack rather than
defend.

Before sunrise, the men from Marseilles and from Brittany, who
formed the vanguard of the insurgents, had reached the Carrousel
and had turned their guns on the palace itself. At that time there
were fewer than eighty members in the Assembly, not enough to
debate the petitions which the crowd had brought with them. The
people were told that since they could not all see the King at the
same time, they should choose a delegation of about twenty who
could present their case for them. But their leaders would not hear
of this proposal. And it was clear that the great part of the National
Guard sympathized with them, and were in favour of taking the
palace by storm.

A municipal officer ran to the King with the news that the insurgents were advancing towards the palace itself.

'What is it they want?' asked Joly the Keeper of the King's
seals.

'Abdication to be proclaimed by the Assembly.'

'And what after that?'

The officer could only bow in silence.

Louis then held a Cabinet meeting with the Queen and his ministers. Roederer warned the King that the attackers would be upon him in five minutes. 'Your only safety lies in the Assembly,' he said. 'The Department advises you to go there immediately. There are not enough men to defend the palace nor can they be relied on to do so.'

The King replied at first that he did not see many people advancing towards the palace, and the Queen declared with spirit that the King had enough troops to defend himself. But Roederer persisted, and Louis, after some hesitation, got up from his chair and said, 'Let us go.' 'Monsieur Roederer,' said the King's sister, 'will you answer for the life of the King?' 'Yes, Madame, with my own,' he replied. 'I will walk immediately in front of him.'

Then Louis XVI left his palace with his family, his ministers and the members of the Paris Department. Placing himself between two files of the National Guard he walked out of the palace and across its garden to the Assembly. As they walked along the path the young Dauphin amused himself by scuffing up a heap of dead leaves with his foot. 'Yes,' said the King in a mournful voice, 'they are falling early this year.' He was met by a deputation of members. 'Sire,' said the President of the Group, 'the Assembly, eager to provide for your safety, offers you and your family a refuge in its midst.' The King and his followers then continued on their way into the hall pursued by threats and insults from the crowd.

'Gentlemen,' said the King on his arrival, 'I have come here in order to prevent a monstrous crime from being committed. I feel sure that I cannot be in safer hands.' 'Sire,' answered Pierre-Victorin Vergniaud who was in the chair, 'you may rely on the firmness of the National Assembly. Its members have sworn to die in maintaining the rights of the people and the constitutional authorities.' The King then took his seat next to the President but he was reminded that the Assembly could not debate in the presence of the King and he then retired with his family and ministers to the reporter's box behind the President's chair while his fate was decided.

But though he had abandoned his garrison in the Tuileries (perhaps he reckoned that their lives were safe once he had left them), he had not given instructions for it to disband and the loyal Swiss remained at their posts. In time the insurgents began to fill

the courtyard and persuaded the artillerymen to come over to their
side. For a time the attackers and defenders stood facing each other
and the Swiss at the windows threw down a few cartridges as a
token of goodwill. But they would not allow the crowd to pass beyond the outer hall of the palace. Fighting broke out and the Swiss
fired on the crowd and succeeded in clearing the courtyard. But
the sound of firing was clearly heard by the deputies who began to
fear for their own lives. Too late the King, from the safety of the
Assembly, gave the order that should have been given before, 'The
King commands the Swiss to lay down their arms at once and retire
to their barracks.' To obey this order now meant certain death.
Some of the Swiss fell dead at their posts. Others tried to retreat
through the gardens but were captured and taken to the Town Hall
where they were massacred. Others sought sanctuary with the
King in the Assembly. In all, six hundred out of a total of nine
hundred perished, and nearly four hundred of the attackers were
killed or wounded.

Then came the turn of the Assembly. The new Commune insisted
on being received there and demanded that the King be deposed
and a National Convention summoned to draw up a new Constitution. Other deputations followed with the same demands until the
Assembly was cowed into submission. They unanimously passed a
measure providing for the summoning of a National Convention,
the dismissal of the ministers accredited by the King and the approval of the measures that the King had previously vetoed. The
new rulers of France insisted that the Army transfer its allegiance
from the King to the Assembly (La Fayette after planning an unsuccessful military coup, deserted to the Austrians). Most of the
former ministers were recalled to their posts. But among them
there was one new face—Georges Danton, the man who had
approved the September Massacres and who from now on was to
play an increasingly important part in directing the course of the
Revolution. He was named Minister of Justice. After this experience the Assembly, its confidence shattered, dared not assemble
and its business was turned over to a special commission which was
in continual conflict with the real rulers of Paris, the new Commune.
But it scored one success. It declared that it had remained permanently in session, and that the sitting of 9 August had not been
concluded but merely adjourned.

For two days after leaving the Tuileries the King and his family remained in the Assembly. At night he and his family slept on mattresses at the near-by convent of the Feuillants. Before the Assembly adjourned he heard that, though he was not to be deposed, he was to be suspended and separated from his son, who was to be educated by a tutor chosen by the Assembly. It was clear that the child was being held as a hostage for the good behaviour of his father and mother. Furthermore the Assembly was made to surrender its prisoner to the Commune who insisted that only the Temple prison, with its unscalable towers, narrow windows and deep surrounding ditch, was secure enough to hold its human prey.

Chapter 6

PREVIEW OF THE TERROR

B Y modern political standards, the royal family's prison life was almost a de luxe existence. They took with them twenty attendants including a kitchen staff of ten. French rolls and decanters of lemonade were taken up for the King's breakfast, fried chicken and sponge fingers for lunch and the Queen had her favourite dish of duck and pâté when she felt inclined. There was no brain washing—no indoctrination. There were no midnight interrogations; no glaring cell lights; no softening up with promises of release; no warnings—except perhaps from the cries of the news sellers in the streets below announcing the imminent demise of the monarchy.

Not unnaturally, to prevent a repetition of Varennes, or something worse, some precautions were observed. The prisoners met only for meals, where their conversation could be supervised. The clean linen and the washing book sent with it were closely examined in case they contained hidden messages, so were any books supplied to the prisoners. Paper, pens, pencils and ink were removed. Knives and forks were take away—as might have been expected—after each meal and in the later stages of his imprisonment the King was not allowed to use his razor except in the presence of two municipal officers.

But no attempt appears to have been made to take statements from the King which could have provided evidence for the benefit of the prosecution. Indeed the new Convention did not meet until 20 September and it was only on the following day that a decisive vote was taken abolishing that part of the Constitution calling for a monarchy.

The 22 September was decreed as the beginning of year one of the Republic. The poll which elected the Convention had been a low one. Only about one million Frenchmen out of the five million who had the franchise had voted. Some right-wing or middle-of-the-road electors abstained through fear, since voting by ballot had been abolished in Paris and in some of the Departments; others in the provinces, who might have stood for election, had already gained much from the Revolution and felt that it would be unwise to involve themselves in the politics of a capital under mob rule. Nevertheless, the deputies chosen were by no means extremists. About one-third of them had sat in the two previous assemblies. Many of them were connected in some way with industry or commerce, and most were of mature age. The ministers, too, were moderates. Possibly the result would not have been greatly different with a higher poll.

It was therefore clear that there would soon be a struggle between this relatively moderate majority, who came to be lumped together as Girondists, and the more advanced revolutionaries whose inspiration was derived from discussions in the Jacobin Club, about what should be done with the King, whether he should be brought to trial and if so who should try him. The monarchists argued that the King could not be tried because, under the Constitution, his person was declared to be inviolable and unless he were to abdicate—which he certainly had not done—there was no way of removing him legally from the throne. But the more radical leaders pointed out that the Constitution no longer held good, since the people had charged the National Convention with altering it and they argued that the National Convention, directly representing the will of the people was competent to try anyone, including the King. They contended also that since all the King's official acts were performed through his ministers, he was not protected from being proceeded against for acts committed, not by his ministers, but by himself acting as an individual. Discussions continued in the Assembly for two solid months, seven hours a day, with speeches published not only in newspapers and pamphlets but also in works one of which ran to eight volumes. At one point a locksmith named Gamain intervened to tell the Assembly of the existence of a secret safe in the Tuileries. As a boy he had been given a room in the palace in order to help the young Louis XVI with his hobby of making locks. Later he had been called in to construct a secret strong-room.

Gamain was convinced that the King had ordered that he should subsequently be poisoned to prevent his revealing the secret of the strong box. In revenge he felt himself free to disclose its existence to Roland, the Minister of the Interior to the Convention. Roland told Gamain to look for the safe and open it. Inside was a mass of private papers including the arrangements for the King's flight, Mirabeau's advice on royalist policy, correspondence with the English Prime Minister Pitt, and suggestions for bribing some of the popular leaders not to take part in the coup which was expected to take place on 9 August. Roland produced these papers to the Convention on 20 November.

But even this evidence might not have decided the issue had it not been for the sheer logic of the case. For as Robespierre pointed out in his speeches of 2 December, the National Convention derived its power from the crowds of sans-culottes (non-breeches-wearers) who had deposed the King. 'If the King is not guilty, those who dethroned him are. . . . The Constitution prohibited everything you have done. . . . Prostrate yourselves therefore before Louis and invoke his clemency.'

It followed that since the Convention was unwilling to prostrate itself, the King *must* be found guilty and must be sentenced as an enemy of the people. Robespierre even argued that a trial was unnecessary, adding that trying the King was like submitting the Revolution to litigation. 'In the case of tyrants,' he cried, 'insurrection corresponds to a trial, his fall from power is the verdict and the liberty of the people his punishment.'

Robespierre's speech concluded:

As for him, I demand that the Convention declares him now this very moment a traitor to the French Nation, a criminal to humanity, I demand that he provides a true example to the world in the same place where the selfless martyrs of liberty died on 10 August. I demand that this memorable event be consecrated by a memorial destined to nourish in the heart of the people a consciousness of their rights and a horror of tyrants and, in the souls of the tyrants, a healthy fear of the justice of the people.

St Just at the same time declared, 'Personally I see no middle way. Either this man ought to reign, or he ought to die.'

On 3 December, however, the Convention decided to stage a State trial. On 6 December a Commission was appointed to frame the charges. They accused Louis of having conspired against the sovereignty of the people at Versailles and at the Bastille, of having committed treason by his flight to Varennes, of having favoured foreign intervention and counter-revolution, of having bribed émigré regiments, of having allowed the French armed services to decay, of having employed a private army against the wishes of the Legislative Assembly and of having ambushed patriots at the Tuileries.

On 11 December the King was brought from his prison to the Convention for questioning. He did not ask to be provided with a Defence Counsel, nor did he complain at being called on to answer questions which he had not had time to study. He gave such replies as he could—by no means always truthful since he disowned all knowledge of the iron safe and of documents in it written in his own hand. He indignantly denied having been responsible for shedding the blood of Frenchmen.

After the hearing, the Convention agreed that the trial should be held and that the King should be allowed to choose Counsel to prepare his defence. Guy-Jean-Baptiste Target, probably the most distinguished barrister of the day and a member of the French Academy, asked to be excused on the grounds of illness and age (he was fifty-nine), but François-Denis Tronchet aged sixty-six accepted and likewise Malesherbes who was still older. They were joined later by Desèze, a barrister from Bordeaux, who made the speech for the defence. Desèze had only a few days in which to prepare his plea and was ordered by the King to make it on a purely legal basis, and not to appeal to emotions which could lead to war between Frenchmen.

At the trial, held on 26 December, Desèze sought to prove that the King had not abdicated and that the Convention had no power to try him. In the presence of the King he argued that the Convention could not be called a court since the accusers and the judges were the same men. He claimed that the King had always responded to the wishes of his people and during the storming of the Tuileries had done no more than defend himself against an armed insurrection with the knowledge and consent of the city and Departmental authorities.

Louis even spoke himself to protest against the charge of having deliberately shed French blood. 'I think that I should have been spared from this reproach by the continual proofs that I have given of my affection for my people,' he said.

But the Convention heard him unmoved and decided almost unanimously that he was guilty. Some of the deputies thought that it would be wise to seek sanction for their actions from the broad mass of the people through a referendum. The proposal was defeated partly because there was a risk of civil war over the issue and partly because of the dangerous principle of one man one vote which would have been involved.

The next point was to decide what sentence should be passed. The Convention was given a night to consider its verdict but the deputies were warned that each would have to announce his decision publicly from the tribune and that the names of those who failed to do so would be posted up as a public token of disapproval.

Voting began at eight o'clock on the evening of 16 January and continued throughout the night and most of the following day. Each of the deputies one after the other stepped on to the platform and announced his decision sometimes justifying it with a lengthy speech. It was a strange and theatrical scene. Ushers showed the mistresses of the Duc d'Orléans to their box as though they had been attending an opera. Ladies in evening dress ate ices and oranges, laughed and talked with their friends, while the men drank brandy and made bets on the outcome. Some deputies were more anxious about missing their dinner than about casting their vote. Others fell asleep and had to be woken when their turn came to vote.

The first count showed a majority of one for an unqualified recommendation that the King should be executed. But another twenty-six more deputies voted for a death sentence with some

form of qualification (such as a suggestion that an appeal be permitted for reprieve), and other republican-minded members of the
Convention who were absent would probably have also voted for a
death sentence. However, in order to discover the will of the Convention more clearly, a second vote was taken to decide whether the
death sentence should be subject to reprieve or not. There was a
majority of seventy against any appeal. Orléans was among those
who voted 'death'.

The King, who had been present during the trial but not during
the voting, was told by the Minister of Justice on 20 January that
he was going to die the following day and received the news without emotion. He asked for three days in which to take leave of his
family and prepare himself with the aid of a confessor for his end.
Only the last two requests were granted. The authorities were
afraid that any delay would encourage attempts to release him
from prison or kidnap him on his way to the scaffold. That Monday
evening he parted from his wife and children, having promised to
see them the next morning. But later, pacing up and down his
room he felt that the final parting would be too distressing for them
and declared vehemently, 'I will not go.' That night he slept peace-
fully. He had already sent for the Abbé Edgeworth, his sister's
confessor, a priest of Irish extraction who had refused to take the
constitutional oath.

The next morning his valet, Cléry, woke Louis at five. Louis
received Communion at six, kneeling before an altar put up on the
chest-of-drawers in his bedroom. To Cléry he handed over the only
possessions that he had been allowed to keep—a ring, a seal and a
lock of hair. Soon after eight, Santerre, the brewer who was to head
the cortège arrived. 'You have come to fetch me,' the King said
and, after handing his will to the Municipal Officer, he called for his
hat and said in a firm voice, 'Let us go.' Louis left his prison about
half past eight in a closed carriage on his way to the Place de la
Révolution which had been chosen as the place of execution since
the broad streets leading to it were easily policed.

The journey of two and a half miles took nearly an hour. The
streets were lined with a double row of soldiers and forty thousand
troops were under arms. The bridges and the main avenues were
protected by cannon. The shops were shut all day. At a street
corner near the Châtelet, a royalist, Baron de Batz, called for
volunteers to rescue the King. His appeals were drowned by the

sound of drums that the municipality had thoughtfully caused to
be sounded continuously throughout the proceedings.

At that hour of the day a cold mist still hung about the Place
de la Révolution. But whole families were there to watch the
spectacle, from the railings of the Tuileries gardens or from any
vantage point they could find. The King got out of the carriage
and, supported by Abbé Edgeworth, walked up the steps leading to
the scaffold. He knelt to receive the blessing of the priest. Then he
stood up and made a sign to the drummers to be silent. 'My people,'
he cried, 'I die an innocent man. I forgive my enemies: and you
also unhappy people.' At this point Santerre gave an order for the
drums to start beating again.

In France, as in many other countries, the 'profession' of public
executioner was a family business and Charles Henri Sanson, who
was to execute his thirty-nine-year-old King, was one of seven
generations of Sansons who followed the same calling. His team
were waiting to act. Three of them seized the King who with some
show of resistance submitted to the indignity of having his hands
bound. To his executioners he was heard to say, 'I hope that my
blood will secure the happiness of my people.' A moment later
Sanson held up his severed head for the crowd to see.

His hat with its tricolour badge was auctioned from the scaffold.
His hair and hair ribbon were sold too. Pieces of his coat and the
buttons from it were handed out to the crowd and his body,
dressed in a white waistcoat, grey silk breeches and stockings, was
taken to be buried in the cemetery of La Madeleine in quicklime in a
grave ten feet deep.

Three days later a proclamation was issued, 'Citizens, the
Tyrant is no more. . . . Today the French people can have no other
thought than liberty.' This then should have been the day of glory.
But the two groups who ruled France, the men of the Gironde and
the men of the Jacobin Club, were not agreed among themselves
about the past, the present or the future of their country.

The Girondists had been the war party and remained all the
more so after the victory of Valmy which they hoped would
enhance their authority. Jacques-Pierre Brissot, one of their
leaders, wrote in November 1792:

> We must never rest until the whole of Europe is ablaze. There
> must be no slackening of our endeavour. We must take the

offensive. We must issue manifestoes in French and Spanish. We must stimulate every mind either to revolt or to accept revolution. If once we push our frontier to the Rhine, if once there are free peoples on both sides of the Pyrenees, then our liberty will be firmly established.

But the Girondists lacked the ruthlessness to take the measures needed for victory. Robespierre had originally opposed war because he felt it was necessary to secure the Revolution first in one country, France, before exporting it. Thus he might in later times have favoured Stalinism as opposed to the Trotskyism of the Girondists. But once war was declared the Jacobins began to take over the leadership. The struggle was prolonged because the Jacobins, the ultimate victors, were in a minority in the Convention. In fact the extremists numbered only fifty out of a total of seven hundred and eighty-two members. Their strength lay in the fact that they knew what they wanted and how they proposed to get it.

The Girondists were for the most part friends of the well-to-do, of wholesalers, bankers, merchants and shipowners. They favoured a republic established constitutionally rather than by violence. The Jacobins on the other hand championed the smallholders, petit-bourgeois and sans-culottes, and realized that victory could not be won without their support.

There has been much learned discussion about what sort and condition of people were included under the description of sans-culottes. Certainly men at the time used sans-culotte in many different senses. Some took it to mean those people who had no other way of making their living than to work with their hands. Others thought that the term included all good patriots, especially those who had not yet profited from the Revolution. More accurately the sans-culottes amounted to a political association of people with different aims and ambitions. But they all claimed the right to work, the right to State assistance, and free education. They were hostile to large capitalists and ready to attribute any misfortune—even the plague—to them. And their widely scattered interests became solidly fused in common indignation over the scarcities of food, fuel and clothing and by injustices of the black market through which these were supplied. This explains the fact that although the majority of sans-culottes were workers and small shopkeepers, quite a few were of independent means.

Eventually it became fashionable to adopt sans-culottism as a way of life. The notice displayed outside restaurants and clubs—'We are all citizens here'—was usually respected. The terms 'Monsieur' and 'Madame' had been banned by the Commune in August 1792, though this was short-sighted because one could thereafter no longer distinguish between married women and unmarried. The idea of calling all people *tu* (instead of some *vous* and others—servants and children—*tu*) had been launched by Louise de Keralio, wife of an advocate from Liège, in an article in December 1790 in the *Mercure National*. She argued that it was absurd to use *vous* when talking to more than one person since its use made it impossible to tell whether one was addressing all or only one of those present. If no one gave themselves airs and if all were addressed as *tu* she reckoned that a new comradeship would soon spring up. Besides, it was fun for employees to be able to *tu-toyer* the boss.

Social habits were roughed up in other ways too. As far back as July 1790 it had been suggested that in future hats were no longer to be removed in token of salute but only when the wearer felt hot or was addressing the National Assembly. It was also suggested about this time that bowing should be banned and that the habit of writing, 'I have the honour to be your humble and obedient servant' even as a mere formality, should be dropped. Prostitution was suppressed as a degrading relic of earlier tyranny.

Styles of dress changed too. Phrygian red bonnets of liberty were officially encouraged at Voltaire's funeral celebrations in 1791.

Seventeen ninety-two was the year of the Carmagnole. The Carmagnole was originally a short woollen jacket of about finger-tip length decked with metal buttons and worn with pantaloons and a waistcoat. It had been introduced to France by Piedmontese workers from Carmagnola. It caught on in Marseilles and was brought to Paris by the Marseillais *fédérés*. The the name was given to an anti-monarchist dance and to the music and words that went with it.

There were other changes in fashion too. Fans became more utilitarian and the decorations on them showed current events rather than shepherds, flowers and butterflies. Jewellery was seldom seen after the Government had suggested that every citizen should make a 'gift of patriotism' for the public welfare. It was safer to wear a souvenir from the Bastille. A year later, in September 1793,

Parisians, including women, were ordered to wear a tricolour cockade on pain of eight days' jail for the first offence and imprisonment till peace was signed for a second misdemeanour. Masked balls had been forbidden by the Assembly in January 1792 perhaps in order to make conspiracy more difficult.

After the September Massacres there was, of course, a reaction against the Commune and the methods which it had adopted to carry out its policy and the Girondists were able to mount a series of attacks against the Jacobins. A week after the Massacres had ended Roland attacked the Commune and its commissioners, or commissars as we should probably call them today. Pierre-Victorin Vergniaud, another Girondist leader, denounced the Commune's special Vigilance Committee and the Commune duly apologized and temporarily dissolved its committee. But the deputies who had been elected in Paris through the influence of the Commune continued to propagate their ideas through Communes elsewhere in France.

After Valmy it proved possible to dissolve the Commune itself. Roland took over the special police and dismissed the Extraordinary Tribunal set up to try the 'criminals' of 10 August. The Girondists succeeded, too, in breaking up the camp set up to repair the fortifications of Paris, the inhabitants of which had become the private army of the Commune.

However, a formidable Girondist attack on Robespierre by Jean-Baptiste Louvet misfired largely because it was not pressed home by the other Girondists. Robespierre was allowed five days to prepare his defence. He made the most of the time and was able to convince the Convention that the thought of becoming a dictator had never entered his mind.

Some months after the King's death the Convention had moved from the Riding School to the Tuileries itself and was installed in the private theatre there. Ten rows of benches, in straight lines curved at the ends, rose one above the other. And extreme Jacobins who sat in the upper benches of the Convention were therefore known collectively as the Mountain. They were able to make an issue over the death of the King. They attacked the Girondists for being half-hearted about the trial and gave them the choice of being labelled as 'royalists' or of following their lead.

The Girondists had indeed doubted the wisdom of bringing the King to trial. They had argued that a trial would increase the risks of intervention from abroad. But the Jacobins never held back.

Indeed they eventually realized that terror, the fear of foreign intervention, a general state of tension and crisis were the very conditions that they needed in order to impose their own dictatorship.

After the execution of the King the Jacobins felt free to turn their full attention to the Girondists and the big battle began. On 1 February, France, already at war with Austria and Prussia, declared war on Holland and England. Towards the end of February a decree was passed to provide for an army of three hundred thousand men, part of which was to be conscripted. Commissars, mainly Jacobins, were sent to the provinces to explain the need for the call-up and to put it into effect. Their rulings could be changed only by the Convention itself. They naturally made good use of the opportunity to build up Jacobin influence through the Jacobin clubs in every city they visited.

The need for strong government and the Girondists' inability to provide it was soon illustrated again when the Republic's best general, Dumouriez, deserted his troops and went over to the enemy. The explanation for Dumouriez's defection is to be sought in two proclamations made in 1793 on the scope and object of the war which France was fighting.

The first of these, issued back in November 1792, proclaimed that the National Convention would grant 'fraternity and aid to all peoples who wish to recover their liberty'; and it ordered the executive power 'to give the generals the orders necessary for bringing aid to such peoples and for defending citizens who have been, or who might be, harassed in the cause of liberty'. Less than a month later the Convention passed a second motion making it clear that the people of the liberated territories would be expected to pay for the upkeep of the armies that liberated them and accept payment in worthless paper money of their goods. The Girondists hoped that in this way they could end shortages at home. But the policy meant that military occupation was envisaged, which made it doubly hard to secure victory. Thus the second decree turned a limited war which could, perhaps, have been supported by France without any great hardship, into an unlimited struggle against any established power where there was discontent. It was clear to Dumouriez that he was not likely to be given the support necessary to carry out the Convention's orders even if he had been in sympathy with their aims, and, on being given orders in February to revolutionize Holland, he declared that the Convention was made up of three

hundred scoundrels and four hundred imbeciles and announced his
intention of starving Paris into submission. When the War Minister
himself and his staff arrived at his camp at the end of March,
Dumouriez told them, 'The Convention is an Assembly of tyrants.
As long as I have a dagger I will not allow it to reign and shed
blood with the Revolutionary Tribunal which it has just created.
As for the Republic, it is an idle phrase. I had faith in it for three
days. But I have since deplored all the successes obtained in so
poor a cause. There is only one way to save the country—that is to
re-establish the Constitution of 1791 and a King.' When they read
him a summons from the convention to return to Paris, he told
them, 'Tigers wish for my head; I will not give it them.' Then,
when the minister tried to arrest him, he handed him and his staff
over as hostages to the Austrians and went over to the enemy.
He died in exile and is buried at Henley.

At the same time another Government crisis over conscription
arose to expose the weakness of Girondist leadership. It was the
hardships caused by the levy of three hundred thousand,which led
to considerable resistance in western France particularly in the de-
voutly Catholic area of La Vendée, where priests had already stirred
up fanatical opposition to the Revolution. The Jacobins' remedy
was to force the Convention to decree the establishment of Vigilance Committees in every Commune from 21 March, a measure
which further weakened the Girondist control over the provinces.

On 10 March a special Criminal Court, afterwards known as the
Revolutionary Tribunal, was set up to deal with counter-revolutionary activities; juries were appointed for a fixed period and
compelled to give their verdict in public by majority vote. (What
would Voltaire have said?)

On 1 April the decree providing for the inviolability of the
Convention deputies was repealed and commissars of the Convention were given power to arrest suspects. A sans-culotte army to
'protect Paris' was authorized.

Five days later the Girondists unwisely agreed to the creation
of a Committee of Public Safety with powers to deliberate in secret
and to override ministers. The Girondists may have hoped that they
would have a majority here as they still had elsewhere, but on voting day not a single Girondist was elected to the Committee. At the
same time arrangements were made by a Central Committee of
commissars of the Paris Sections for a new anti-Girondist coup. On

28 May this Central Committee organized a snap election, declared that the Commune was abolished and set themselves up in its place.

The Girondists organized one counter-blow. Gaudet, a Girondist deputy, recommended moving the Convention bodily to Bourges and when this failed to get support, set up a Committee of Twelve to protect the Convention against 'conspiracies'. On 24 May this Committee suggested, in the hope of forestalling midnight coups, that in future the Sections should not be allowed to continue their meetings after ten in the evening. The Committee imprisoned Hébert, already a prominent Commune official and spokesman for the sans-culottes, for a provocative article and also arrested Dobsen, a President of one of the Sections, for his refusal to produce the accounts of his Section.

But these actions came too late to save the Girondists. They had bungled the King's trial, the war and the economy and they had quarrelled with the people. On 28 May the Girondists were compelled to release their two prisoners. On 31 May and 2 June an organized mob invaded the Tuileries, surrounded the palace, blocked all exits and compelled the Convention to suspend twenty deputies, two ministers and most of the Committee of Twelve. That night they were placed under house arrest.

The eclipse of the Girondists left three men in control of the French Revolution. The first of these—Jean-Paul Marat—being the agitator-in-chief. Marat, son of a Swiss mother and a Spanish father (who had moved to Sardinia after having adopted the Calvinist religion), was forty-six years old when the Bastille fell. In his twenties he had lived in Soho studying medical science. In those days Joseph Farington, the diarist, described him as 'a little man, slender, but well made. Of a yellow aspect, he had a quick eye. He had a great deal of motion, seldom keeping his body or limbs still. He was thin, discontented, and abused the establishments which existed.'

Fabre d'Eglantine, another revoluntionary, noticed his short thin body, big shoulders and strong arms which allowed him to make effective oratorical gestures. He had a bony face, acquiline nose, piercing greyish-yellow eyes and a wide mouth creased by a nervous twitch. He usually wore the red handkerchief head-dress of his native island.

When first heard of in France in 1777 Marat appears as a

physician attached to the Life Guards of the Comte d'Artois—in
the thick of the establishment of the day. He had also built up
among aristocrats, such as the Marquise de Laubespine and the
Duc de Choiseul, a thriving private practice on the strength of a
secret tincture which he used to cure chest complaints but which
when analyzed was found to consist of chalk and water. He
affected an imaginary coat of arms with a Latin motto. He was
ambitious in more than one way and waged a guerrilla campaign
against the French Academy of Science which refused to recognize
the worth which he ascribed to a paper that he had written on
Newton's optics.

The Revolution therefore found him more ready than ever to
'abuse the establishment' and he did so by founding a paper *L'Ami
du Peuple* in which he was happy to write that to ensure public
order it would be necessary to cut off two hundred thousand heads
and that a man who is starving has the right to cut another man's
throat and devour his living flesh.

In July 1792 we find him arguing that the Revolution has been
sustained only by the outcasts of society, the labourers, artisans,
shopkeepers, farm labourers and ordinary people, because those
with education who had taken part in the Revolution had done so
merely to exploit its strength to instal themselves in the places of
those who had been proscribed. In August this most suspicious of
men was appointed to the Watch Committee of eleven in charge of
the Paris prisons. With help from the Sections, Marat prepared the
list of suspects who were to be murdered in the September Massacres and profited by them to seize the royal printing presses for
his paper.

He was impeached before the Assembly as being responsible for
the excesses of the September Massacres but was acquitted after he
had threatened to blow his brains out before the eyes of his accusers.
After his acquittal he was elected President of the Jacobins, and
the Girondists again attacked him and accused him before the
Revolutionary Tribunal of having declared in a circular that the
supporters of the counter-revolution were to be found in the
Government. In turn Marat played a leading part in organizing the
demonstrations which overawed the Convention into proscribing
the Girondists. He even succeeded in getting arms, which should
have been sent to the front, turned over instead to his own street
mobs since to his view the protection of Paris came before all else.

With his hollow croaking voice, his affectedly dirty clothes and his repulsive skin afflictions, Marat could never have been a great leader but as the prophet of doom he was an essential part of the Revolution.

His death was as bizarre as his life. At half past seven on the evening of Saturday, 13 July, a young woman wearing a dress of Indian muslin, a pink gauze scarf and a green hat with black tassels, called at 30 rue des Cordeliers, the residence of citizen Marat, claiming that she could reveal plots that were being hatched in her native city of Caen. Charlotte Corday, the well-brought-up daughter of a poverty-stricken but aristocratic Norman squire, had intended to spend her days as a nun but was turned out into the world when the Revolution closed all convents. She was convinced that Marat was a monster and that posterity would praise the man or woman who put an end to his life. She prepared for the murder that she was about to commit with care and deliberation. She told friends at home that she was leaving to go to Argentan to see her father. She told her father that she was going to England because no one could live happily in France. And, to get an introduction to the Convention where she hoped to find Marat, she espoused the cause of a friend, Alexandrine de Forbin, whose pension had been cancelled because she had formerly left the country. When she reached Paris, Charlotte learnt that Marat was too ill to go to the Convention and so, instead, she called early at Marat's house and left a note saying that she had useful information for him from Normandy. In the evening she returned again determined to see him. She had even taken special care with her appearance, and with her clear skin, blue eyes and newly dressed silky chestnut hair she looked—for she was a tall girl—at her statuesque best. In one hand she carried a green fan, and, pinned to the inside of her dress a paper headed 'Address to the French People' explaining the motives for her deed and declaring that none of her friends or relatives knew anything of her plans. Inside her dress was also a kitchen knife with an ebony handle and a blade six inches long which she had bought that morning in a shop in the Palais-Royal. The knife rested in a green cardboard sheath.

Her well bred looks and clothes made her an object of suspicion in Marat's working-class quarter and she would probably not have got inside the door of his flat if two other people had not called to see Marat about the paper that he was in the process of getting out.

One wanted his signature on an invoice and the other some copies of the paper for the War Office.

In Marat's front hall, Charlotte was confronted by Madame Pain, the porter's wife, Jeannette Maréchale, Marat's cook, and Simone Evrard, his mistress whom he claimed to have married 'in a ceremony before the Supreme Being'. The three women told Charlotte that it was impossible for her to see Marat. By this time, however, the sound of raised voices had reached Marat, who was in his bathroom separated from the hall by the dining-room and an ante-room. He could hear the young woman with the cultivated voice asking if he had got her note—which indeed he had—and his curiosity was aroused. He asked for the caller to be brought in. The next issue of his paper would be all the more influential if he could print the names of the Girondists who were plotting in Normandy. Marat received his visitor sitting in a high-walled copper bath which he had hired in the hope that soaking in it would help to cure the chronic ulcerating skin disease from which he suffered. The bath covered him up to above the navel and a plank had been placed across it to allow him to read and write. He must have been a revolting sight. But Charlotte with the greatest composure began to answer his questions about the conspirators of Caen.

As she told her story, Marat wrote by the light of an orange-tinted window behind him. Once they were interrupted by Simone Evrard who made an excuse to ask Marat whether some almond water that she had prepared for him was the right mixture. At the same time she took from the bathroom window-sill a plate of veal and rissoles that she planned to serve for dinner. As she left, she noticed that the chair on which Charlotte Corday was sitting seemed dangerously close to Marat. Not long after, from outside the door, she heard Marat crying for help. In one swift movement, Charlotte had taken the knife from its green cardboard sheath, and plunged it between Marat's ribs into his heart. A surgeon could hardly have done better. It was over so soon that Marat was able to utter only a few words before he was dead.

Everyone who saw her afterwards was amazed at Charlotte's coolness. She neither hurried from the bathroom nor made any attempt to escape. She denied all suggestions that the murder had been planned by the Girondists and repeated that she had come to Paris only to murder Marat and save her country. She was not averse to publicity and with some complacency allowed her portrait to be painted in prison.

She remained equally calm during her trial and even when she had to put on the red shirt that murderers were compelled to wear on their journey to the guillotine. She refused the offer of a seat during her journey to the scaffold and stood up in the cart for all to see. She insisted on inspecting the guillotine, stepped up to the platform without hesitation and clung almost with pleasure to the plank to which she was bound before the blade of the guillotine fell.

Pierre-Victorin Vergniaud, the Girondist leader, who could hardly speak a sentence without uttering an epigram and who realized that a witch hunt would follow Marat's death, summed that matter up when he said, 'She has killed us but she has shown us how to die.'

In return, Marat's funeral, designed and presented by Jacques-Louis David, was a demonstration of how to be buried. His coffin was followed by young girls dressed in white, by the whole of the Convention and by representatives of the Sections. Incense was sprinkled, revolutionary hymns sung and Marat's heart was suspended in an urn from the ceiling of the Cordeliers Club.

The Girondists were not the only ones to suffer from Marat's assassination. The consequences followed right down the political line. The far right were accused by the moderate right of having been responsible, the moderate rights by the moderate lefts and so on right through the spectrum and the deed left the two remaining giants of the Revolution, Robespierre and Danton, eyeing each other with the deepest suspicion.

There has probably been more controversy over Robespierre than about any other figure in the French Revolution. To some he has appeared as the selfless patriot; to others a petty intriguer and would-be tyrant.

In deciding which of these two images is the truer, we have to allow for the fact that Robespierre's enemies, by outliving him, had the last word. He was survived by many who believed that he had been planning to send them to the guillotine and it was natural both for them and for those who had encompassed his death to justify their conduct by blackening his character. After his death few contemporaries were ready to defend his policies or to be associated in any way with the dead leader.

Let us first begin by describing the man. He is shown at his best
in his portrait painted by Boilly a few years before the outbreak
of the Revolution. According to this, Robespierre, then twenty-
five, had a face of distinction and refinement, an impressive face
perhaps slightly heart-shaped, with a firm chin and large eyes sur-
mounted by arched eyebrows. Other contemporaries were less
flattering and Merlin de Thionville, one of the military commissars
of the Convention, declared that the big luminous eyes slightly
askew, and the small cat-like nose, inhumanly pale skin and indeed
Robespierre's whole face, reminded him of a cat's for it could look
wild and ferocious as well as amiable. Robespierre was certainly
not a large man nor did he have the deliberate movements of one.
His step was rapid and jerky. His manner was aloof; his laugh dry
and forced rather than genuine, and the impression that he was a
difficult man to know was no doubt increased by the fact that he
habitually wore tinted glasses, to which he added a pair of eye-
glasses when he wanted to look more closely at his audience. His
weak eyesight afflicted him with a nervous blink.

His voice was thin and his delivery unimpressive and hesitating,
so much so that his audiences habitually wondered whether he had
finished what he was saying or whether a few more words were to
come.

François-Maximilien-Joseph Isidore Robespierre was born at
Arras on 6 May 1758 four months after the marriage of his parents.
His mother died when he was six and his father deserted the family
a year later. Young Maximilien was brought up by two aunts and
his grandfather. It was enough to make any man discontented with
his lot.

However, at the age of eleven he attracted the attention of the
Bishop of Arras and like that other young man of talent, Camille
Desmoulins, was awarded a scholarship under royal patronage at
the College of St Louis le Grand. There Robespierre was allowed to
read an address on the occasion of the King's visit, for which he
received a reward from the royal purse. His most valuable contacts
there, however, were with the traditional Jesuit methods of
thought. From these he learnt not only how to argue but how to
reduce his arguments, usually based on ideas provided by others, to
the simplest possible form. At fifteen he had read Rousseau and he
almost won a prize offered by the Academy of Metz for a theme
which could well have appealed to any Revolutionary lawyer—an

attack on the law then in force which made a man's family punishable for the crimes which he committed.

When he opened his career as a lawyer in 1780 his first case was on behalf of Charles-Dominique de Visséry de Bois-Valé, an elderly lawyer of St Omer, who had installed one of Benjamin Franklin's new-fangled lightning conductors on his house. His neighbours in the Marché-aux-Herbes objected on the ground that this would attract disaster. Robespierre was able to point out that three similar lightning conductors had already been installed at Dijon, including one on the bell-tower of St Philibert. His client, he maintained, was thus supported by excellent precedents. The opposing lawyer argued that though some lightning conductors could be beneficial, the one installed by de Visséry might not be properly designed and that in any case the discharge of electricity into the earth might cause earthquakes. Robespierre was able to convince the judge on both counts and won his case. His practice, however, did not grow as fast as he had hoped.

He was not elected to the dining club of the leading barristers of Arras and began to suffer feelings of resentment against both his fellow attorneys and his fellow citizens. He was incapable of making close friends and though in late years he talked eloquently of 'the people' and was jealous of anyone else who claimed to understand them, he recoiled from intimacy with any particular one of them. He never married.

From Rousseau he had learnt that his own discontent could find a political solution. In 1789 he wrote the *Cahier of Complaints* forwarded to the King on behalf of the cobblers of Arras and he was elected to the National Assembly as a deputy of the Third Estate for Artois.

It would perhaps be over-simplifying matters if one said that thereafter his policy was one of protecting the people by removing from power not only the aristocrats but any of the bourgeoisie who could be considered his rivals for power. It would be over-simplification because these removals helped to strengthen the Republic. For example it was he who suggested in May 1791 that no member of the Constituent Assembly should be elected to the Legislative Assembly. This deprived the new Assembly of any experienced members who could have combated the influence of the clubs on which Robespierre intended to base his power. It allowed the Jacobins to get in more new members favourable to their way of thinking. But it also speeded up the Revolution.

In June 1791 Robespierre was elected Public Prosecutor to the new Criminal Court of the Seine—ready to strike at his enemies. Like Stalin he rose to power through the quarrels of others. The monarchists were weakened by the Girondists, the Girondists by Marat and Danton. Later Danton attacked the extremists led by Hébert, and thus laid himself open to the charge of being too lax.

Robespierre in time learnt to speak effectively and his two speeches to the Assembly calling for the execution of the King were almost unanswerable. On 27 July 1793 he joined the Committee of Public Safety and presided over its deliberations. Although he had once been opposed to capital punishment (as a young man he had refused an appointment as criminal judge because, he said, he could not bear having to pass sentence of death on a human being), he now came to believe that only blood-letting purges could cleanse the country of its impurities. From time to time men like Lindet, Isnard and Carnot began to ask themselves how much longer government by bloodbath could continue. At one time even Robespierre himself, while planning the death of his old schoolmate Camille Desmoulins, promised his faithful followers of the Mountain that 'once a few more serpents had been crushed' victory would be theirs.

But in fact Robespierre was incapable of ruling by persuasion and recognized only two undefined standards of conduct— 'revolutionary' and 'counter-revolutionary'. Shortly before his fall he was still denouncing a conspiracy against the Government which apparently was of such wide proportions that he felt unable to name its authors.

Then, of course, there was his personal vanity. His lodgings with the Duplay family at 398 rue St Honoré were modest . . . his bedspread had been made out of an old dress belonging to Madame Duplay. But the apartment was crowded with pictures of the leader, and Robespierre had grown used to receiving cringing servile letters from those wishing to ingratiate themselves with him, epistles written in a style which, though no more idolatrous than those addressed to the late King Louis XVI, were hardly republican in tone. And it may well have irked Robespierre to think that he who was treated like a God by the people should be treated almost as an equal by the other members of the Committee of Public Security.

How then could such an unlovable man remote from his followers and without close friends have built up such a position for himself? One explanation is perhaps that the policy pursued by Robespierre was logical. Often his arguments were unanswerable. His progress towards the ideal Republic could not be called in question. It was possible also for him to argue as dictators often have that it was his duty to use violence to found the Republic to safeguard liberty . . . that in the heat of battle against the counter-revolution it is impossible to enter into public debate . . . that when a régime is the guardian of freedom no one can complain if he has no rights . . . that although a people's sovereign will may exist, as long as people are hungry there can be no true reflection of it, that the conditions for expressing it must be created gradually by such means as popular education (and the elimination of the opposition) and that in the meantime the people's sovereign will must be represented by enlightened leadership.

Perhaps some of his attraction lay in the fact that his style of dress was almost unique. He was the only one of the few revolutionary leaders to continue wearing the clothes that had been fashionable before the Revolution—the tail coat and breeches topped by the carefully powdered hair. Indeed his enemies insisted that he spent an hour a day on his toilet. Did he perhaps convey to many doubters that the man with the most advanced revolutionary principles could look respectable and perhaps be respectable?

He also appeared disinterested and indeed incorruptible. No one could accuse him of lining his own pockets or of living extravagantly. He never kept a mistress, or permitted himself a love affair. Perhaps the people saw in him the man capable of absolving them from the crimes which they saw committed or perhaps even had helped to commit in the name of liberty, a man capable of reconciling the horrors of the Revolution with a code of honour, a man who could reproduce in practice, the ideals that men had read of only in the works of philosophers.

Robespierre had convinced himself and was able to convince others that his plan was to instal the rule of virtue, although virtue was to go hand in hand with terrorization because it would be impotent without it. His approach was summed up in the speech which he made before the Convention on 26 July 1794 when he said:

There exists a deep feeling, tender, compelling, irresistible,
the torment and delight of generous hearts, a profound hatred of
tyranny, a compassionate concern for the oppressed, a sacred
love of one's country, a more sublime and sacred love for
humanity, without which a great revolution is no more than a
sudden crime that destroys another crime; there exists this selfless ambition to found the first republic in the world; this egoism
of men uplifted who find a divine pleasure in the peace of a clear
conscience and in the enchanting spectacle of happiness of all.
You feel this in that moment which burns in your souls; I feel it
in mine.

Equally compelling are his words on the moral code surrounding the cult of the Supreme Being—the gospel of reason which
Robespierre wished to substitute for the religious fanaticism of
the past.

Nature is the true priest of the Supreme Being; the Universe
is his Temple; virtue his cult, and the happiness of a great people
assembled before his eyes to knit together the beloved links of
universal brotherhood and to offer to him the homage of pure
and receptive hearts constitute his festivals.

But there was illogicality too in Robespierre's methods. When
the Girondists wanted to hold a referendum on the question of the
King's execution, Robespierre argued that it would be unwise to
appeal to the people because 'Virtue has always been a minority on
this earth'. Yet a year later he threatened to appeal to the people
when asked to revoke his most extreme terrorist measure.
And though he could perhaps have justified these inconsis-
tencies of logic to himself, there were others whom he failed to convince. The chief of these, of course, was Georges-Jacques Danton,
the outsize, loud-voiced countryman from Arcis-sur-Aube in the
Champagne province. He had a vast frame, navvy's hands, big
head, pock-marked skin, twisted lip, and bashed-in features. He
was said to have been kicked by a bull. He lost his father when he
was three years old and was educated in a religious seminary at
Troyes. He came to Paris aged twenty-one, studied law in Cham-
bers and became engaged to Gabrielle Charpentier, the daughter of
the proprietor of a prosperous Right-Bank restaurant where he
often dined and played dominoes. With her dowry and the aid of a

loan from his father-in-law he bought himself an appointment to
the Law Courts.

The newly marrieds set up house in the Cour du Commerce on the
Left Bank in the Cordeliers District and Danton soon became a
member of the Society of the Friends of the Rights of Men and
Citizens. He became friendly too with Camille Desmoulins and his
wife, Lucille. Danton was not one of the philosophers but his was a
cultivated mind. His library included not only Blackstone's legal
works but Dr Johnson's dictionary and even Richardson's novel
Clarissa. He talked Italian with his mother-in-law and English
with the agitator Tom Paine.

But politics to Danton were not so much an opportunity of
putting ideologies into practice as of assuring himself a successful
career. And for some time his services—and he was a forceful
speaker able to put across ideas in language that all could understand—were at the service of the highest bidder.

Examination of Danton's personal accounts show that in some
way he mysteriously acquired a fortune not accounted for by his
earnings and that he was able not only to pay off his loans but also
to buy three separate pieces of property. There is reason for thinking that he received money as early as October 1789 from the King's
Foreign Minister, Montmorin. Mirabeau claimed that he had paid
Danton a large sum from the fund entrusted to him by the King
and the Spanish Ambassador was also reported to have offered him
money to intercede for the King's life. Admittedly these bribes do
not seem to have won over Danton to the royalist cause and from
the first he appears to have taken a radical line. It was Danton who
pressed for the house-to-house searches that preceded the September Massacres and who was thereby saddled with much of the blame
for the excesses. At the time of the right-wing reaction which followed the Massacre of the Champ de Mars, Danton thought it safer
to leave Paris. But it is difficult, even after allowing for the standards of those days, to make him a hero as some historians have tried
to do. Indeed though many men of all persuasions behaved with
heroism during the French Revolution, it is hard to point to any
one and say, 'This was one of the Great Men of all time.'

Danton nevertheless was a far-sighted and practical man of
action. He was one of the first to demand the dethronement of the
King, and helped to organize the attack on the Tuileries of 10
August 1792. On the following day he was elected Minister of

Justice and President of the Executive Council of the Assembly.
He helped to organize the opening victories of Dumouriez that so
disconcerted Robespierre. Men whom he had picked from among
his friends on the Commune were sent as commissars to the provinces to explain the significance of the events of 10 August and the
elections for a Convention that were to follow. He was the moving
spirit behind the establishment of the Revolutionary Tribunal and
was head of the original Committee of Public Safety. While there,
he began realistic moves to break up the coalition of hostile powers
with which France was faced. But though he argued for moderation
at home on the ground that no foreigners would do business with
maniacs, his hand was forced by the outbreak of civil war in France.
In these circumstances he was even denounced at his own club, the
Cordeliers, for his lack of revolutionary fervour.

Danton's wife died in February 1793, unhappy because politics
allowed her to see less and less of her husband and because of the
reputation which he had begun to earn. And four months later Danton married a sixteen-year-old girl, Louise Gély, a devout practis-
ing Catholic and the daughter of an Admiralty clerk. Louise insisted as the price of her hand that she should be married in church
after Danton had received absolution from a non-juring priest. The
marriage was happy and this may well have led Danton to think of
retiring from politics with the wealth that he had managed to
acquire during his four years in politics. But for that, as we shall
soon see, it was already too late.

Chapter 7

THE NIGHTMARE

And now the Terror was surely approaching. For three months after their expulsion from the Convention, the Girondists were kept in suspense. Etienne Clavière, the Minister of Finance, and Henri Lebrun, the Minister for Foreign Affairs, were allowed to continue in office. The others were permitted to speak and write against their enemies. And indeed if only they had been united they might well have completely rehabilitated themselves. Unfortunately twenty of the twenty-nine who had been proscribed, escaped to the provinces. Several tried to mount an armed rebellion against the dictatorship of Paris and of the Jacobin leaders in the Convention. The rebels were supported in the south, west and especially in the north-west of the country by the upper middle classes who had had enough of the Revolution, by the local patriots who did not fancy being kept in subservience to a distant capital and by troops led by royalists who were prepared to fight a civil war. They were defeated partly by measures announced from Paris which committed the smallholders, shopkeepers and minor officials more closely to the success of the Revolution. Taxes were lowered, official salaries raised, and more land was doled out to the peasants. And when it came to the pinch the royalist troops were no match for the fervid republicans.

In August 1793 the Government had decreed the Levée en Masse, applying for the first time in modern history the principle of general conscription. The whole nation—including scientists and factory owners—were drawn into the national effort. The decree read simply:

> From this time on until the enemy has been driven from the territory of the Republic, the French people are permanently requisitioned for army service. The young men will be sent to the battlefield; the married men are to make arms and bring up supplies; the women are to make tents and clothes and serve in hospitals. The children are to make bandages and the old men are to report to the square to inspire the soldiers with courage, to cement the unity of the country and keep alive the hatred of Kings. National buildings are to become barracks; armament works are to be set up in public places and the soil of cellars shall be washed in lye to extract saltpetre [used for gunpowder] from them. . . . No one may arrange for a substitute to carry out the duties to which he is assigned. Officials in the public service are to remain at their posts. The levy is to be general. Unmarried citizens or childless widowers, from eighteen to twenty-five years are to go first. They are to meet, without delay, at the Chief Town of their district where they must undergo physical training every day while waiting to be mobilized. The Committee of Public Safety is responsible for taking all necessary measures to establish at once the production of arms of all kinds in accordance with the enterprise and energy of the French people. Accordingly it is authorized to set up any establishments, production centres, workshops and factories necessary for the execution of such tasks and to requisition throughout the entire extent of the Republic, the craftsmen and workmen who can contribute to their success.

It was high time for such measures, for Dumouriez's desertion in the spring of 1793 had laid France wide open to invasion by the English and Austrian armies. That summer, the English forces, under the Duke of York, made for Dunkirk, which they needed as a supply port, while the Austrians captured the northern fortress of Valenciennes, and later invaded Alsace. Mainz was betrayed to the Prussians, and Spanish armies invaded the country at both ends of the Pyrenees. Unrelenting civil war flared across the wooded landscape of La Vendée while revolts against the central Government, inspired by the Girondists, blazed in cities such as Bordeaux, Marseilles and Lyons. By September, Britain had enlisted Russia, Sardinia, Naples and Portugal as well as Holland, Spain, Prussia and Austria, in a coalition against France. Only the victories of Hondschoote and Wattignies saved France's north-eastern frontier.

During the autumn of 1793 tremendous efforts were made to improve the armies. The volunteer battalions were merged with the regulars. New leaders, some of whom became Napoleon's marshals, were promoted.

By the spring of 1794 a new spirit was discernible, and Mercy d'Argenteau, the Austrian Ambassador, who had moved from Paris to Brussels, sent home to his Foreign Minister, the following very pertinent but far from reassuring report to explain why the French troops 'although badly organized and led, although poorly drilled and undisciplined, can resist the best armies in Europe':

> France should be regarded as entirely subservient to the Convention, and all attempts to break the accord which reigns between the nation, its Committee of Public Safety, its clubs and its delegates to the Departments and the armies, would be illusory. Any attempt to detach the soldier from the cause of the Convention would be equally unfruitful. He could not find abroad what he finds in France: freedom, good money, quick promotion, subsistence, help of all kinds and unpunished excesses.

After listing the soldier's rations—which included brandy twice a week and a pint of vinegar per twenty men when drinking water was unpalatable or during heat waves, the Ambassador continued:

> The regularity with which he gets bread is shown by the fact that it is always given out on the evening before it is due. . . . When his kit becomes worn, the items are replaced without waiting for the normal renewal date. His pay is in assignats, but this is no loss to him because the law compels people to sell to him at the official price. He is excused any offence provided that he is a patriot.
> The soldier has no enthusiasm for military manœuvres. He

learns willingly to make use of his arms and looks on everything else as useless.

Account is taken of all his demands. The officers and under-officers look after him since (under the system of promotion by election) they hope for—or already owe—their advancement to him.

The death of a general is unavoidable every time this is needed to cover up the faults of the men, and the Convention believes that there is always something to be gained by replacing a general.

The representatives of the Convention are to the armies what the Committee of Public Safety is to France. Their authority is unlimited; they can cancel even a new decree if it is harmful in the circumstances prevailing.

No foreign newspapers reach the troops and, besides, soldiers take little part in political events. There is no tendency on the part of the generals to join up with the forces of foreign powers.

In the interior of the country, terror paralyses all opinions that are not republican and revolutionary. Everyone fears for himself or his dependents. There are fears above all that any insurrection would lead to the massacre of the vast number of people confined in prisons as hostages. Everyone has severed his connections. Societies no longer exist. A single Jacobin makes millions of men tremble.

We must pause for a moment here to explain the existence of the Committee of Public Safety, whose crest incidentally, provided one of the earliest, if not the earliest examples of the famous motto 'Liberty, Equality, Fraternity'. It was the successor to the Committee of General Defence formed in January 1793 when France was faced by a united and hostile Europe. After Dumouriez's desertion it was replaced in April 1793 by a less unwieldy committee of nine members forming the First Committee of Public Safety. Their task was to speed up the war effort and they acted as a War Cabinet, and even dealt direct with foreign Governments.

When some of its members disagreed early in July on matters of policy, Robespierre's supporters seized the chance of reorganizing it and of stepping into power themselves. The second or Great Committee of Public Safety consisted of twelve members who were re-elected *en bloc* every month. On 27 July Robespierre himself joined them as unofficial spokesman. The work of the various Government departments was divided up among sections presided over by one or more of the members. The proceedings were secret and no minutes were kept of debates but the decisions were signed by those who had agreed to them. Naturally Robespierre and the other members of the Committee of Public Safety played an important role in the liquidation of the Girondists.

The news that the rebels had suffered defeats both in Brittany and Normandy reached Paris almost on the day of Marat's assassination. This conjunction was, as Vergniaud had prophesied, fatal for the Girondists. On 28 July they were declared outlaws, to be hunted down. Those that could be found were subjected to a mass-trial of the kind we have grown used to in Communist dictatorships. Fifty thousand leaflets justifying their arrest were printed and distributed in advance. The party as a whole was accused of conspiring against the State and those who had not themselves committed any crime or held any counter-revolutionary views were guilty by association with those who might have done so. Since the State was trying the Girondist party as a whole and not any one individual, the charges were vague. But anyone who had opposed any phase of Revolution—including of course the execution of the King—or who had been on speaking terms with anyone who had expressed anti-Jacobin views or who had encouraged separatism, was to be regarded as a criminal.

The Girondists however, were good orators and their trial in Paris threatened to last almost indefinitely. The prosecutor's witnesses insisted on bolstering their evidence by tracing the history of the Revolution from its very beginnings and the prisoners themselves were no less prolix. Antoine-Quentin Fouquier-Tinville (original name Fouquier de Tinville), the Public Prosecutor, pointed out that after five days only nine witnesses had been heard, and that under these circumstances he almost despaired of getting a conviction.

Spurred by these promptings, the Convention felt constrained to pass a law which provided that if a jury, after hearing evidence for three days, declared themselves to be 'sufficiently enlightened', the President of the court could declare the trial closed.

That settled the fate of the Girondists. Charles-Eleanor Dufriche Valazé stabbed himself with a dagger when he heard the sentence of death. Lasource told his judges, 'I die at a time when people have lost their senses; you will die when they recover them.'

The other Girondists who had been declared outlaws could be shot without trial. A few escaped. Wimpfen who had led the rebel troops in Normandy hid successfully in Bayeux; Louvet concealed himself in the Jura mountains and Meillan in the Pyrennes. Some tramped through Brittany disguised as republican volunteers. Salle and Guadet remained concealed in an attic at St Emilion where they were discovered in June 1794. Valady was recognized and shot as an outlaw in Perigueux. Cussy was captured in Bordeaux. Pétion, Buzot and Barbaroux (to whom Charlotte Corday had written her last letter) were concealed by a friendly hairdresser in St Emilion until June 1794 when fear of discovery led them to try and escape to Spain. Barbaroux attempted to shoot himself after being captured bear Castillon but was taken alive to the guillotine while his friends Pétion and Buzot committed suicide in a pine forest near by. Chambon was discovered and shot dead in the village where he was hiding. Condorcet, who had produced a draft constitution of 368 clauses and suggestions for the reform of public education, committed suicide in prison by taking poison; Clavière stabbed himself after being captured.

The most famous woman Girondist was not allowed to escape. Madame Roland, born Manon Philipon, was the daughter of a master engraver and the granddaughter of a cook. As a girl she took with her to church a volume of Plutarch disguised as a devotional work and laughed when her mother told her that babies grew under gooseberry bushes. She was an intellectual snob. She became a social snob and a resentful one too, after a childhood visit to Versailles where she was lodged in one of the palace attics and suffered from the supercilious glances of aristocrats. She described herself in her memoirs as having a vivid complexion, good teeth, an engaging smile and elegant long fingers 'indicating intelligence and grace'. She had a good opinion of herself and expected others to share it. She was easily impressed and saw herself in many different roles. It was natural for her to try to enter politics. She married Jean-Marie Roland de la Platière, a smug and prosy prodnose who was then an inspector of commerce some twenty years older than herself. Next she became the Lyons correspondent of Brissot's newspaper *Le Patriote Français*. Her husband was elected to the Lyons Municipality and, on a visit to Paris, met Brissot through her. When a lengthy financial negotiation brought the Rolands to Paris in 1791 they installed themselves in lodgings near the Pont

Neuf. Brissot and his circle were only too glad to have somewhere other than the Jacobin Club in which to discuss politics and Madame Roland's salon soon became popular and famous.

She persuaded her husband to throw up his position in Lyons and settle permanently in Paris. Through Brissot's influence Roland was appointed chief of the Jacobins' Correspondence Committee, the body through which all propaganda letters passed from the mother club in Paris to the branches in the provinces.

Not long after, Roland was appointed Minister of the Interior and the Rolands were able to set themselves up in a magnificent private house that had formerly belonged to Louis XVI's Finance Minister, Charles-Alexandre de Calonne. Madame Roland's salon became more influential than ever and she began to take a personal hand in managing the affairs of her not too brilliant husband.

She made preparations to run the Bureau de l'Esprit Public which was charged with maintaining public morale, and even made a speech at the Bar to the Assembly. But she was too much of a prim blue stocking to make friends with Danton, too fastidious to ally herself with Marat, and was distrusted by Robespierre as one of Brissot's warmongers. Thus when the Girondist Government fell in June 1792, largely as we have seen through an impertinent and doctrinaire letter drafted by herself, Madame Roland and her husband were without friends.

Roland was reappointed Minister of the Interior under the Convention Government but was compelled to resign in January 1793 when Robespierre and Danton challenged him to publish the accounts of the Bureau de l'Esprit Public. He escaped from Paris at the time of the expulsion of the Girondists from the Convention. His wife stayed on in Paris disenchanted with the Revolution. 'I should like to see my trees and my garden,' she lamented, 'after so many fools.'

She was thrown into prison and became a heroine not merely in her own imagination but in reality. Beugnot, the Girondist deputy who survived the Terror to write his memoirs, was captivated by her large blue eyes, her fair hair, her face, her hands and her figure, by the musical quality of her voice, by the grace and elegance of her speech and by her natural wit. Divorced from politics she became a sensitive and enchanting woman. Her cell became a kind of salon and her appearance in the prison courtyard was enough, Beugnot relates, to put even harlots and pickpockets

on their best behaviour for fear of displeasing her. They turned to
her for advice, consolation and hope. On the day appointed for her
trial Madame Roland dressed herself with care in a white muslin
dress set off with a black sash. Her hair was elegant and her face
smiling. She attempted no heroics and her only thought appeared
to be to comfort her fellow prisoners and to raise their spirits. She
was executed on 8 November, and when her husband heard of it
he left his hiding place in Rouen, walked into a field and shot himself.

If Madame Roland was good enough for the scaffold, so, too, was
the Queen. Marie Antoinette was kept in the Temple for more than
six months after her husband's death. The Dauphin had been
separated from her on the night of 3 July 1793 and handed over to
Antoine Simon, a cobbler and friend of Marat who could be trusted
to see that the boy was brought up as a good republican to despise
his parents. Prison food, prison air and lack of exercise soon undermined his health which the republicans—or for that matter the
émigré royalists—were in no way concerned to preserve. The
Queen herself was transferred in August from the Temple to the
Conciergerie, that gloomy building once a royal dining hall and
storehouse on the Ile St Louis on the Seine. It was then being used
as a prison as it lay next door to the so-called Palais de Justice. At
first the Queen was lodged in the Council Chamber of the building
while rooms were prepared for her in the pharmacy. She was
allowed a serving woman, the post being given first to Mère
Larivière, whose son was warder at the Conciergerie, and later to
Madame Harel, wife of a security police officer. Her food was
simple—coffee or chocolate and a roll for breakfast, soup, chicken
and desert, or something similar, for lunch and much the same
menu, cooked by M. Richard the prison registrar for dinner. She
was never allowed to leave her room with its thick double door and
treble locks, and her toilet chair was brought in to her every morning and removed after use. Her chief amusement was to watch her
guards playing piquet. She was shielded from the cells where
straw was the only bed or where fifty-four women competed for
nine mattresses. But she was cut off, too, from the companionship
of the Cour des Femmes in which the women washed themselves
and their clothes.

Her trial was hurried on for at least three reasons. Firstly, the
Government wished to satisfy the ever-present hatred of the

monarchy, which was held responsible not only for hardships and
food shortages but also for the threatened invasion of France.
Secondly, it was thought that a trial and execution was the only
way of killing the ever-present rumours that an escape was being
planned. But the third reason was Robespierre's own. He was
afraid that Danton would be able to use the Queen as a trump
card in breaking up the foreign coalition against France and he was
determined that no rival of his should get the credit for a success of
this kind.

On 3 October the Convention ordered the Queen's trial. Less
than two weeks' preparation was allowed. Even Fouquier-Tinville,
the prosecutor, did not receive the documents, numbering about
nine hundred, supporting the Acte d'Accusation until 14 October,
the day appointed for the Queen's first public hearing. She attended
dressed in her widow's weeds. The Queen's defence to the charges
was that she had consented to her husband's acts as a wife only and
not as a Queen. On the following day the prosecution called new
witnesses, but it needed neither their testimony nor evidence of the
Queen's loose living, said to have been provided by the Dauphin, to
convince the public of her guilt. The jury began their deliberations
at one in the morning. Three hours later the death sentence was
pronounced.

Marie Antoinette was driven to the scaffold not in a carriage, as
her husband had been, but in an open cart, where all could see her
hands bound behind her, her shaven locks, her white linen mob-cap
and dress and black cloak. Her self-possession remained with her to
the last.

The Duc d'Orléans, despite the fact that he had voted for the
death of the King (or perhaps because this showed he might have
an interest in the throne) followed the Queen on 6 November
and Madame Elisabeth, the King's younger sister, six months
later.

But despite the public's hatred of the monarchy and all that it
stood for, such butchery would not have been tolerated if it had been
carried out by the methods used in the September Massacres or
even by the headsman's axe. The guillotine with its mechanized
impersonality, its efficiency and its silence was an indispensable
instrument of the Terror. In two years and three months it dispatched 2,831 victims in Paris and five times that number in the
provinces where portable models were frequently set up. It took

the machine only half an hour to dispose of the twenty-one proscribed Girondists and on a particularly good day in June 1794 the
figure rose to sixty-one decapitations in forty-five minutes.

The idea of a mechanical head-chopper was suggested as far back
as October 1789 by Dr Joseph Ignace Guillotin, a Paris doctor. But
similar ideas had already occurred to the Italians and the Germans
and, as far back as 1661, the Earl of Argyll had been beheaded in
Edinburgh by a machine constructed for the purpose.

In welcoming the guillotine the French, however, were looking
to the future rather than the past. In the past, beheading by sword
had been a death penalty reserved for the well-born and carried no
personal stigma. Common criminals could be put to death by being
broken on a wheel as part of a public spectacle. This class distinction was ended in May 1791 by an Assembly decree ordering that
all those sentenced to death should in future have their heads
chopped off, as a maximum penalty. But how was this to be done?
The axe would be a return to the days of the Middle Ages. The
sword was almost as barbaric. Besides it could be used only once
without re-grinding and involved the victim being held firmly in
position.

But a machine could solve the problem and would make it unnecessary in future for an executioner personally to strike the
physical blow ending the life of one of his fellow men. Accordingly
in March 1792 the Assembly consulted Dr Louis, the Permanent
Secretary of the Academy of Surgery. In his report, Dr Louis
declared it to be well known to anyone who had studied the subject,
that even the finest knives act like saws and that it was a mistake
to expect them to cut with a direct blow. A convex blade was, he
said, necessary. He added that the human neck consists of a series
of overlapping bones which are difficult to penetrate and said that
it would be unwise when death sentences were to be carried out to
rely on the skill of a human being who might be influenced by moral
or physical considerations. It would be easy to construct a machine
which would function reliably and which could be tested first on
live sheep.

Nicolas-Jacques Pelletier, found guilty of robbery with violence
in the rue Bourbon-Villeneuve and executed on 25 April 1792, was
the first victim of the guillotine. The *Chronique de Paris* wrote,
'The people . . . were not at all satisfied. They had seen nothing.
The whole thing was over too quickly. They broke up disappointed.'

And indeed the instrument was so silent that it seemed to be performing a service rather than encompassing the death of a human being.

Only three muffled sounds could be distinguished—the first, made when the plank, with the victim bound to it, was slid into position, the second when the yoke or collar which held the victim's head was closed and the third when the knife made its swift descent.

The guillotine was set up first in the Place du Carrousel, renamed the Place de la Réunion—conveniently near the Revolutionary Tribunal, its main source of livelihood; but, at the request of the Convention, it was later moved to the Place de la Révolution where the crowds were more easily controlled.

The system which was to provide the guillotine with its fodder was no sudden improvisation. The Comité des Recherches of the original Constituent Assembly had disregarded the rights of individuals by breaking into houses, opening mail and acting as a secret police force. And the Legislative Assembly, on the last day of its life in September 1792, had decreed that every citizen must be provided with a card issued by the Section in which he lived, vouching for his patriotism.

A new flood of decrees followed in March 1793. On the tenth of the month the Revolutionary Tribunal was set up to deal with 'counter-revolutionary activities' and to regularize slaughter as the only debt which the people acknowledged to be owing to its enemies. The decree which established the Tribunal provided for paid jurors who should arrive at their decisions by voting aloud in public and by absolute majority. There was no appeal from their findings.

Furthermore, contrary to the principles advocated by Robespierre himself in earlier days, the property of those convicted was confiscated, leaving the victims' families dependent on State aid.

On 21 March, Watch Committees were set up in each Section. All foreigners were to register themselves and those not possessing property in France were to find six sureties for their good behaviour. Every male aged eighteen or over was to confirm before his Commune or his Section his place of birth, his means of livelihood, and the performance of his duties as a citizen. These statements had to be confirmed by four citizens who had lived in the Section or Commune for not less than a year.

A week later émigrés were banished permanently from French
soil and declared to be civilly dead. Their property was confiscated.
Emigrés included all French subjects who could not prove con-
tinuous residence in France since 9 May 1792 as certified by eight
citizens who were not relatives, tenants, servants, debtors, creditors
or agents of the individual concerned. A flourishing black market
business in false certificates of residence soon arose. In June, about
sixty Departments were in revolt against the Convention.

Then in September 1793 after the royalists had handed over the
port of Toulon to the British, a new series of dictatorial measures
was passed. On 5 September, Government by Terror (i.e. by
intimidation) was declared to be the order of the day, that is, the
business of the Convention. The Revolutionary Tribunal was
divided into four sections so that it could handle a large number of
criminals. In October the Constitution of 1793, which the Jacobins
had prepared in a week in order to have an alternative to Condorcet's Girondist product, was neatly discarded by a decree declaring
that the Government of France was 'revolutionary [i.e. directly
under the Committee of Public Safety] until the peace'.

The Communes had already been granted authority to act as a
police force in dealing with crimes against the State and any
'active citizen' could bring any person 'strongly suspected' of a
crime against general security before the Commune.

On 17 September the Convention agreed to the Law of the
Suspects or, as we should probably say, Suspected Persons, who
were to be put in prison immediately. Robespierre played a
prominent role in drafting this measure. Suspects included 'those
who by their conduct, associations, talk, or writings have shewn
themselves partisans of Tyranny or Federalism and enemies of
liberty', also those to whom certificates of citizenship had been
refused, those who had been unable to justify their means of existence and to prove that they had carried out their obligations as
citizens. Volunteers absent from the front without leave were to be
treated as émigrés. The Vigilance Committees of which there were
perhaps ten thousand by now in France, could themselves order
the arrest of suspects, including all not wearing the tricolour.

Travelling commissars were sent on tour, armed with wide
powers to liquidate any counter-revolutionaries without reference
back to Paris. After a journey of this kind in October 1793,
Pierre-Gaspard Chaumette, former President of the Insurrectional

Committee of the Commune got the Commune to agree that certificates of citizenship should be refused to:

Those who at popular meetings impede progress by malicious speeches, turbulent cries or menaces.

To those more prudent, who talk mysteriously of the misfortunes of the Republic, lamenting the fate of the people.

To those who have taken no active part in the Revolution but who, to excuse themselves, lay emphasis on the contributions they have paid, on their patriotic gifts, on their service in the National Guard either through a substitute or by other means.

To those who though they have done nothing against the Revolution have done nothing to promote it.

To those who do not attend the meetings of their Sections excusing themselves on the ground that they do not know how to speak or that their business affairs prevent them.

To those who speak in scornful tones about the lawful authorities, the emblems of the law, the popular societies and the defenders of liberty.

This would surely present the people with enough severed heads to assure them of the Government's zeal. Later on Chaumette himself was included in this list.

Even before the Great Terror had begun there were those who feared it would go too far. At the beginning of October 1793, three of the Paris Sections asked the Convention to declare that every prisoner was entitled to insist that the Committee should provide him with a copy of the deposition which had led to his arrest, and that the Justices of the Peace and police commissioners should be called on to decide without delay on the detention or release of suspected people.

A decree providing for this was passed—and ignored. The promoters of the Terror asked sarcastically whether public security had been established sufficiently securely for it to be possible to release counter-revolutionaries.

Robespierre supported the denunciators, and talked of 'the simple and generous citizens of the Revolutionary Committees who showed so much courage in laying themselves open to the full fury of the aristocracy'. He added that, 'those who were ignorant of the subtleties of chicanery were paralysed in the execution of their task by the obligation of stating in writing the basis of their moral conviction'. He asked, when public notoriety accuses a citizen of crimes for which there exists no written proof, but the proof of which exists in the heart of all indignant citizens, are we to return to the former judical system?'

Suspects when questioned were faced with a formidable array of challenges. They were asked, 'Where were you on 10 August 1792? And on 31 May and 1 and 2 June 1793? What have you done for the Revolution? Give a list of your possessions in 1789,' and so on.

Behind all this activity was a conviction, fostered by Robespierre among others, that if only enough blood were shed, the State could be purged of traitors. Fouquier-Tinville, the Public Prosecutor, a large, heavily built man of forty-seven, with dark black hair and forbidding eyebrows and a loud voice, who had been put on the road to power by Camille Desmoulins, hoped to step up the number of traitors sent to the guillotine (whom he insisted on keeping separated from common criminals) to two hundred per week. It was he who obstinately transported the dead body of the Girondist deputy Valazé in a cart to the guillotine so that it should not be said that he escaped fulfilling the sentence passed on his colleagues. Fouquier kept in touch with ministers, with the two main committees (the Committee of Public Safety and the Committee of General Security which dealt with long-term counter-revolutionary activity), as well as with those who had interrogated the prisoners, in order to be able to name those who were to appear in court on the following day and to advise the executioner accordingly.

When he left his office at the Conciergerie, Fouquier wore a long black coat and a hat with a turn-up brim, decked with black plumes and a tricolour cockade after the style of the French King Henry IV. He co-operated closely with the President of the Revolutionary Tribunal, an elegant young man of twenty-four named Nicolas-François-Joseph Herman, who felt moved to write to his brother who had asked him for employment: 'You should know that an official has no relatives or friends.'

In the Tribunal the usual routine was for the judge to hear the preliminary evidence and formulate the charges. Then the prisoner was interviewed and witnesses heard. After which the jury deliberated and delivered its verdict.

Most of the cases were taken in the chamber known as the Hall of Liberty, in which Louis XIV had once said, *'L'Etat c'est moi.'* Bu

at the height of the Terror, an extra room known as the Chamber of
Equality was brought into use. Charlotte Corday was among those
tried there.

Prison life was by no means intolerable for those who had plenty
of money. Coittant who was confined in the Port Libre Prison along
with the poet Vigée and twenty-seven former tax farmers, recalled
that at the end of the corridor on the first floor there was a large
hall, known as the salon, where six tables of six places each were
laid for dinner every evening for the richer prisoners.

To pass the time Coittant edited a daily prison newspaper
announcing the names of new arrivals and rumours of arrests elsewhere. The men prisoners composed odes of gallantry to the
women, declaring that it was pointless for the warders to have
taken away dangerous weapons such as scissors and pen-knives
from Lise and Chlöe while leaving them their enchanting smiles and
great big eyes. Others organized tables for whist, piquet or chess.

The more affluent sent home for wines that they had put by in
their cellars. Frequently their jailers were drunk with wine provided
by the prisoners and quite incapable of verifying whether their
charges were still in captivity.

It happened that towards the end of the Terror two women
named Biron were imprisoned in the Conciergerie. One day Fouquier gave orders to fetch 'the Biron woman' for trial. He was told
that there were two women of the same name and was asked which
of them he had intended to call. 'Take them both,' he said—and
they were guillotined the same afternoon. Madame Mayet was
executed in mistake for Madame de Mayet, and André Chénier,
the poet, was confused with his brother Sauveur. But indeed without photographs or fingerprints or indeed warders capable of reading, some lapses in identification were inevitable.

There were so many people in prison that only a few could be
dealt with. Each morning the jailer called out the list of those whose
cases had come to the top of the folder and who were to be transferred to the Conciegerie for trial and almost certain death. Those
who were lucky not to be drawn in this lottery of blood surrendered
themselves once more to the only pleasures they were capable of en-
joying.

Many of the condemned reacted with indifference, light-hearted-
ness or even bravado. Colonel Vaujour, told that he would be
executed at two in the afternoon, was heard to remark, 'What a

pity. That's when I usually eat. However, I'll have my meal earlier today,' and he was still eating when they came to fetch him.

The Princesse de Monaco put extra rouge on her cheeks to make sure that the crowd should detect no sign of weakness in her on her way to the scaffold. When the Maréchal de Mouchy was called to take his place in the tumbril, he recalled, 'When I was fifteen I went into battle for my King. At eighty I go to the scaffold for my God. I am not unfortunate.'

There was an appreciative audience whose attention was devoted to the prisoners from the time of their arrival at the prison doors until their departure. The very staircases of the Conciergerie were crowded with spectators to whom a duchess or former bishop represented a collector's item.

The rue St Honoré was known as a good place from which to watch the tumbrils on their way to their death tryst and Gisors, the architect commissioned to restore the Tuileries for the Convention, complained that the work was delayed because the workmen took time off to watch the executions.

For those who had time to wait—the executions unfortunately did not always take place at regular hours—there was the Cabaret (i.e. Inn) de la Guillotine. In token of their patriotic feelings—or of their unappeased hatred—the crowd made known their assessment of the prisoners, denouncing them as infamous brigands, assassins, barbarians, hypocrites, throat-cutters, agents of tyranny or the like.

The executioner, Sanson, that hard-worked man, benefited less than might have been thought from his increased responsibilities. He had only two carts of his own and had to hire any others from outsiders who insisted on being well paid for allowing their vehicles to be used for this traffic in blood. Sanson's other expenses included nails and wood for the maintenance of the scaffolding, ropes for binding the prisoners, and wicker baskets to catch their heads. Then, perhaps because it was thought that no State servant should profit from the death of his fellow men, or perhaps because goods had become scarcer, the executioner was deprived of his right to keep the clothes of his victims. They were sent to hospitals or to prisons where at least one ghoulish jailer's wife insisted on ordering the inmates to deck themselves out in them.

But life was not much more pleasant even for people outside prison. Between May and July 1793, assignats had fallen to a

fifth of their original value. The theatres showed only what was
acceptable to good Jacobins. Shops shut early. It was illegal to
carry a parcel after dark. People went home and barricaded themselves in their houses lest they be arrested on suspicion by one of
the night patrols. It was dangerous to be found with a guest in the
house (he might be a conspirator). People went to bed early because
of the difficulty of procuring candles. Nearly everything that the
factories produced was requisitioned for the Army.

The common people, so often described by Robespierre as
'generous', had no generosity to hope for. Their last chance
vanished when Robespierre egged on Danton to attack and liquidate Jacques-Réné Hébert and his fellow-travellers, the Enragés,
who believed literally in government of the people, by the people,
for the people. Hébert, the son of the Deputy Mayor of Aleçon,
Normandy, was the King of the sans-culottes. A failure up to the
age of thirty-two, he was forced to accept a job in a Variety
Theatre handing out passes to box owners. With the outbreak of
the Revolution, he took to writing and soon found himself famous.
Though capable of expressing himself in a cultivated and even
subtle style, he preferred to punctuate his sentences with four-letter
farmyard expletives. He named his one-man newspaper *Père
Duchesne* after a Comedie Française character who was especially
fond of giving plain-spoken advice.

To the Jacobins, the sans-culottes and the Enragés had become
as obnoxious in the early months of 1794 as their predecessors had
been four years earlier to La Fayette and Bailly. If one allowed them
to run the war, there would be little hope of winning it. The
Government might not even survive. So what could be more
sensible than to liquidate their movement?

Accordingly the leading Hébertists were accused of spending
their time in idleness and intrigue, of encouraging civil war, of
promoting famine, of planning to assassinate the members of the
Convention and to destroy the Republic and replace it with a
government of tyrants. François-Nicolas Vincent, one of the
Hébertist leaders, was reported as having made fun of the costumes
of the deputies, and Ducoquet, another leader, was said to have
confiscated a rabbit, a turkey and three dozen eggs which ought to
have been sold for public consumption. Out of these and similar
offences a composite charge was made out. The Hébertists went to
the guillotine on 23 March, as the Girondists had before them, and

were replaced in the Sections by Robespierre's own men. It was the
first faint sign that the onward march of the Revolution was coming to a halt.

A week later the Government decided to strike against the other
potential opposition leader—Danton. For some time Danton had
drifted away from the main current of the Revolution. His influence at the Cordeliers Club had been lost to the Hébertists. He
was excluded from the new Committee of Public Safety when this
was reorganized on 10 July. More and more he began to tire of
emergency meetings which interfered with his happiness at home.
In October 1793 he retired to the country determined to lead the
life of a squire and to take no more part in politics. He was horrified
when he heard that the Girondists, against whom he had fought,
were to be executed *en masse*. 'Those men in Paris will murder the
Republic,' he declared.

Soon after, he was warned that his own life was in danger and
on 17 November he hurried back to the capital. He hoped there
was still time to stay the course of the Terror before his own head
was forfeit. In the Convention on 1 December he criticized the
commissars for the massacres committed when they were establishing the reign of Terror in the provinces.

That same evening he made a bid to restore his influence in the
Jacobin Club. He defied his listeners to prove any flaws in his
patriotism. At once, Robespierre was on his feet. He offered to
stage the investigation which, he suggested, Danton was anxious to
have and went on to list the accusations which, according to
Robespierre, 'some people' were making.

No one else came forward to press any charges. And indeed
Camille Desmoulins's new newspaper, the *Vieux Cordelier,* which
supported Danton's policy of clemency, achieved an immediate
success.

Desmoulins called on the Government to open the prisons and
release two hundred thousand people held in them as suspects.
'Today,' he wrote, 'a miracle happened in Paris. A man died in his
bed.' Robespierre realized that this amounted to an attack on
those—including himself—who had filled the jails, and he demanded that Desmoulins be denounced at the Jacobin Club and his
paper burnt.

Once more, after the arrest of the Hébertists, Danton spoke
in the Convention in favour of ending the Terror. Twice he

approached Robespierre personally. But Robespierre indignantly denied that any innocent people had perished and insisted that Danton's concern for suspects was a proof of his own lax principles.

Robespierre then prepared a list of charges which could be made against Danton and handed them to Louis-Antoine-Léon St Just who had first supported Robespierre over the trial of the King and whom Robespierre now asked to take charge of the Danton case. These charges were read by St Just at the Jacobin Club on the night of 30–31 March at a joint emergency session of the Committee of Public Safety and the General Security Committee. A great majority of both Committees signed the warrant for Danton's arrest. He and Desmoulins were rounded up the same night.

The next day Robespierre and St Just announced Danton's arrest to a Convention too terrified to resist in case they themselves were denounced next.

Robespierre refused to allow Danton the privilege of being heard at the Bar of the Convention. 'We will have no more privileges here,' he proclaimed, 'and no more idols.'

Robespierre, through his position in the Committee of Public Safety, through his unemotional, almost inhuman, detachment from his fellow human beings and through his ability to represent himself as supporting the cause of morality against evil, had acquired an almost hypnotic influence over the Assembly.

His audience knew that an attack by Robespierre on anyone was equivalent to a sentence of death and that he was fully capable of turning the most innocent phrase of an opponent into a confession of the deepest guilt.

Once Robespierre had spoken against Danton, whom he described as a false and rotten idol, no one dared to rise to his defence. Then St Just read the charges which he had prepared and promised that if the Convention would agree to this final purge, only true patriots would remain and the Convention would be freed from similar purges.

Two days later Danton was transferred from the Luxembourg to the Conciergerie in preparation for his trial. Fouquier-Tinville was told that death would be his own lot if he failed to secure a conviction.

Danton for once seemed in a state of irresolution. At first he appeared to think that Robespierre would never dare to have him tried and condemned. But he told Thomas Paine who was also in

prison under suspicion, 'They are sending me to the scaffold. I
shall go gladly.' He felt that it was better to be guillotined than to
guillotine. Nevertheless he was determined to fight his accusers,
particularly since they had done him the injustice of trying him
and his followers in the same dock with a gang of forgers whose case
occupied the best part of two days. At last, when the public, to
whom Danton hoped to appeal, had grown tired of waiting, his
case was called. Danton's main defence was an impassioned and not
unsuccessful appeal to the gallery.

Herman, the President of the court, countered by claiming that
calmness rather than violence was a proof of innocence. He insisted on cutting short Danton's speech and refused to allow him to
call any witnesses until after the other prisoners had been cross-
examined. But Danton's co-prisoners proved just as difficult to
handle as Danton. Something desperate had to be done if the
defendants were not to be acquitted.

Fouquier-Tinville wrote personally to the Convention warning
them that the defendants, by insisting on calling their witnesses
and by appealing directly to the people were attempting to take
the case out of the hands of the Revolutionary Tribunal. He said
that under the present system of laws he could not prevent them
calling their witnesses into court.

Robespierre and St Just accordingly fell back on a plan, well-
known to dictators, of alleging that a plot had been prepared to
overthrow the Revolutionary Tribunal and that the Public
Prosecutor had been forced to suspend the trial until he had obtained new support from the Convention. St Just told the Convention that the form of defence which the accused had adopted
showed that they must be guilty and demanded that the Convention agree to pass a measure stating that 'any prisoner under a
charge of conspiracy who resists or insults national justice shall at
once be debarred from pleading his cause'.

After this, no more was heard in court of the accused's defence
or of the witnesses they would like to have called; the trial closed
at the end of the fourth day. The prisoners were removed from
court while the jury deliberated. But to make sure that the verdict
was satisfactory, Herman and Fouquier-Tinville themselves visited
the jury with a letter, the contents of which are unknown to this
day but which, it is widely believed, revealed that Danton had at
one time been in correspondence with the royal family.

After this there could be no doubt about the verdict. The sentence of death was read in the courtroom after the prisoners had left. They were told even before they were back in their cells and were immediately prepared for the guillotine with their hair shaved at the back of the neck and their hands tied behind their backs. Desmoulins screamed and raved on his way to the guillotine, but Danton was able to joke, until he realized that he would never see his wife and two sons again. At the last moment, however, he recovered himself. 'Come now, Danton,' he said, 'there must be no weakness.' He turned to Sanson the executioner and said, 'You must show my head to the people. It is worth it.'

Danton's death together with that of seventeen others accused with him, should have ended the Terror. Instead, government by fear was intensified in the weeks that followed. A managed economy was needed even after those who had opposed it had vanished. There was no possibility of new elections since the present emergency Government had already been approved and legitimized 'until the peace'. It had even been agreed that the Committee of Public Safety should be responsible for replacing those deputies who had been guillotined. Now, in April 1794, all Government Ministries were abolished and both the executive and legislative powers of the Government were from that time forward completely under the control of the Committee of Public Safety, and in the provinces under the Watch Committees authorized by law in March 1793 but formed, in many cases, earlier.

Life was dangerous even for the Jacobins, since they might at any time be expelled from the club under one of Robespierre's periodic purges. It was a precarious existence even for the revolutionary leaders themselves since a near dictatorship is more easily overthrown than a popularly elected Government. The Revolution had in fact reached the stage where each of a number of leaders was prepared to denounce others in order to seize power. Robespierre began to have genuine and perhaps even justified fears of dying by the hand of the assassin.

On 4 June 1794 he had been elected President of the Convention by the unanimous votes of 485 deputies. Six days later a law known as the Law of 22 Prairial was passed (Prairial was one of the thirty-day months in the new republican calendar); it imposed the most rigorous dictatorship France ever knew up to the time of the German occupation in the Second World War.

It classed as an 'enemy of the people anyone who spreads false
rumours in order to divide, disconcert or discourage citizens, anyone who confuses public opinion, anyone who depraves morals,
anyone who adulterates the purity of republican principles'. It
included all who had approved of tyranny and federalism by word
or deed or by their personal friendships, all dismissed or suspended
officials, all nobles or émigrés, all those who had failed to take up
useful employment. The Parliamentary immunity of the deputies
was in fact suspended though this was vigorously denied by the
Bill's promoters. Officials guilty of maladministration, all who
compromised liberty or the unity or safety of the Republic, all who
weakened the national war effort or reduced its food reserves, were
now criminals.

Article Nine allowed any citizen to seize and bring before the
magistrates conspirators and counter-revolutionaries. The Committee of Public Safety, the Committee of General Security, the
commissars of the Convention and the Public Prosecutor could
bring suspects directly before the Revolutionary Tribunal. Later,
all cases including provincial ones were centralized through Paris.
No preliminary interrogation was needed before bringing the suspect to trial. Denunciation was sufficient. (Robespierre in particular supported this as indeed the other clauses of the Law which
were largely drafted by him.)

The practice of having a Defence Counsel was also forbidden on
the ground that this offered a platform for royalist propaganda and
that in any case only the privileged could afford to pay for it. The
law, it was said, provided patriotic juries in defence of patriots
who had been slandered but no assistance for conspirators.

Any evidence which could gain 'the assent of any reasonable
mind' was to be regarded as proof of guilt. The juries were to vote
their verdicts in public and out loud. These verdicts were to be
ruled by the consciences of the jurors 'enlightened by a love of
their country with a view to the triumph of the Republic and the
ruin of its enemies'. There were only two alternative sentences—
acquittal or death. There was no appeal.

Article Twenty of the law annulled all laws not in accord with it
in so far as counter-revolution and the Revolutionary Tribunal
were concerned.

During the Grande Terreur which followed between 10 June and
27 July, which date Robespierre disappeared from the scene,

nearly one thousand four hundred victims were guillotined. Much
of the evidence came from prison spies introduced among the
prisoners by Fouquier-Tinville.

It is difficult to be sure whether this continued slaughter arose
principally from a conviction that rule by shock was the only
practical policy, or from a feeling that the Republic could survive
only if it were purified, or from fear that its leaders might be
assassinated by royalists (who did not in any case deserve to
live), or from anxiety lest the people became dissatisfied with
their leaders, or from a love of power, or from a form of psy-
chotic sadistic lust which only the regular shedding of blood could
satisfy.

Different leaders no doubt acted differently for different reasons.
Jean-Baptiste Carrier, who gave orders for five hundred peasant
boys and girls to be clubbed to death in a field outside Nantes and
who organized mass drownings off rafts in the River Loire could
only have been a maniac. Likewise Joseph Lebon, who made a
point of watching the guillotine at work in Arras every day from a
window with his wife sitting by his side, and invited the executioner to join him at lunch afterwards.

In Paris, St Just (originally Louis-Antoine de St Just), an
equally enthusiastic advocate of mass slaughter, was a far more
complex character. The Angel of Death, as he was nicknamed, was
as austere, as fanatical and as pitiless as Robespierre himself. But
in contrast to Robespierre, he was self-confident and a man of
action, capable of putting into practice the doctrinaire but frequently juvenile convictions which filled his mind. It was he who
advocated that death should be the penalty for anyone who struck
a woman. On one occasion he was foolish enough to write, 'I think
I may say that most political errors come from regarding legislation as a difficult science.' A late-comer to the Revolution (he was
still under twenty-five when the Legislative Assembly was elected
and was therefore too young to represent his native city of Soissons), he retained his aristocratic manners and dress. And his
boyish face and dark good looks contrasted with his ruthlessness towards all who doubted that terror was the equivalent of
justice.

St Just's scheme for redistributing property by taking it away
from the rich and giving it to the poor is sometimes mentioned as
an early example of Communism in action. Under St Just's

measures, passed in February and March 1794, the dossiers of all
those who had been in prison since 1 May 1789 were to be forwarded to the Committee of General Security and lists prepared
of 'recognized enemies of the Republic'. The property of these
enemies was to be valued and forty thousand municipalities in
France were to provide lists of deserving patriots. The Committee
of Public Safety was to marry the two lists together.

The Jacobins may well have supported these measures as a
matter of practical politics, in order to deprive the Hébertists—then
about to be purged—of the support of the sans-culottes. But to St
Just the redistribution of property was one of the steps on the way
to the establishment of his ideal political Republic. It was his way
of affirming the Revolution by turning the ruin of those who opposed it to the profit of those who supported it. And to him there
was only one method of doing so.

'The way to frighten all ill-disposed people,' he declared, 'and
to make them see that the Government has its eye on everything is
to punish a small offence in each walk of public life.' Or again,
'We make too many laws and two few examples. . . . Would those
who reproach us for our severity prefer us to be unjust? . . . Be
inflexible: indulgence is to be feared because it threatens the
country. . . . The Republic consists in the total destruction of what
is opposed to it. . . .'

St Just's political reasoning was that since there is only one
truth, there cannot be legitimate differences of opinion as to what is
right. 'The sovereignty of the people demands that the people be
unified,' he said. 'It is therefore opposed to factions, and all factions
are a criminal attack on sovereignty.' He believed that there was an
ideal State leading to man's fulfilment, that liberty could be
established according to certain permanent principles and that the
opportunity for achieving liberty might never return.

Behind this lay a conviction that the Revolution could come to
an end as soon as all were equally devoted to their country and its
laws, a piece of optimism matched by the Russian Communist
prognostication that once true Socialism had been established the
State would be able to wither away. But neither St Just nor his
fellow Jacobins explained how a minority dictatorship could claim
to represent the will of the people, or how, if the people were not
sufficiently far-sighted as to recognize their own interests, one
could be certain that the Committee of Public Safety would be able

infallibly to define and recognize the public will. And *who* was to give the signal for the Revolution to stop?

Moreover, visions of the perfect political Republic was only one of the Government's preoccupations. The religious problems of millions of Frenchmen were those of the Government too. Both Robespierre and St Just favoured a Republic founded on virtue, and Robespierre, in his report of 5 February 1794, on the moral principles that should guide the Convention, wrote:

> In our Republic the sole ambition will be the desire to deserve glory and to serve the nation. Souls will grow greater through the constant sharing of republican sentiments. The arts will add lustre to Liberty which in turn will ennoble the arts. Commerce will become the origin of public wealth instead of the monstrous treasure of a few families. We wish to substitute morality for selfishness, rectitude for vain distinctions, principles for habits, duty for etiquette, love of glory for love of money, merit for intrigue, and the delights of contentment for the staleness of self-indulgence.

The new Republic, Robespierre said, would replace an easy, frivolous and discontented people with one that is happy, powerful and brave.

These were signs of revolutionary Messianism of the kind which demands not only the acquiescence of those ruled but as in Communist China and elsewhere today, their participation. But even the constitutional priests who had sworn loyalty to the State were quite unable to respond to such an appeal and, towards the end of 1793, the more radical revolutionaries, such as Anaxagoras Chaumette in the Paris Commune and Joseph Fouché in the provinces, had been conducting a campaign of dechristianization. This campaign affected not only the orthodox Catholic priests, those servants of Kings, but also the constitutional clergy, who were suspected by the soldiery of fomenting civil war. Sometimes the purges were helped by Protestants, ex-priests or members of popular societies.

The Church plate and other 'utensils of the cult' were commandeered for the benefit of the Republic as once the Church lands had been; and inquiries were held in cases where these treasures had disappeared without a presumption of theft. Church bells continued to be melted down to make coins and the bell-ropes were

sent away for use by the Navy. Surplices became shirts for soldiers
or bandages. Religious books yielded paper for wrapping food—or
for cartridges; coffins supplied lead for bullets. Rheims cathedral
was turned into an army granary.

All these measures could perhaps have been justified by reasons
of necessity. But in addition there were attacks on everything
Christian. Religious monuments including crosses were pulled
down; the Auberge de Jerusalem became the Auberge du Bonnet
Rouge and children were no longer christened with the names of
saints but rather with Roman names such as Brutus or Gracchus.
Even cities called after saints were re-named, for saints were a
'*culte des imbéciles ou des hypocrites de la légende*'. Dunkirk became
Dunlibre, St Malo became Victoire Montagnarde; St Leonard in
Angers became Fruit Sucré; and at one time there were Frenchmen
living in such places as Haricot, Asperge and Absinthe. Priests
were encouraged to marry as a demonstration of their patriotism.
In Paris some of the Sections, prompted by the Commune, re-
nounced Christianity and closed their churches, or re-named them
Temple de la Raison.

On 6 November 1793 a deputation from the inhabitants of
Mennecy came to the Convention wearing ecclesiastical robes saying that they had no idols but Marat and Lepelletier (who, like
Marat, had been struck down by an assassin). On the following day
Archbishop Gobel of Paris formally abjured the Christian religion
before the whole Convention. Three days later the Feast of Reason
was celebrated with a civic mass in Nôtre-Dame. A danseuse named
Aubry from the Opéra portrayed the Goddess of Reason and after
the ceremony she visited the Convention with her followers, receiving a kiss from the President and a seat by his side.

It was clear that the Government would have to take action.
Robespierre could not afford to allow the religious beliefs of the
capital to be controlled from the City Hall. The Hébertists had
been executed on 23 March. Soon afterwards the Government decided to make a powerful effort to capture the support of Hébert's
sans-culotte followers.

Robespierre favoured some kind of deity as an aid to good order
and stability. A Supreme Being had been mentioned in the French
Declaration of Rights as well as by Gabriel Bonnet de Mably whose
writings anticipated some of Communism's main principles. The
existence of a Supreme Being would give the State a monopoly of

popular festivals, would enable it to harness, for its own uses, all the fanaticism formerly devoted to the Catholic faith, would help to reconcile the people to the loss of their Church and perhaps absolve them in their own eyes from any guilt that they might feel for having contributed to the excesses of the Revolution. At ceremonies in honour of the Supreme Being, French, which the State was promoting as the national language, would take the place of Latin used at Mass. The Clubs would offer a forum in which sins could be confessed and absolution given and Hell could be replaced by prison, exile or other penalties at the disposal of the authorities. The change might also serve to persuade public opinion outside France, that the Revolution was becoming respectable.

The recognition of a Supreme Being coincided with Robespierre's desire for centralization. In the provinces matters had been getting out of hand. Local councils were celebrating unauthorized festivals on unauthorized days and guidance was needed on such weighty matters as whether it was undemocratic to kneel or whether Marat or someone else should have pride of place in the new Saints' Calendar. The cult of the Supreme Being would therefore enable Paris to assert her authority in spiritual as well as in material affairs.

Robespierre with his usual artistry of words, presented the Supreme Being as a symbol of the self-realization of the French people. He proclaimed that atheism was not revolutionary but on the contrary aristocratic and he made clear that the priests who had formerly installed themselves in Heaven in order to rule on earth could not expect the new cult to rehabilitate them. 'Fanaticism', which in revolutionary jargon meant conventional religion, was to disappear for ever.

In his address inaugurating the Supreme Being, Ropespierre argued that mankind had made enormous progress in the material sense. Cornfields had replaced forests, new worlds had been discovered, new ways of communicating ideas through the printed word had been devised and now the other phase of world revolution—in the political spheres had just begun—with France some two thousand years ahead of the remainder of the human race.

Elsewhere in Europe, a labourer is an animal prepared for the pleasures of the well-born; but in France the well-born seek to transform themselves into labourers and workmen and cannot even secure this honour. The rest of Europe cannot conceive that it is possible to exist without Kings or nobles; we cannot imagine living with them. The rest of Europe pours out its blood in order to enchain humanity and we do so to break those chains. ... Yes, this delectable land which we live in, which nature caresses, is made to be the domain of liberty and happiness; this proud and sensitive people is truly born for glory and virtue. ...

Oh my country! If Fate had caused me to be born in a strange and distant land, I would have prayed continually to Heaven for your prosperity; I would have shed soft tears over the story of your struggles and your virtues; my soul would have followed attentively with restless enthusiasm all the movements of your glorious revolution; I would have envied the lot of your citizens and of your representatives. I am French; I am one of your representatives. ... Oh sublime people. Accept the sacrifice of my whole being; happy the man who is born in your midst. Happier still he who can die for your happiness.

The French people, no doubt, found it hard to resist such an appeal particularly since it was accompanied by an assurance that the State still regarded their souls as immortal.

Having made these points as sponsor of the cult of the Supreme Being, Robespierre outlined its provisions to the Committee of Public Safety. The document setting out the articles of belief which was voted without discussion, declared in its opening clause that the French people recognized the Supreme Being and the immortality of the soul. Other articles made clear that the cult involved the duty of detesting bad faith and tyranny, of punishing traitors, helping the unfortunate, sympathizing with the weak, defending the oppressed, doing all possible good to others and being just towards all.

A list followed of festivals to be held in honour of such themes as The Supreme Being and Nature, The Human Race, The French People, The Benefactors of Humanity, The Hatred of Tyrants and Traitors and qualities such as Modesty, Motherly Tenderness, etc. etc. Two hundred thousand copies of Robespierre's report were printed for circulation and the big launching festival fixed for 8 June.

The arrangements for this drama were placed once again under the artistic direction of Jacques-Louis David. David, like many other revolutionary leaders, had been born into the bourgeoisie.

His father was killed in a duel when he was nine years old and he was brought up by his uncles. His artistic talent was soon apparent and at his third attempt he won the Prix de Rome, that coveted award which allows the artist to visit Italy and study its treasures. The sketches that David made in his note-book on his first trip abroad were a source of inspiration to him for the rest of his life. At thirty-three he became an associate member of the French Academy and two years later a full member. He married the daughter of the contractor for the King's Buildings who brought him a very substantial dowry. There thus were good reasons why he should have been satisfied with his position under the old régime. But like many other perfectionists, he was a quarrelsome and easily discontented individual. He was involved in a law suit with a soldier who recognized his portrait as the face of Christ in a painting executed by David for the Marquise de Noailles. He failed to gain the directorship of the French Academy in Rome and ascribed this, probably with some reason, to the manœuvres of the 'old gang' of traditional Court artists.

And in 1789 when the King asked him to paint a picture of Coriolanus (the Roman patrician who had humbled the plebs in 500 B.C.) he obliged instead with one of the Roman lictors bringing back to Brutus the bodies of his sons. The moral of the painting seemed to be that Brutus was ready to sacrifice his sons for the Republic, while the French King condoned the extravagances of his own relatives. The Court banned David's painting from being shown at the French Academy.

No doubt the near-monopoly exercised by the Court painters helped to convince David that there would have to be great changes including political upheavals if art in France were to be really free. He was a man of ardent enthusiasms and not readily amenable to reason or compromise. The Revolution was clearly to his interests. It was evident too, that the elaborate and artificial rococo style was as distasteful to David as the artists who had made use of it. He himself succeeded in combining the simplicity of the classical style with a natural realism which could tell a story without words.

The Jacobins were not slow to realize the value of such an artist in communicating a political message to people, many of whom could scarcely read, and in February 1790 David was elected to the Jacobin Club.

A tumour in his right cheek impeded his speech and prevented

him from being a great orator. But there was no doubt about his
patriotism. He had voted for the King's death without delay or
appeal. He voted for a republic at the first meeting of the National
Convention. He served on the Committee of General Security and
supported the Mountain.

For four years he worked almost exclusively as the chief visual
propagandist of the Revolution. In July 1791 he had staged the
ceremony at which Voltaire's remains were laid to rest in the
Panthéon. A figure representing Voltaire alive was carried at the
head of the procession sitting in a sedan chair while twelve grey
horses, four abreast, drew the coffin on which rested a second wax
figure of Voltaire dead.

Among David's many pageants was the festival held in April
1792 in honour of the mutinous soldiers of the Châteauvieux regiment. His was the design for the uniform—tricolour sash and
plumes—worn by the deputies sent by the Government on special
missions to the provinces. In August 1793 he was charged with
organizing a dictatorship of the arts.

That same month he organized the Festival of Unity and In-
divisibility (against federalism and royalism) for which the people
were asked to rise at dawn so that the sun's first rays should light
their gathering. On such occasions the programme of the proces-
sions was published in advance in the newspapers. Extra provisions were allotted to the markets.

But the Festival of the Supreme Being on 8 June was undoubtedly David's greatest production. It took place on a gloriously
sunny day. Paris was decked with roses sent from gardens for miles
around. Drums sounded the reveille; bells rang; cannons were
fired. The guillotine was shrouded in velvet for a day. Citizens from
forty-eight Sections gathered in two columns close to the Tuileries,
women to one side, men to the other, six abreast. Young men and
women marched between the two columns carrying the Section
banners. The women carried bouquets, the men oak branches.

At midday the members of the Convention appeared in a body
wearing for the first time, according to some accounts, their official
uniform consisting of a blue coat, short breeches, sash and hat with
tricolour plumes, each with a bouquet of wheat, flowers and fruit
in their hands. Robespierre, who four days earlier had been voted in
as President of the Convention, was at their head. The deputies
grouped themselves in an amphitheatre with their backs to the

Tuileries. An orchestra played an air of welcome. Then Robespierre held up his hand. The vast crowd was silent. He spoke of the Supreme Being who had created men to help each other and to achieve happiness through the path of virtue. A hymn was sung led by the choir of the Paris Opéra. Robespierre took a torch and set fire to a cardboard figure representing Atheism. Egotism and Insincerity were scorched if not burnt too. A statue of Wisdom emerged from the ashes. Then another speech was delivered by Robespierre whom Boissy d'Anglas compared to Orpheus instructing mankind in the principles of civilization and morality.

A second hymn followed and the procession then moved off led by representatives of twenty-four Sections with the members of the Convention in the middle and the remaining twenty-four Sections at the rear. Also, in the midst of the procession was a magnificent wagon draped in red and pulled by eight white oxen with gilded horns. The wagon carried a sheaf of wheat, a printing press and a tree of liberty. The cortège wound its way along the river-bank towards the Champ de Mars. As it passed Les Invalides, the pensioners saluted the Convention and swore that they were ready to die for liberty.

An impressive mountain had been erected on the Champ de Mars with a tree of liberty at the peak. Robespierre, stepping like a dancing master five yards ahead of the other deputies, led the Convention to the summit. Musicians and choirs numbering several thousands took up their position. Incense was burnt. More hymns were sung in alternate verses by men and women. Promises were made to sweep away the crimes of tyranny. The young men drew their sabres, the girls threw their bouquets in the air and an artillery salvo was fired to represent the nation's vengeance over its enemies.

For a moment it seemed as though Robespierre had succeeded not only in dominating the Convention but in rallying the orthodox Catholics to the standard of the Revolution. His success could then have served as a lesson to future dictators in their dealings with the problems of religious faith.

Who could then have foreseen that within two months Robespierre himself would have been carted to the guillotine and that the chance that he thought he saw of a republic based on virtue would have vanished, never to return?

Chapter 8

THE SLOW AWAKENING

DURING that brilliant, burning spring of 1794 yet one more change had come over the minds of the citizens of Paris. Since the beginning of May they had seen more people than ever before 'sneezing into the sack' or 'putting their heads on the window-sill'—which in current slang meant being guillotined. This was partly because since 8 May all cases of conspiracy were transferred to Paris in order to stoke up the Terror (or was it as some say, to control it better?)

But, in addition, the proportion of prisoners acquitted fell, and those condemned seemed less and less obviously guilty—since more and more of them clearly belonged to the lower middle and working classes. Moreover, it was also evident that the authorities, in order to maintain the rule of Terror, had begun to guillotine teenage prisoners as well as veterans in their seventies. Even Frenchmen whose patriotism was undoubted began to be bored with the monotonous repetition of public death, and the public reached the point of preferring an acquittal to a conviction.

The seamstresses of the rue St Honoré no longer dropped work to watch the tumbrils go by. The inhabitants of central Paris began to protest against the rivulets of blood coursing through the streets and complained that cattle refused to walk across the Place de la Révolution.

Indeed after the Festival of the Supreme Being, the guillotine was transferred first to the Place de la Bastille and then to the more remote Barrière du Throne Renversé (now the Place de la Nation), where a specially dug ditch caught the blood of the one thousand three hundred victims dispatched there in six weeks.

The deputies of the Convention were no more secure than the ordinary people and so became less and less enthusiastic over rule by Terror. Their immunity as the nation's representatives had been removed in April 1793; restored the following November and —though they were assured to the contrary—apparently removed again by the Law of 22 Prairial. Even the members of the Committee of Public Safety trembled at times, for within a fortnight of joining it, Robespierre claimed to perceive traitors conspiring against the interests of the people within the midst of the Committee itself. (And no one even then had dared to stand up and deny this.)

Robespierre's qualities as a leader, or perhaps one should say as a politician, were limited by the fact that he had never relied greatly on the arts of persuasion as a means of policy. And in the final resort, he was prepared to establish his ideal republic by plotting the deaths of those who were not as enthusiastic about it as himself, regardless of personal loyalties. Denouncing your former friends is not an endearing trait, especially if you say that you are doing so from the highest motives. Moreover, no one, from the deputies downwards, who had gained power in the five-year struggle for survival, wished to lose his position, still less his life, because Robespierre claimed to have higher ideals than his fellow men. Robespierre's colleagues did not all claim high mindedness and injustice was not what spurred them to oppose the tyrant; it was fear that they might lose their own heads. Stalin's collaborators must have felt the same.

Government spies were everywhere and their activities in the Section added to Robespierre's unpopularity. Robespierre was also becoming unpopular too in official circles. The Committee of General Security, which dealt with the long-term defence of the Republic against counter-revolution, was resentful because

Robespierre had removed Danton's case from its jurisdiction and handed the papers to St Just. They were displeased because the control of the Revolutionary Tribunal had been to some extent taken out of their hands and given to the Police Bureau of the Committee of Public Safety. They also clashed with the Committee of Public Safety over the prosecution of government officials, which, the Committee of General Security claimed, was exclusively a matter for themselves.

The introduction of the Supreme Being into the National Convention turned out to be a costly blunder for Robespierre. For the French Revolution was not a religious movement comparable with Islam and it was impossible for any man to attempt to turn it into a religious revival—especially one in which, for political reasons, he would have a monopoly.

Then there was Robespierre's personal position. He himself may not have favoured the cult of personality with which he came to be surrounded, but some Frenchmen, even though now members of a republic, could not bear to be without some figure whom they could address with the same fawning obsequiousness which they had formerly observed towards their seigneur. In the eyes of the more independent, such homage was an additional offence, for which Robespierre must be held responsible.

Robespierre's 'image' was seriously damaged by the case of Catherine Théot, a mystic who was so unrevolutionary as to proclaim the coming of a new Messiah. Police found a letter concealed in her mattress in which she had written that Robespierre was the Messiah. They also discovered that a Chartreuse monk, Dom Gerle, who had obtained a certificate of good citizenship with Robespierre's help had visited Théot. From this it did not require much imagination to suppose that Robespierre had actively encouraged the propagation of the idea that he should be accorded popular veneration. Robespierre was able to prevent the case of Catherine Théot from being transferred to the Revolutionary Tribunal from the Committee of Public Safety. But it was his last big triumph in the Committee.

Robespierre's closest colleagues were no more attractive than their leader. St Just was cold and impersonal. And who could trust the judgement of a man who had plans for insisting in his ideal state that everyone from the age of twenty-one must publicly declare his friendships once a year? And Georges Couthon, a

partially crippled deputy from Auvergne, who was Robespierre's
other chief confident, was not a man with whom one could come to
an understanding. A poor man's lawyer, he had himself made the
most devastating attack on the rule of law, declaring that judicial
truth was neither moral nor natural but a collection of dogmas
and ritual designed to secure the inviolability of conspirators. He
argued that justice should instead be placed in 'pure Republican
hands'. Couthon had also proclaimed that 'a revolution like ours is
only a rapid succession of conspiracies'.

On top of this, it was becoming clear that the military emergency
which had originally justified the Robespierre dictatorship had
passed with the victory of the French over the Austrians at
Fleurus near Charleroi whereas the economic crisis, which the
dictatorship had claimed to be able to solve, still persisted.

The Jacobins had promoted their first price control measure
known as the Maximum in May 1793 to gain the support of the
sans-culottes against the Girondists. It applied to flour only. As
was to be expected, no one would sell at the reduced prices and the
supplies, so badly needed, promptly disappeared from the market.
So the next move was a series of laws which prohibited hoarding
and encouraged Government requisitioning.

'Hoarding' included failure to display goods which had been
bought for sale; allowing food or goods to perish and failing to declare stock in hand. The regulations were enforced by an army of
spies who were allowed to keep a third of what they discovered. At
the same time (September 1793) about forty other items, including
clothing and footwear as well as food, drink and fuel were added.
Prices in most cases were fixed at a third more than those of 1790;
wages at a half more. At first the penalty for breaking these regulations was death.

But food became scarcer and scarcer as civil war interfered with
ploughing, sowing and tilling. All over France the young men were
taken from the plough to the barrack square. Worse still, Government contractors, who had a million men spread over twelve
armies to feed, paid exorbitant prices and siphoned off supplies
which would otherwise have gone to civilians in the big cities.
To make good the shortage, bread rationing was decreed in
the second half of 1793 and came into force on Christmas Day.
Potatoes were planted in the Luxembourg gardens. Farmers were
encouraged to concentrate on growing grain, which not only

impoverished the soil, but also interfered with the supply of meat.
In April 1794 meat rationing had to be introduced. But this too
was only partially successful as butchers insisted on selling heads
and hooves with good meat in order to maintain their profit.

After the Government's first efforts to control prices had failed—
mainly because the authorities insisted on all transactions being
carried out in assignats—a new price structure was worked out. It
was based on the local cost of production to which amounts were
added for the middleman's margin and for transport costs adjusted
according to whether main roads, by-roads, or rivers—upstream or
downstream—were used. But the new scheme took six months to
prepare and proved as ineffective as the earlier systems had been.

Most people preferred, when they were short of food, to make a
trip to the countryside and pay what was asked rather than to
queue all night waiting for the official market to open. Yet the
Government in their announcements claimed that queues were unnecessary. In May the Paris municipality issued a proclamation to
the good citizens of Paris and had it posted up in each of the
Sections:

> Fearing that commercial supplies might not be sufficient to
> provide food for this vast city, Cradle of the Republic, the
> National Convention and the Committee of Public Safety have
> taken the necessary measures to provide Paris with supplies of
> its principle needs. Why then these gatherings at the doors of
> butchers' shops and other retail stores? No one who recognizes
> his true interests, would wish to remain an instrument of male-
> volence, for it is ill-will alone that provokes such scandalous
> meetings. The aristocracy smiles complacently at the activities
> of traitors and agents of despots who have united against our
> liberty and who infiltrate such meetings, sustaining them and
> seeking to arouse the hopes of foes whom we have beaten to the
> ground, by kindling in our midst a dangerous and ill-founded
> defiance of authority. You will recognize these treacherous
> agents among those who form the hard core of these daily
> gatherings; far from joining them, the law charges you with the
> duty of denouncing them. Carry out this duty without demur; it
> will be your victory over the aristocracy, over intrigue, over cor-
> ruption; continue to deserve the title of republicans by showing
> an unconquerable firmness and calm.

Marie Antoinette, had she been so minded, could hardly have put it better.

In the spring of 1794 the Government found that wages too were as difficult to control as prices. First it was the tobacco workers who demanded—and were refused—a pay increase. A week later the transport workers asked for higher rates and were told that their labour had now been requisitioned as a matter of national importance. The bakers' apprentices followed suit and were warned that their conduct made them liable to be treated as suspected persons. The pork butchers and the munitions workers were no less grasping. No one was satisfied with the revised scale of wages announced by the Government on 2 July (and revised by the Committee three weeks later).

There were signs, even, that the common people were preparing once more to conspire against the Government. Claude-François Payan, the man whom Robespierre had appointed as Agent of the Nation in the Paris Commune, decided that the Sections must be weakened lest they rise again. He abolished payments which had hitherto been made for attendance at Section meetings. He closed down many of the popular societies and declared that the Soupers Fraternels, or open air popular banquets, at which people had been encouraged to share their food were breeding 'a false sense of security' and should be discontinued.

This then was the atmosphere in which the overthrow of Robespierre was prepared. Even the leader himself feared the worst. He showed signs of instability and wept at times. He needed the relaxation of exercise but hesitated to take it for fear of assassination. The sight of two colleagues talking fraternally together was enough to arouse his suspicions that a plot was being hatched against him.

After the Théot affair he presumably wanted no more personal publicity. For a while he stayed away from both the Convention and the Committee of Public Safety. He was nevertheless planning to re-establish his influence even more strongly than before over the mesmerized groups of deputies and committee men. But now for the first time he had to act as a conspirator. In the past he had been able to move openly against the King and against the Girondists because he could rely on the mob to support his actions. This time, he was plotting against men and organizations from whom his intentions had to be concealed.

Robespierre's new move was against such people as Marc-Guilliaume-Albert Vadier, whom he had never forgiven for his malicious report on the Théot case and Jean-Henri Voulland, an active member of the Committee of General Security. It involved an intensive purge of the Convention too and on 1 June, Robespierre went so far as to tell a deputation from the Department of l'Aisne that 'the Convention in the situation in which it now stands, putrid with corruption, and incapable of rehabilitating itself, cannot save the Republic. Both must perish.'

Robespierre's plan was to overawe the Convention and, if he could not himself browbeat them into acquiescence, he would do so through the Committee of Public Safety of which St Just and Couthon were members, through the Commune, now staffed by Robespierre's men, through the National Guard commanded by François Hanriot, as well as through the Revolutionary Tribunal with its new President, Dumas.

Some of the men whom Robespierre was planning to send to the guillotine were well aware of the danger in which they stood. Among them were two members of the Committee of Public Safety, Jean-Marie Collot d'Herbois, who still had a strong following among the sans-culottes, and his friend Billaud-Varenne. Jean-Lambert Tallien, who had been sent by the Convention to Toulouse and had found himself a treasure that Robespierre had never possessed—a beautiful ex-aristocrat mistress—knew that he was on the list.

Joseph Fouché, a member of the Convention who had presided over the massacres in Lyons following the revolt there, realized that he too was one of those to be proscribed. He had fallen out with the provincial Jacobin leaders and was recalled to Paris, along with the various commissars, to account for his actions. On reaching Paris Fouché decided to side-step Robespierre and appealed directly to the Convention for justice. When this approach failed, since the Convention was not yet ready to take the lead against Robespierre, Fouché called on Robespierre himself, again without success. Indeed Robespierre soon after publicly attacked him in the Convention as being an atheist.

But the fatal error that Robespierre made in promoting the cult of the Supreme Being was never more clearly exposed than when Fouché, the atheist, was elected President of the Paris Jacobin Club. Robespierre was able to get him expelled, but the feeling had by now begun to spread abroad far and wide among the deputies at the Convention that if they did not get rid of Robespierre he would soon get rid of them. Lazare Carnot, the stalwart member of the Committee of Public Safety, who had done so much to establish the new revolutionary army was one of those who realized that he was in peril. His success in the military field had made Robespierre regard him as a possible rival. Paul-François-Jean-Nicolas Barras, ex-aristocrat from the French Colonial army who had originally supported the Terror, was another. Joseph Cambon, who acted as financial adviser to the Government, was also one of Robespierre's suspects. And so was Louis Legendre, who had been unwise enough on one occasion to speak up for Danton in the Convention.

Gradually it leaked out that matters were to be brought to a head on 27 July, known in the new calendar as 9 Thermidor. But Robespierre attempted to strike first. The day before, he walked into the Convention early in the day and launched his attack.

'Citizens,' he began, 'I will leave others to paint flattering pictures for you; instead I will tell you some home truths. . . .'

He then congratulated France on the fact that her revolution was unlike those of the past, which had been concerned merely with changing a dynasty or with transferring power from one source to another. The French Revolution, he claimed, was the first to be based on 'the rights of humanity and the principles of justice. But,' he said, 'conspirators have infiltrated themselves into the movement and are seeking to overthrow the defenders of liberty by labelling them as tyrants.'

'I am going to unveil abuses which tend towards the ruin of the country and which your honesty alone can repress. And if I say something at the same time about the persecution to which I have been subjected, you will not hold it against me. . . .'

Next he justified the Terror. 'What are the great deeds of severity for which we are being reproached?' he asked. 'Who were the victims of it? Hébert, Ronsin, Chabot, Danton, Lacrois, Fabre d'Eglantine and some other accomplices? Are we being reproached for their punishment?' The latest crimes against the liberty of the people prove, he said, that the Government, so far from being harsh, had not been severe enough.

Robespierre went on to say that the enemies of the Convention had been spreading rumours that the Committee of Public Safety and Robespierre himself intended to proceed against a number of deputies, including some who were irreproachable and others who, through some mistake, had suffered the consequences of circumstances or human weakness and who were to be regarded as conspirators. He said that the Committee had received reliable reports stating that because of the fears aroused by these rumours, a large number of deputies no longer dared to sleep at home.

What could be the object of such falsehoods? What men other than criminals had been accused by the Committees? Had not the Convention consented to their punishment and had not the people applauded it?

'As for the National Convention, my first duty and also my first inclination is a boundless respect for it. Without wishing to absolve crime; without wishing to justify here the deadly errors of some; without wishing to tarnish the glory of the energetic defenders of liberty, or to diminish the lustre of a name sacred to the annals of the Revolution; I say that every representative of the people whose heart is pure, ought to resume the confidence and dignity appropriate to him.'

This told the deputies nothing about Robespierre's intentions towards them, and other parts of the speech were equally perplexing. For Robespierre went on to say that he did not impute the crimes of Danton and Hébert to men of good faith who had been deceived by them or had been enticed by them from the strict paths of righteousness.

Then he returned to defending himself. 'They call me a tyrant. . . . If I was that, the kings that we have conquered, far from denouncing me, would lend me their guilty support. . . . But where is the tyrant who protects me? What group do I belong to? It is you! What group since the start of the Revolution has brought down parties and wiped out acknowledged traitors. It is you. . . .'

Then more self-pity. 'What am I, the accused man? A slave of liberty, a living martyr of the Republic. Every criminal abuses me; actions which are perfectly harmless and legitimate when performed by others, are crimes in my case; others are forgiven their misdeeds but my zeal is treated as a crime. . . . Here revolutionary institutions [i.e. the Committees and the Convention] are openly slandered; people try to incite hatred against them by committing excesses. . . . Those who slander the Republic and those who make it hated by acts of oppression are the same men.'

He complained that when anything went wrong, Robespierre was blamed. The nobility were told, 'It is he who has proscribed you.' While at the same time the patriots were told, 'He wants to save the nobility.' Everyone who complains is told, 'Your future depends on him alone.' The Revolutionary Tribunal is called a Tribunal of Blood created by Robespierre alone and Robespierre is said to believe that the Convention contained within itself 'some men unworthy of it'.

I am accused unofficially and by insinuation of being responsible for all the good and all the bad that has been done. My colleagues are told faithfully all that I have said and, above all, all that I have not said.

Any suspicion that someone else might have contributed to a displeasing occurrence, is carefully put aside; I am supposed to have done everything, insisted on everything, ordered everything; for one must not forget my title of dictator.

Robespierre then said that he did not dare to name at this moment and in this place the conspirators within the nation who were working on orders from 'the Duke of York and Mr Pitt' but he was prepared to say that among them were 'the impure apostles of atheism and immorality'.

How can I recount or guess all the various impostures which have been secretly put about in the National Convention and elsewhere to make me hated and feared? I will limit myself to saying that for more than six weeks, because of the character and the force of the slander, because of my inability to do good and to hinder evil, I have been forced to give up my work as a member of the Committee of Public Safety. . . . I prefer my status as representative of the people to that of member of the Committee of Public Safety and I place before everything my status as a man and a French citizen.

However that may be, it is now six weeks since my dictatorship expired, since when I have had no kind of influence over the Government. Has patriotism been the better protected? Have the conspirators been more timid? The country happier? I hope so. . . . [Having defended himself, Robespierre then called for a new mandate for an intensification of the Terror.]

People have told you that all is well in the Republic. I deny it. How can those who the day before yesterday predicted frightful

storms see only passing clouds today? How can those who told
you earlier 'I declare that we are standing on a volcano' maintain
today that our path is strewn with rose petals . . .

The counter-revolution has installed itself in the Finance
administration. It is concentrating on a new counter-revolutionary system, disguised in a façade of patriotism. Its aim is to
foment speculation, to exhaust public credit by dishonouring
French loyalty, to favour rich creditors, to ruin the poor and
drive them to desperation, to multiply the numbers of the discontented, to despoil the people of the national treasure, and to
bring on imperceptibly the ruin of the public weal. . . . [Here
Robespierre named a few of the 'guilty men' including Cambon
and Mallarmé.]

This is one part of the conspiracy. And who must be held
responsible for these evils? We ourselves with our lax weakness
towards crime and our culpable abandonment of the principles
which we ourselves have proclaimed. . . . All kinds of groups
swarm in the midst of a great Revolution. How can they be suppressed without the full fervour of justice? If righteousness does
not prevail, crime and ambition must reign. . . . Let the reins of
the revolution fall but for a moment and you will see a military
despotism take them up and the head of the conspirators will
overthrow the despised Convention. . . . Yet the guilty men have
established the principle that to denounce an unfaithful representative is to plot against the Convention itself.

Finally he turned to the scope of the purge which he hoped to
carry out, beginning with the Convention.

If someone here proposed an amnesty for treacherous deputies
and suggested placing the crimes of all representatives under the
protection of a decree, we should all blush with embarrassment.

What shall we do then? Our duty. Let us admit that a conspiracy against public liberty exists; that it owes its strength
to a criminal coalition which pursues its intrigues in the very
midst of the Convention; that the members of this coalition have
accomplices in the Committee of General Security and in the
office of this Committee which they control; and that the enemies
of the Republic have placed this Committee in opposition to the
Committee of Public Safety, making thus two Governments;
that members of the Committee of Public Safety have entered

into this conspiracy and that the coalition formed in this way seeks to do away with the nation and its patriots.

What is the remedy for this evil? It is to punish the traitors, to reform the bureaux of the Committee of General Security, to purge the Committee itself, to subordinate it to the Committee of Public Safety, to place the Government as a whole under the supreme authority of the National Convention . . . and to crush all factious groups under the weight of the national authority so that the power of justice and liberty can be built on their ruins; these should be the principles. If no one can proclaim them without being called a self-seeker, I shall conclude that these principles are banned, and that tyranny reigns among us, but not that I should keep silent; for who can object to a man who is in the right and is ready to die for his country. . . .

There was a deep and prolonged silence after Robespierre had finished speaking because the purge that he demanded was fundamental, and he had set no definite limits to it. Few of the deputies could be certain whether they themselves were on the danger list or whether the list included merely the man sitting near by or even someone on the far side of the hall.

At last Lecointre, the deputy for Versailles, rose and proposed, as was normal, that the speech should be printed. An angry buzz at once arose within the body of the Convention. Burdon de l'Oise, one of the deputies who sat with the Mountain, and who had been a follower of Danton, suspected that his name was on Robespierre's list, rose and openly opposed the publication of the speech, claiming that it contained many unproved accusations. Though he was temporarily overruled, it was clear that the Robespierre hypnotic spell over the Convention had been broken. Vadier led a new attack. And Cambon, whose name had been singled out by Robespierre, followed up:

'Before my name is dishonoured, my voice shall be heard by France,' he cried. 'It is time that everyone here should know the whole truth. One man has paralysed the will of the National Assembly. That man is Robespierre!'

Robespierre appeared to have been struck dumb. For Billaud-Varenne was the next to force his way to the tribune. 'The mask must be torn off,' he cried, 'no matter whose face it hides. I would rather that my dead body should serve an ambitious man for his

throne than that I by my silence should become the accomplice of
his crimes.' Stanislas Fréron, once a schoolfellow of Robespierre,
went so far as to propose that the two Committees of Public Safety
and General Security should be dissolved.

'The time has come to revive liberty of opinion,' he cried. 'I
move that the Assembly revoke the decree which gives the Committee power to arrest the representatives of the people. For who
can speak freely while he is in fear of being arrested?'

But the discussion of so fundamental a step would have dis-
tracted attention from the main issue—the counter-attack on
Robespierre, and Etienne Panis, a member of the Committee of
General Security, returned with a direct challenge. 'Robespierre
has prepared a list of victims,' he cried, 'and my name is said to be
on it.' An immediate outcry followed. Robespierre was urged to
announce the names of those whom he had accused. 'Let us hear
the list. . . . We want the list of names,' the deputies clamoured.
And here the Incorruptible made a fatal error. He said, 'I will make
known the list at the appropriate time.' Perhaps he felt it safe to
leave the accusations to St Just who was to speak on the following
day. Perhaps he had not really made any firm decision, or perhaps
he felt that, by keeping the Convention in the dark, he would take
away from its deputies their last shreds of courage. His knowledge of
men, however, was poor. Withholding the names led the deputies
to believe that most of them must be on it. And they voted that
Robespierre's speech should *not* be published and circulated at once
but should be referred to the two Committees for consideration.
Robespierre protested. 'What!' he cried. 'I have been courageous
enough to put before the Convention truths which I believe
necessary for the safety of the nation and you send my speech to be
examined by the very men I have accused.' But his protest was
ignored.

That evening the Robespierrists tried to recoup their strength
in the Jacobin Club. His trusty followers listened to him declaiming
his whole speech of some twelve thousand words all over again and
some of them vowed to drink hemlock with Robespierre if they
failed on the morrow to secure the impeachment of the traitors.
Collot d'Herbois and Billaud-Varenne who had gone there in the
hope of learning more of Robespierre's plans, were thrown out.

The two Committees also met but it was an aimless exercise because everyone knew that in a room adjoining the Committee of

Public Safety, St Just was spending most of the night drawing up the accusation, based on Robespierre's list, that he would make a few hours later in the Convention. He, too, refused to make known the names of those he proposed to attack. 'You have withered my heart,' he told inquirers. 'I propose to open it to the Convention.' It was a certain way to unite the other members of the Assembly, including the Right, the Centre and the Left, against Robespierre.

Next morning, on a day hot enough to scorch all tempers, the final drama began. Robespierre, wearing his 'uniform' of a turquoise-blue coat and cream-coloured breeches had arrived early and had taken a seat near the front of the hall, doubtless so that he could hurry quickly to the speaker's platform in an emergency.

Shortly before noon those who were about to be accused saw St Just rise and walk to the tribune. 'This is the moment,' said Jean-Lambert Tallien. His mistress was in one of Robespierre's prisons in hourly fear of death and he had evidently been chosen to lead the anti-Robespierre forces. St Just began by proclaiming that he belonged to no party and this gave Tallien the very opportunity he needed.

'I demand to be heard,' he cried. St Just protested but Collot d'Herbois, who was President, silenced St Just with the President's bell. Everything had clearly been arranged in advance. Tallien then pursued his attack, complaining that one after another people were claiming to be members of no party.

'No good citizen can hold back his tears when he considers the disastrous state of public affairs,' he cried. 'We see nothing but disunity. Yesterday a member of the Government broke away from it in order to accuse it. Today someone else does the same. Men endeavour to attack each other, to add to the woes of the country and to precipitate it into the abyss. The veil must be torn away.' A chorus of agreement rose from his supporters. Billaud-Varenne then rose and spoke from his seat. 'Yesterday,' he said, 'the Society of Jacobins was filled with hired men who entered without cards; in that society a plan for murdering the members of the National Assembly was prepared; yesterday too, I saw men mouthing the most atrocious insults against those who have never faltered during the Revolution. Today I see one of those men who threatened the Republic sitting in the Mountain.' 'Arrest him, arrest him,' cried the chorus and in a moment he was whisked off by the serjeant, to the Committee of General Security. 'This is the moment for speaking the truth,' Billaud continued. 'The Assembly would mistake both the course of events and its own position if it failed to recognize that it must choose between one of two massacres. It will perish itself if it weakens.'

Philippe Lebas, one of Robespierre's satellites, tried to get a word in. He was pushed aside, and Billaud rushed to the Tribune and launched a personal attack on Robespierre. The whole Convention was now watching the Incorruptible. Cries of 'Down with the tyrant' began to be heard. Then Tallien spoke again.

'Just now,' he said, 'I demanded that the veil should be torn away. It gives me great pleasure to see that it is now wholly torn asunder. The conspirators are unmasked. They will soon be destroyed and liberty will triumph. I, too, was present at the meeting of the Jacobins; I trembled for my country. I saw the army of this new Cromwell forming and I armed myself with a poniard to stab him in the heart if the National Convention lacked the courage to decree his impeachment.'

He drew the dagger which had been sent him as a distress signal from prison by his mistress, brandishing it before the eyes of the deputies.

Robespierre, hearing himself described as Cromwell started from his seat and ran forward and tried to climb the steps of the tribune. He was shouldered away. The deputies then voted that Hanriot, who was known to be ready to lead 'Cromwell's' army, should be arrested. The motion was carried to cries of *'Vive la République'*.

Billaud next asked for the arrest of Dumas, the Robespierrist President of the Revolutionary Tribunal, and two other prominent Robespierrists, Boulanger and Dufrèse. Once again Robespierre tried to speak and once again he was silenced by the President's bell. Then Louis Louchet, a little-known deputy from the Aveyron jumped to his feet and shouted, 'I demand that Robespierre be arrested.' His proposal was acclaimed by the deputies of the Mountain who roared, 'Down with the tyrant.' Robespierre made one final effort to save himself. 'President of Assassins,' he cried, turning to Thuriot, a Dantonist, who was acting as Deputy President in place of Collot d'Herbois, 'for the last time will you allow me to be heard?'

But Thuriot continued to sound his bell to the evident approval of the deputies and Tallien, claiming that Robespierre had just insulted the Convention, put the proposal for his arrest to the vote. Robespierre appealed to the spectators in the public gallery to listen to him. When they remained unmoved, he turned to his former friends of the Mountain. He was deathly pale and for once almost inarticulate. 'He is choked by the blood of Danton,' cried one of his enemies. Then he stumbled towards the Centre and besought them as 'pure and virtuous men' to give him the hearing that assassins on the other side of the house had denied him. But the Centre saw that Robespierre's cause was lost, and that it was safe for them to disown him completely. He sat down bewildered on a bench.

His younger brother, Augustin, leapt to his feet. 'I am as guilty as my brother. I share his virtues. I will share his fate,' he said. The Convention was happy to oblige. It decreed the arrest of both Robespierres, Couthon, Lebas and St Just. Robespierre hardly seemed to realize what was happening. He seemed too dazed to comprehend the order for his arrest which an usher handed to him. He was hustled to the Bar of the Convention where the warrant was read to him. Then he was taken away with the other prisoners. His rule had lasted for exactly one year.

By this time it was half past five, half an hour after the usual hour for dinner, and the Convention, nearly beside itself with relief and joy, then made a cardinal error.

It declared a two-hour recess during which the deputies, good trenchermen then as now, could have their dinner. And while they were tucking in, the Commune, still loyal to Robespierre, was acting. As early as two o'clock tale-bearers in the public gallery had run to warn the Commune that trouble was afoot. Fleuriot, the Mayor, sent orders to all prisons in Paris forbidding them to lock up Robespierre. He called for reinforcements from the Jacobin Club, sounded the tocsin, closed the barriers, called a full Council meeting and tried to rally the Section leaders. He sent for the cannon which had been so successful in putting Louis XVI to flight two years earlier and got ready to administer a revolutionary oath to all concerned. But Hanriot was missing. He had already drunk himself silly early in the day and, after hearing that his arrest had been decreed, had made off to the Place de la Nation with the final batch of Robespierre's victims who, on the plea that justice could not wait, were sent on their way regardless of the arrest of Dumas. When Hanriot got back towards eight o'clock in the evening, he

was recognized by two deputies in the rue St Honoré. Gendarmes
arrested him in the Palais-Royal where he was trying to assemble a
mob. He was tied up and left under guard in the office of the Committee of Public Safety.

Robespierre, who had been sent to the Luxembourg Palace, was
freed and, before the Convention knew it, a Robespierrist posse
arrived at the Tuileries, found their way to the room where Hanriot was guarded and released him as well.

Too late the Convention realized that by their sloth they had
allowed themselves to be outmanœuvred. Soon they were surrounded by men commanded by Hanriot. And Hanriot, still no
doubt drunk, had no hesitation in ordering his artillerymen to
direct their cannon on the Chamber where the deputies were sitting.

Only one thing saved the Convention. The artillerymen refused
to obey Hanriot's order to open fire. Hanriot then marched them
back to the Hôtel de Ville. The spirits of the deputies, who had
thought at one time that they were to be massacred in cold blood,
revived. They responded by declaring Robespierre, Hanriot and
the members of the Commune to be outlaws and liable to be shot on
sight without trial. Then albeit tardily, they began to assemble
their own protective force, of which Paul-François Barras, who had
assisted in lifting the siege of Toulon, was put in charge. Commissars were sent to the Sections to gain recruits. A posse of deputies, wearing their official uniforms, carrying torches and protected
by gendarmes, toured the streets and read the decree outlawing the
Commune. Since the trial of the Hébertists, the sans-culottes had
been almost leaderless. The citizens were divided in their opinion
and undecided as to whether the Convention or the Commune
would be likely to prove the winning side. Robespierre's popularity
had declined with the continuation of the Terror, the failure to halt
inflation and the new salary limits so recently announced. Twenty-
seven of the Sections sent deputations to the Communes asking for
instructions, but only thirteen of them sent fighting units. The
Commune seemed to be bereft of definite plans. Robespierre did
not readily take to the role of outlaw. He had eventually set himself up in the Mayor's residence where he was out of touch with the
City Hall. He did not arrive there until eleven o'clock, by which
time a thunderstorm accompanied by heavy rain had destroyed the
spirits of his adherents waiting outside the building. Meanwhile

the news had percolated that the Convention's forces had a leader and a rallying point.

Detachments of armed men began to arrive at the Convention to pledge loyalty to it. By the time Robespierre had reached the Hôtel de Ville they were ready to march on it. By the time they arrived there the Hôtel de Ville was undefended. The loyalists swarmed in unopposed. Augustin Robespierre flung himself from a third-floor window to escape capture. Hanriot tried the same unsuccessful escape route. Philippe Lebas shot himself. Couthon crawled out of his chair and hid under a table, where he was discovered and badly knocked about.

Robespierre's jaw was shattered on the left side by a bullet for which a gendarme named Meda claimed credit. The tyrant's shirt was covered with blood, his stockings had slipped down his legs, he was without tie or hat. His clothes were torn and covered with dirt, his hair dishevelled. He was taken to the Convention who refused to receive him and from there to the Committee of Public Safety, where he was laid out on a table, his head supported on a wooden box containing samples of army bread. He remained there for nearly six hours, taunted by the kind of crowd that he had so often inflamed against others. At noon he and twenty-one others were taken to the Conciergerie for identification and thereafter as outlaws immediately sentenced to death without trial. The guillotine was sent for and transported specially from the Place de la Nation to the Place de la Révolution so that the good people of Paris could watch this specially attractive mass execution.

Towards six o'clock in the evening the cavalcade of three tumbrils set out on its way to the scaffold. Robespierre seemed oblivious of everything around him. His jaw was supported by a bandage wound round his head. Couthon, who was incapable of standing, lay on the floor of the cart, as did Hanriot and Augustin Robespierre. Some of the crowd threw their hats in the air as the tyrant passed; others danced round the cart or cursed the man they had once fawned on and pursued him with insults to the very scaffold. Thoughtfully the cavalcade stopped outside Robespierre's lodgings in the rue St Honoré. A bucket of blood was fetched from the nearest butcher's shop and thrown at his door. Robespierre was the last but one of the group to be executed. And except for the fact that the executioner at the last moment tore away the bandage holding his jaw, he might have died as bravely as any aristocrat.

At last the Terror was over. It would perhaps be an over-simplification, though not a gross one, to say that the French Revolution lost its way and petered out after the death of Robespierre. Eighty-three of Robespierre's followers were guillotined on 27 and 28 July. Those other few deputies capable of leadership, who had survived the years of bloodshed, had lost their bearings. They had to answer with respect to Robespierre the same kind of question which Khrushchev faced after the death of Stalin, namely, 'If this man was such a monster, why did you not get rid of him before?'

And what should be their reply to St Just's postillion who had sat two or three times as a juror at the request of the Committee of General Security and who justified himself by saying, 'Why should I not have had the confidence of a man who had the confidence of the Government?'

Both the Jacobins and the Commune were utterly discredited. Justice for aristocrats as well as for sans-culottes became a possibility. Almost immediately after the end of the Terror, Jacques-Charles Hervelin, a drummer living in the rue Jean-Pain-Mollet, was actually brought to trial on a charge of having fried and eaten the heart of the Princesse de Lamballe during the September Massacres.

The Convention took over the direction of the Commune within a month and later appropriated its police force. The tocsin was removed from the Hôtel de Ville and taken to the Convention, a measure equivalent in modern times to seizing the broadcasting station. As a precaution the Headquarters Staff of the National Guard was changed every ten days. Within four months the Jacobin Club was closed on the pretext that it provoked rowdyism.

No doubt the members of the two committees hoped to retain their privileged positions there. They feared that if the government by terror was abandoned completely there might well be the danger of a counter-revolution, leading to their own death as well as that of the Republic. But the Convention had been frightened once too often and was determined on a policy of self-preservation. It decreed that one quarter of each committee should be replaced every month and that their duties should from that time on be shared with the Committee of Legislation.

Bertrand Barère, one of the permanent members of the Committee of Public Safety, proposed, firstly, that the Revolutionary

Tribunal continue its work of purifying the nation and, secondly, that it should still be aided by Fouquier-Tinville. Neither of these suggestions was adopted. The Revolutionary Tribunal lost its special powers three days after the death of Robespierre when the Law of 22 Prairial was repealed. Fouquier-Tinville, despite his pleas that he had had no part in denouncing, arresting, imprisoning, judging or sentencing the victims of the guillotine, was sent there himself. Ninety-four citizens of Nantes, who had been sent to Paris for judgement there, were brought before the Revolutionary Tribunal and after a prolonged public trial acquitted.

When the time arrived for one-third of the Committees to be replaced under the new law, their posts were taken by reliable moderates and Collot d'Herbois and Billaud-Varenne, finding themselves heavily outnumbered, resigned.

The new party of moderates known as Thermidoreans, encouraged a species of informal militia known as the Jeunesse Dorée recruited from the bourgeois classes. The Jeunesse wore open coats with square shoulders and low-cut shoes; their hair hung low at the sides and was curled up behind into tresses. They carried short sticks weighted with lead. By breaking up the bust of Marat in the Théâtre Feydou, they led the removal of his remains from the Panthéon and it was they who protected the Convention when the outer Sections of the Faubourg St Antoine and St Marceau tried the following March to prevent the arrest and trial of Billaud-Varenne, Collot d'Herbois, Barère and Vadier.

But one perennial problem remained. That of feeding Paris at prices that people could afford. On 1 April 1795 mobs once more invaded the Convention crying 'Bread and the Constitution of 1793'—which would of course have meant the end of the Convention. They were dispersed by the National Guard, but the Convention was provided with an excuse to sentence Barère, Collot d'Herbois and Billaud-Varenne to transportation. Collot soon died of yellow fever, but Billaud-Varenne settled down as a farmer in the tropics with a devoted negro girl named Virginie and spent the rest of his life there.

A more serious assault on the Convention took place the following month when fighting in and around the Tuileries lasted for three days. The Convention was saved largely through the firmness of its President, Boissy d'Anglas, who insisted on remaining at his post and refused to suspend the session. For the first time since the Fall

of the Bastille Army detachments were called in to restore order.
Six of the deputies, who had been rash enough to support the demands of the insurgents, were sent to the guillotine.

Yet there was no intention of abandoning the Republic. Louis
XVI's heir was still in prison when he died of tuberculosis in June
1795. The Comte de Provence, who then became his legitimate successor, thereupon issued a manifesto showing that he was a true
Bourbon who had learnt nothing and forgotten nothing from the
past six years.

So once more on August 1795, a new republican Constitution was
devised and decreed. It handed over the legislative power to two
Councils, one known as the Council of the Five Hundred, who acted
as a House of Commons and initiated legislation and a second, consisting of two hundred and fifty members aged forty and upwards,
known as the Council of the Ancients, who acted as a House of
Lords. Five Directors were charged with the duty of putting the
laws into effect. They were to be chosen by the Ancients from a list
of fifty drawn up by the Five Hundred. They were to appoint
ministers but were not entitled to sit with the Legislators nor to
command troops in person nor to control the budget. And one of
them was to retire each year.

The first five Directors were all men who had voted for the death
of the King. They therefore provided the rest of the Government
with a guarantee against the restoration of the monarchy and made
possible the emergence of conservative bourgeois groups.

Continuity with the old Convention was provided by a decree
sponsored by Pierre Daunou and others which required that two-
thirds of the new Council should be chosen from the members
of the Convention. A referendum was called to approve the Constitution and the 'two-thirds' decree. It was the decree that nearly
wrecked the whole Constitution and almost handed Paris back to
mob rule. Neither the conservatives nor the remnants of the sans-
culottes favoured it, and the sans-culottes also resented the fact
that the new Constitution no longer provided votes for all, but restricted votes that really mattered to 'those best educated and
most interested in upholding the laws', i.e. the property owners.
Such notions were rejected by two-thirds of the Paris Sections, and
an Insurrectional Committee, similar to those which had helped to
overthrow the monarchy and later the Girondists, was revived and
supported by the majority of the Sections.

On 5 October an Army of more than twenty-five thousand men once more advanced on the Convention, determined to impose their will on it. Barras, who had been so successful on 9 Thermidor, was appointed to co-ordinate the Government's defence, and, at his suggestion, a young officer who, like Barras, had distinguished himself in the siege of Toulon, was given the job of setting up artillery posts round the Convention. His dispositions were efficient and thorough. Moreover, when the clash came he had no hesitation in opening fire on the mob. The young officer's name was Bonaparte. From that time on, the Constitution was saved, rioting became unfashionable and the Army entered French politics.

The new Constitution came into effect on 26 October, when the long-lived Convention dissolved itself. Its final act had been to re-christen the Place de la Révolution as the Place de la Concorde. The change was symptomatic. For the composition of French society itself had once more begun to alter. A new, affluent society made up of speculators who had profited through buying national property, of opulent war contractors and black-market food profiteers controlled in turn by the kind of women who prosper under such conditions, came to the fore.

The Government, too, was changing. The elections of May 1797 introduced a monarchist element into the two Councils and led to friction between them and the Directors. There could hardly be a compromise between monarchists and republicans since neither the peasants nor the newly rich bourgeoisie could consent to a return to the old régime. Three of the Directors, more republican in outlook than their colleagues, favoured a *coup d'état* against the Councils and soon realized that they could depend on the republican-minded Army to support them. On 4 September the three Directors with the help of the army turned the two Councils out of the Tuileries and transferred them 'for their own safety' to the Odéon and the School of Medicine. Some members from each Council were sentenced to transportation together with the two other Directors, Carnot and Barthélemy.

Once again the Army had entered politics and the surviving Directors became more and more dependent on it. Once again the Government had become 'revolutionary', that is, unconstitutional. But in the meantime France had taken a foreign-policy decision of vital importance. She had resolved as a matter of national pride to force Austria to agree to the French occupation of Belgium. This

in turn meant that an attack would have to be made on Austria's
possessions in north Italy. In March 1796 Bonaparte was given
command of the Army of Italy. None of the generals whom he
commanded knew him. Some thought that his appointment had
been procured through the influence of the beautiful wife whom he
had recently married, and his frail and haggard appearance was not
one to inspire confidence. However, as Masséna remarked, once he
had put on his general's hat, he seemed to have grown two feet. He
spoke with such authority and good sense that it was impossible not
to defer to his judgement. He captured the hearts of both his men
and their commanders. His plan was to strike first at the Sardinian
possessions in the west of Italy, so that having subdued them he
could safely turn eastwards. Within twenty days of opening his
campaign he had compelled the Sardinians to sue for peace, to hand
over Nice and Savoy, and to dismantle the fortifications on the
Alpine passes. He was thus free to attack the Austrians without
leaving a hostile power behind him. On 8 May, Bonaparte skilfully
misled the Austrians with a feint attack, got his troops across the
great natural barrier of the river Po, and compelled the Austrians to
retreat to the Tyrol. In two other campaigns that year he won
victories at Castiglione, Arcola and early the following year at
Rivoli. By April the Austrians were forced to make peace and to
surrender Belgium to the French Republic.

In December 1797 Bonaparte was given command of something
still more important to his future—the Army of the Interior, as the
prelude to an attack on England. In May 1798 he left France for
Egypt which was to be used as a base from which to seize the
British possessions in India. He found the Egyptians easy enough
to conquer but Nelson surprised the French fleet at anchor in
Aboukir Bay and destroyed it. Few of the forty-thousand troops
which Bonaparte had taken with him saw France again.

But the situation at home had grown so perilous and the country
had been so nearly overrun by a combined force of Russians and
Austrians that there were sighs of relief when Bonaparte himself
arrived back in October 1799. He was promptly hailed as the
founder of a new Empire, and his brother Lucien was elected to be
President of the Council of Five Hundred. On 6 November the two
Councils honoured Bonaparte with a State banquet.

Bonaparte clearly felt that the time had come for him to fulfil
his destiny. His proclamations showed his impatience with the

surviving Directors. 'What have you done,' he asked, 'with that France which I left so prosperous in your hands? I left you peace; I find you at war; I left you victories, I find nothing but defeats. I left you the booty of Italy and I find nothing but penal laws and misery. What have you done with the hundred thousand Frenchmen whom I knew and who were my comrades in glory? They are dead! This state of affairs cannot last.'

Soon a conspiracy was on foot for Bonaparte to seize power. It was promoted by the same Sieyès, the former Abbé, whose pamphlet in 1789 had awakened the ambitions of the Third Estate to declare itself the National Assembly. Sieyès thus baptized and buried the Revolution.

The Abbé—who was also a Count—had withdrawn from politics after the French Church had been 'nationalized' and emerged again as a political figure only after Thermidor. During the Terror he was saved by his cobbler who declared, 'I mend his boots and I can answer for him.' He was perhaps the first to appreciate that in a hostile Europe, France could survive only if she were truly militarized and he realized too that this could be done only under a far stronger administration than was provided by the Directorate.

It was Sieyès, himself a Director, who persuaded members of the Council of Ancients on 9 November that they were once more in danger from a Jacobin plot and that they should pass a decree under a clause in the Constitution which came into effect in times of public agitation, that both Councils should be transferred to St Cloud and that General Bonaparte should be entrusted with the task of taking them there under his protection.

Sieyès and his friend, Roger Ducos, then resigned from the Directorate, Barras followed their example and the other two Directors were held under guard in the Luxembourg Palace. Thus the two main elements in the Government, the Directors and the Councils, were hamstrung.

The next afternoon the 10 November 1799 the Ancients met in the Gallery of Mars at St Cloud and the Five Hundred in the Orangerie, to the strains of the *Marseillaise*. Bonaparte and his troops together with Sieyès and Ducos were on hand too.

But music did not soothe the feelings of the deputies, and there were angry outbursts in the Council of Five Hundred. Hearing this Bonaparte appealed to the Council of the Ancients:

Representatives of the people, you are in no ordinary situation; you are standing on a volcano. Yesterday when you summoned me to inform me of the decree for your removal and charged me with its execution, I was content.

I at once assembled my comrades; we hastened to your aid. But now I am overwhelmed with slander. People talk of Caesar, Cromwell and military Government! If I had wanted to suppress the freedom of my country, I should not have attended to the orders which you gave me. . . . Representatives of the people: I swear to you that the country has not a more zealous defender than I am; but its safety rests with you alone! There is no longer a Government; four of the Directors have handed in their resignations; the fifth has been placed under surveillance for his own security. The Council of the Five Hundred is divided; nothing remains but the Council of Ancients. Let it adopt measures. It has only to speak; I am ready to obey its orders. Let us save Liberty. Let us save Equality.

Then a republican deputy issued a challenge, 'General, we applaud your words. Swear with us to obey the present Constitution which alone can maintain the Republic.'

For a moment Bonaparte, who had every intention of overturning the Constitution, was taken aback. But he was soon in command again. 'The present Constitution no longer exists,' he cried. 'You violated it on 18 Fructidor; you violated it on 22 Floréal; you violated it on 30 Prairial. The Constitution is invoked by all factions, and violated by all; it cannot be a means of safety for us because it no longer receives any respect from anyone; the Constitution is being violated. We must have another compact and new guarantees.'

These words won the day and the members of the Council rose to their feet cheering. The Council of the Five Hundred was less docile. It refused to receive Bonaparte declaring him an outlaw and howled down Lucien Bonaparte, its President.

There was only one way to deal with the situation and Bonaparte used it. His soldiers rescued Lucien from the Orangerie and Lucien, mounting a horse, proclaimed that the Five Hundred were at that very moment being terrorized by the daggers of a few extremists. He told the soldiers that he would return to the Orangerie and would call on all loyal representatives to follow him out of the hall. 'As for those who remain in the Orangerie, let them be expelled by force. Those brigands are no longer representatives of the people but representatives of the dagger.'

Then Bonaparte spoke, 'Soldiers—I have led you to victory; may I rely on you?' Cries of *'Oui! Oui!'* and *'Vive le Général!'* answered him. 'Soldiers,' he continued, 'there were reasons for expecting that the Council of Five Hundred would save the country; on the contrary, it is plagued by internal strife. Agitators are trying to stir it up against me. Soldiers, may I rely on you?' Again those reassuring cries filled the air. 'Well then I will make them see reason,' said Bonaparte and gave orders for the hall to be cleared.

That evening three consuls, Bonaparte, Sieyès and Ducos, were appointed as a provisional Government, with orders to prepare a Constitution. It only remains to say that the new Constitution established a dictatorship in which the First Consul Bonaparte assisted by two others controlled both the Government and the Army. The Consuls appointed the Senate, and the Senators appointed the Legislators. Yet so strong was the desire of the French people for stable government that the new Constitution was approved by a million more Frenchmen than had voted for the people's Constitution of 1793.

On 16 July 1801 with Napoleon's approval a concordat restoring the position of the Catholic Church in France was signed. The agreement was celebrated by a special service in Notre-Dame in the presence of the entire Government. Bonaparte drove to the cathedral in the coach used by former French monarchs, and in the same splendour that had been enjoyed by *le roi*. A special Mass was celebrated by the Pope's cardinal-legate and the people were once more addressed in Latin.

That evening the Tuileries gardens were 'floodlit' and there was an evening concert. But the soldiers, still republican in outlook, were not so happy. When Bonaparte got back to his apartments, he questioned General Delmas on the matter. 'What did you think of the ceremony?' he asked. 'A fine piece of showmanship,' came the reply. 'Nothing was lacking but the million men who were slain in destroying the very thing you are re-establishing.' Napoleon was unmoved.

In May 1802 he was made First Consul for life and two years later the Pope himself came to Paris to crown him as Emperor of the French. After fifteen years of treachery and bloodshed *Le Jour de la Gloire* had at last arrived. The real revolution remained unachieved.

APPENDICES

APPENDICES

Appendix One

A NOTE ON THE FRENCH
AND RUSSIAN REVOLUTIONS

WHAT distinguished the French Revolution from other political
upheavals that the world has seen and what were its special
characteristics? Was it merely an unprecedently violent and prolonged uprising or was it something unique in nature which permanently altered the course of world history by introducing new
political doctrines, new forms of revolutionary organization, new
conceptions of leadership, new means of persuasion and communication, new methods of revolutionary administration and new
economic policies, to be regarded as the fore-runners of modern
Communism?

And what, if any, was the relationship between the French
Revolution and the Russian? Did the political explosions that took
place in Paris lead through some kind of delayed chain reaction to
the Russian uprising in the same way as a hurricane in the West
Indies can cause a ground swell hundreds of miles away and, if
there was no direct connection, did it inspire or influence the
Russian Revolution by example?

At first when one compares the French Revolution with the

upheavals that took place in Russia there are superficial points of resemblance, which if one considered them alone might lead one to think that the Russian Revolution was from its circumstances a repetition of the French.

In Imperial Russia, as in France, the revolutionaries faced an absolute monarchy in which the ruler appointed his own ministers, and ran the national budget out of his privy purse. There were many parallels, too, between Nicholas II, last of the Tsars, and Louis XVI. Both were weak and well meaning, modest, relatively thrifty and pious. Each had taken a foreign wife whose character was stronger than her husband's. In each case there had been a long delay in providing an heir to the throne and the Prince when he appeared was a near invalid.

In both cases the monarchy had been weakened by a previous war (in Russia's case the Russo–Japanese war, in France's the American War of Independence) and in each case the pace of the revolution was hastened by further hostilities (in Russia's case the First World War, in France's by the hostile coalition formed against her).

In each case women, complaining of food shortages, triggered off disorders which ended in the Army disobeying orders to fire on the rioters, and in each case this led to the capture of the main arsenal by the rebels and thus to the fall of the Government.

In each case there was a bourgeois revolution, represented in Russia by Kerensky's Provisional Government of March 1917 and in France by the Girondist Government and in each case the bourgeois Government was forcibly turned out. In each case the original bourgeois Government was prepared to spare their ruler's life and in each case their successors were not. In each case there was bitter civil war and attacks on organized religion. In France, as in Russia, the victors of the Revolution hoped that the people of other countries would rise against despotism and were, to some extent, disappointed. Finally, in each case necessity compelled those who had struggled for liberty to consent to a dictatorship.

Apart from these superficial resemblances, both French and Russian leaders followed similar ways of propagating their beliefs through clubs and popular societies, popular festivals locally and nationally, community singing and through their attempt to replace religious worship by a State-aided substitute.

But there are fundamental differences too between the nature of the two cataclysms. In the first place, the Russian Revolution was organized largely by leaders in exile who dared not return to their own country except in disguise. Not even Lenin and Trotsky operated under their own names.

The timing, too, was different in as much as Russia at the time of her revolution was already engaged in fighting in the First World War in alliance with Britain, France and other countries and since the war was an imperialist and not a people's war, Lenin made what peace he could without any regard to national honour or prestige. Trotsky, a civilian, was Russia's Napoleon. Another matter of timing: it was not until a fortnight before the October Revolution that Lenin, still in disguise, succeeded in persuading the Bolshevik Central Committee to agree to seize power from the Provisional Government by means of an armed rising. All rather different from the techniques used to overthrow the Girondists.

The theories which inspired the two revolutions were necessarily different since the musings of the French philosophers who believed they could reason out the perfect political system were but loosely related to the actual situation in France and were still less closely connected with the sort of economics which interested Karl Marx. The relatively industrialized society of Imperial Russia was hardly comparable with the relatively primitive economy of France in which it would have been virtually impossible to organize a widespread coordinated strike of the kind which took place in Petrograd in March 1917.

Numerous eighteenth-century French writers realized that unequal distribution of property was inimical to universal happiness but few were prepared to argue that it must be forcibly redistributed before there could be political equality. It is true that Church property was 'nationalized' in France, but the main object of this move was to raise money for the budget, and when the State disposed of Church property it was perfectly happy to see it pass into the possession of other landowners, preferably in large lots since these were more easily conveyed. Equally, St Just produced a scheme for taking property from the rich and giving it to the deserving poor. But this was a sentimental device designed rather to encourage the friends of the Revolution than to perpetuate economic equality.

Thus the French Revolution was several removes away from the Russian and the resemblance between them is partly accidental.

In between the two, Karl Marx had lived and died, Europe had
been convulsed by the upheavals of 1830 and 1848 and also by a
world war.

On the other hand both Marx and Lenin studied the French
Revolution closely (and Lenin paid particular attention to its
'successor', the uprising of the Paris Commune in 1871). The Russians, perhaps with the idea of discovering established precedents
for their own struggles (or perhaps with a view to showing how
much more logical modern Communism is than the eighteenth-
century variety), subsequently conducted a good deal of research
into the political theories that inspired the French Revolution.
The Frenchman who has probably received most attention from
them is François-Noel Babeuf who launched the Conspiracy of
Equals against the Directory in 1796.

Some of the most precious Babeuf manuscripts are now in the
Institute of Marxism–Leninism, maintained under the protection
of the Central Committee of the Communist Party of the Union of
Soviet Socialist Republics in Moscow.

Babeuf, a man of no special distinction, described as having
chestnut hair, a beard, a large long nose and long chin, was born on
23 November 1760 in Picardy, the fertile grain-growing province
centring round Amiens. He was the son of a village labourer and
lived in poverty for the whole of his life. Already at fourteen he
began earning a living as a feudiste or clerk engaged in tracing and
verifying land titles and feudal claims. The work gave him an insight into the injustices of the French property system and an
abiding hatred against the near-slavery to which it subjected the
vast majority of Frenchmen. But when feudalism was abolished
during the early days of the Revolution, Babeuf found himself without a job.

He was happy to participate in the château-burning and destruction of feudal and other records which was one of the features
of the country life of the time. He became editor of a local paper,
the *Correspondant Picard*. With the dismissal of royal officials
and the fall of the monarchy, Babeuf found himself with important
responsibilities covering the sale of State property and the confiscation of émigré estates. In January 1793, however, he was
accused of having falsified the certificate of ownership of a piece of
national property. He was charged with the offence and suspended
from his post. He escaped to Paris, leaving his family to starve

and found work in the Commune food office. But he had to spend two years fighting and re-fighting his case before he finally succeeded in having the sentence quashed. He was in prison during the Terror and by the time he was released the most exciting phase of the Revolution was over. The reaction then set in. There was no more chance of public office for a man with Babeuf's record and he turned once more to a life of revolutionary agitation. By the end of 1794 his political views had almost crystallized. He felt convinced that the Revolution had not been completed and that it was his duty to lead on where others had stopped short.

What did Babeuf believe? He clung to the principle of absolute equality to such a degree that in his view all men should receive equal wages. In *The Manifesto of the Plebs* he wrote, 'There is absurdity and injustice in the claim that a man whose job calls for more intelligence, concentration or strain should receive more reward for it.' He denied that a day's work by a watchmaker deserved to be rated twenty times as highly as that of a ploughman and claimed that the superiority of talent or industry is nothing but a 'specious lure which has always undeservedly helped the plots of those who conspire against equality'. All competition he declared, should be forbidden since the person who tries to do the work of several is aiming at taking more than his share of goods from the community, i.e. from his fellows.

It was this acquisitive spirit which in Babeuf's view led to all the misery of his time. It led first to private property, then to inherited property, and finally to a state in which the poor were led to believe that their condition is a natural one due to their own incompetence and lack of ability, and that they must therefore submit to laws which keep them permanently in a position of inferiority.

So far, however, these beliefs have not taken us much further than previous theories put forward by Rousseau, Diderot, Helvetius and Mably. But whereas these theorists believed that private property must exist if there were not to be anarchy and must be respected in order to check covetousness, Babeuf followed Morelly whose Code of Nature, published in 1755, concluded that private property must be abolished. But Babeuf went further even than Morelly. He realized that it was necessary to have something more than a political system. The people of France were, he believed, in a state of physical and moral slavery. Their perpetual adolescence and ignorance prevented them from recognizing their rights and their inertia prevented them from recovering them. An enlightened vanguard was thus required to establish this system even though the majority of the people were too hidebound to realize the need for it. In the field of economics, Babeuf's idea was that individuals should no longer work for themselves but should bring their produce to a common pool from which it would be handed out to all and sundry according to their needs. He realized, also, that this in turn meant State supervision of the numbers employed and control of the type of goods produced. Here a planned economic order is linked to the planned political order to which so many eighteenth-century philosophers had confined themselves. Babeuf argued that State-controlled industry would be preferable to private enterprise. 'Will industry perish,' he asked, 'if it is no longer allowed to proceed blindly, to take risks, and to make mistakes through mischance or because of over-production? Will it fail through being intelligently managed and stimulated in response to the needs and well-being of all?'

But for modern Communists the additional fascination of Babeuf lies in the left-wing conspiracy which he directed and the methods which he proposed to use in order to launch the world's first Communist state. The conditions for this were in some respects ideal. The makers of the Constitution of 1795, by forbidding the popular societies to have any effective political organization, had laid open the way for an underground movement and a Secret Directory. Babeuf, now in hiding, began to publish his remarkably influential periodical the *Tribun du Peuple*. He wrote in an agreeable and lively style. Conditions for obtaining a hearing for his views were also good in as much as the Government, by abolishing price controls, had added to the profits of the speculators and the miseries of the poor. In the spring of 1796 most prices were thirty times what they had been in 1789 and some were a hundred times their former level. It was not a moment for kind words.

The *Tribun* had nearly six hundred regular subscribers of whom about sixty per cent were in Paris; among them were municipal officials and soldiers as well as the foremen, shopkeepers and the other petit bourgeois who had once formed a section of the sans-culottes.

In the spring of 1796 the Government passed new laws providing the death penalty for those who advocated a change of Government.

They confirmed a decree of 18 March 1793 establishing the death penalty for those who called for a redistribution of property and equally for those who criticized the Government. A section of the police, stationed at Grenelle, who were favourable to Babeuf's ideas, mutinied. The leaders fled and joined the conspirators in hiding urging that power should be seized by force.

At this point Babeuf's plans ran into difficulty. He realized that most of the people he wished to liberate had in fact become tired of the struggle for freedom and would rather not make the effort that a totally new system of life would demand. Indeed they might not understand the necessity of giving up all property, or of making any moral sacrifice whatever in the interests of a better existence. The ideal method of taking control would be for the enlightened vanguard to convert the people gradually to the cause of revolution by open propaganda. But the Government would never allow this to happen. A second possibility would be for a group of revolutionaries to seize power by means of a conspiracy, without having prepared any of the people in advance for the policies which it was intended to carry out. But in this case the new leaders would be behaving like brigands rather than statesmen. Eventually a middle course was decided on. Part of the country could be intensively prepared for the final revolution and a coup carried out there. The leaders could then demonstrate their theories on this well-prepared territory and thus convince those living in the unenlightened areas that they too must be liberated.

It was realized that such a coup could not be bloodless because the mass of selfish people would not surrender their private acquisitions without a struggle. But this was inevitable. If such changes could have been made without violence there would have been no excesses during the French Revolution.

Paris was chosen as the limited area but even here the followers of Babeuf were not by themselves numerous enough to carry out a coup unaided. They were forced to ally themselves in a kind of popular front with former Jacobins who claimed to be the successors of Robespierre and whose policy was to call for a return to the Constitution of 1793.

But the Babouvists had very different ideas as to what would happen if the coup was successful. From that day on the citizens of France would not automatically include those born within her frontiers but would consist only of those who shared in the work

needed to satisfy the wants of their fellow men. All those who
refused to shoulder their responsibilities would be banished.

All citizens would be formally enrolled and given cards in much
the same way as Communists are today. They would not have to
prove political reliability other than by showing that they no
longer possessed private property. Non-citizens would have to bear
the whole burden of taxation apart from a cut of ten per cent
levied on the gross national income which would be devoted to defence. No debts were payable to those not carrying cards nor were
the non-citizens allowed to offer money or goods to citizens. Non-
members could not take posts either in the Army or the Civil Service. By this means the party would, it was hoped, have been firmly
established in a matter of years if not months.

Since no inheritance would be permitted in Babeuf's community,
all property would eventually belong to the State, but those with
private possessions would be encouraged to surrender them
voluntarily in advance by being subjected to heavy taxation, by
being excluded from public office and by policies which would make
it impossible for them to have servants and other luxuries which
made possible the enjoyment of their possessions.

In return for fulfilling their norm, all workers would be guaranteed an assured standard of living. All meals would be eaten
together. Money would be forbidden. Long-distance transport
would be free. Free washing and lighting would be provided and
enough food to provide a modest and frugal way of life. Medical aid
would be free too. The State would be the only agency permitted to
trade abroad. Foreign imports would be limited, to avoid encouraging luxury. Industry would not be allowed to produce anything superfluous to the needs of the community. Nor would ad-
vertising that created fictitious needs be permitted. In schools only
subjects useful to the Republic would be taught. Frivolous books
and art not devoted to the public welfare were to be discouraged.
All good Communist policy.

In each Commune the citizens would be divided into classes, one
for each useful occupation and the members of this group would
elect their own magistrates who would be responsible for production, storage and distribution of the products as well as for the
welfare of the producers. The magistrates would fix the norms for
each type of work, control travel permits, introduce new methods
of production including mechanization in order to lighten the

burden of labour and to increase leisure. Not until he had reached the age of forty would a man be free to choose his occupation. Thus economic dictatorship begins to take the place of political socialism at which earlier French philosophers had aimed. Apart from the magistrates there would be no *élite* party members. The membership of the party would eventually expand to include all inhabitants and propaganda would no longer be needed after the coup had been successful and would therefore cease with it.

This helps to explain why Babeuf accepted so many conspirators who could have no real enthusiasm for his aims. It also explains why his experiment would almost certainly have failed even if he had been successful at first in seizing power.

There is much dispute among scholars as to how far Babeuf alone can be held responsible for these ideas. Certainly policy was discussed in a kind of central committee in which several other individuals played a prominent role. One of these was Philippe Buonarroti generally regarded as the chief theoretician of the party whose work *Conspiration pour l'Egalité*, published in Brussels in 1828, set out in detail the aims of the conspiracy, albeit thirty years later. Exactly how closely these corresponded to those of Babeuf himself at the time of the conspiracy it is hard to be sure. Georges Lefebvre, whose name is still pre-eminent among historians of the French Revolution, believed that Babeuf was more directly inspired by the three-year system of communal agriculture that he had seen in Picardy than by visions of industrial Communism. However, Babeuf as the chief agitator in the conspiracy of the Equals, is still regarded as the embodiment of one of Communism's earliest myths.

The mechanics of the coup by which power was to be seized in May 1796 were organized in some detail. A Committee of Insurrection barely more than six strong directed the operation. Paris was divided into twelve districts each with its agent who knew neither the names of the members of the Committee nor those of the other agents. Contact between each agent and the Committee was maintained through a third party. The agent's job was to direct propaganda through newspapers, leaflets, posters, to initiate discussions in clubs and cafés—especially if they were frequented by soldiers—and in private houses, to report on the state of public opinion, to collect intelligence and counter-intelligence of the Government's plans, and to suggest the names of those who might be recruited as leaders.

An announcement proclaiming a state of insurrection was prepared. It declared with something less than candour that the purpose of the revolt would be to restore the Constitution of 1793 and
called on the populace to make their way to the nearest of a list of
assembly points where they would find commanders, distinguished
by tricolour badges in their hats, ready to lead them. People and
disaffected troops were then to march on the main Government
offices including the National Treasury and the Post Office, and
seize them. Government troops were to be invited to come over to
the insurgents by persuasive orators—including women—and by
rumours insisting that they had done so. If the Government tried
to suppress the revolt, barricades were to be erected to prevent
loyal troops from circulating and they were to be attacked in the
streets with stones and from the roof-tops with boiling oil. All five
members of the Directory were to be killed and seven ministers—
an enterprise which would start the new régime off on the right
foot, as it were, by restoring an atmosphere of terror. As in previous
phases of the Revolution, the people should be induced in the heat
of the moment to engage in crimes which would commit them to the
revolt and make it impossible for them to draw back afterwards
in the cold light of reason.

The people's gratitude was to be bought by an immediate distribution of food and clothing; goods at the pawnshops were to
be returned to their owners without charge, as a measure which
would help to undermine respect for private property. Having
hoisted themselves to power the next step of the leaders would be
to ask the people to approve of 'certain improvements' to the
Constitution of 1793. After that the Revolution would be on its
way.

Babeuf had no objection to the Government knowing that some
kind of conspiracy was being hatched against them, provided that
the names of those taking part remained secret. He thought that it
would serve to unnerve the Directors. Unfortunately Grisel, a
Government agent, had succeeded in infiltrating the inner circles of
the Babouvist Equals, and passed on his knowledge to Carnot, who
at that time was the presiding member of the Directory.

And at the very moment when the enthusiasm of the plotters
was boiling over—they were already preparing the proclamations
to be issued after the success of the coup—police seized the headquarters of the conspiracy.

'Why do you obey your masters?' Babeuf asked the officer who had come to arrest him, at his hovel in the Champs-Elysées.

But the soldiers and the people were tired of fighting and the court were not interested in Babeuf's plea that he had used only the language of earlier philosophers and patriots. And of course it is just because he did *not* use the same language that he interests us today.

Babeuf's conspiracy caused little stir at the time when the political tide was running so strongly towards the right-hand end of the spectrum and it was not until many years later that its connection with modern Communism was fully evident.

On the other hand it has been argued that the French Revolution did have a considerable influence on the modern bourgeois world—in the spheres of commerce and industry—more perhaps than it did on Communism itself, and this argument we shall now examine.

When Arthur Young toured France he found that the system of weights and measures 'exceeds all comprehension'. The livre (pound weight) was different in Paris, Lyons and Marseilles. The *arpent de Paris*, used for measuring land was equivalent to about thirty-four acres, but the *arpent des eaux et forêts* worked out at fifty-one acres. There were twenty-six different land measures in the Haut Garonne alone. The *boisseau de Paris*, a unit of liquid measure, differed from the *boisseau de Bordeaux*. And so on *ad infinitum*.

The standard measures for verifying weight, volume and surface area were kept locally and were by no means constant—a situation which led to fraud and litigation. It was difficult to transport grain freely from one part of the country to another without the risk of having to measure and remeasure it. Reforms had been urged over the previous four hundred years. The problem was to fix on a unit of length based on some natural law and to relate it to surface area, volume and mass employing the same decimal scale as was used for counting ordinary numbers.

Gaspard Monge from Beaune in Burgundy, the son of a tinker, for whose mathematical genius a professorship of hydraulics had been specially created at Paris University, was appointed in 1790 a Commissioner charged with drawing up a decimal system.

It had become essential for scientists to have more accurate measures than those hitherto employed. The stars had been

suggested as a point of reference. From them the astronomers had
been able to derive a reliable time standard and they knew the
length of a pendulum required to swing once a second. Unfortunately the swing was found to vary at different latitudes. So another
approach, a timeless one, was tried. Almost on the eve of the flight
to Varennes, Lavoisier, the famous French scientist, whose experiments led him to discover about the same time as Priestley in England and Scheele in Sweden the presence and properties of an unknown gas called oxygen, received a report from the Royal
Academy of Science, advocating a measure based on the relationship between the volume and weight of a quantity of water at its
maximum density. A draft proposal for a metric system was ready
by 1 August 1793. It was based on a length known as a meter
equivalent to the forty millionth part of the distance round the
earth. But a few days later the Academies were suppressed.
Lavoisier himself was arrested and guillotined for having raised the
money for his experiments by buying a tax farm; and nothing
more happened during all the time that Robespierre was struggling
for his Republic of Virtue. The search was not resumed until April
1795.

Nearly fifty more years passed before the metric system was fully
in force. So the exact amount of credit due to the Revolutionary
leaders for their introduction of the metric system remains in
doubt, though they certainly created the national unity needed for
its adoption.

The law substituting the franc for the livre was passed under the
Consulate and incidentally amounted to a revival of the practice
under Louis XIV when the coinage was also counted in francs.
Marianne, the embodiment of la Belle France, was first used as a
term of disparagement in 1794 by opponents of the Terror, so there
was nothing revolutionary here. As for administration, the first
idea of the revolutionaries was to divide France into equal Departments measuring forty-five miles square. Nature's mountains and
rivers soon put a stop to this nonsense.

The new French calendar which indeed was produced by the
revolutionaries themselves to replace the former almanac, which
they regarded as 'superstitious', had only a limited success. It was
adopted on 10 October 1793 in a law which said that the new era
had begun on 22 September 1792, the date of the autumnal
equinox. From that time on each month was regarded as having

thirty days and was divided into three periods of ten days of rest at the end of each. The days were re-named Primidi, Duodi, Tridi, etc., up to Décadi. (Strenuous efforts were made to cure the French of the superstitious habit of celebrating Sunday as their day of rest.) At the end of each year, five extra days, known as 'Sans-culottides', were added to bring the total for the year up to three hundred and sixty-five. Leap years were allowed for, but they were added at the end of the third revolutionary year and thereafter every fourth year, instead of at the end of February. Another catch was that 'our' calendar did not treat the year 1800 as a leap year whereas the French did. The names for the months were attractive and described the moods of Nature which were to be expected in them in France. Disregarding the effects of leap year they corresponded to our months as follows:

Vendémiaire	add	21	to get the corresponding day in September
Brumaire		21	October
Frimaire		20	November
Nivôse		20	December
Pluviôse		19	January
Ventôse		18	February
Germinal		20	March
Floréal		19	April
Prairial		19	May
Messidor		18	June
Thermidor		18	July
Fructidor		17	August

Despite the logic of this arrangement, the revolutionary calendar failed to catch on outside France for two very simple reasons. The first was that people had no wish to give up resting every seventh day, and the second was that the names of the months were quite unsuited to the world south of the equator where the climate works in reverse and where Thermidor, the hot month, is likely to occur in winter. The revolutionary calendar was discontinued on 1 January 1806.

Inside France, one of the big successes of the Revolution was the progress made towards the use of a single French language in place of the various patois and other near-languages such as Gascon, Languedocien, Picard, Basque, and Flemish.

This concern for uniformity was prompted partly by the feeling that all liberated Frenchmen should speak the same language as brothers and partly by a fear that those who clung to local dialects were reactionary and liable to become allied to enemies beyond the frontiers. Certainly the Assemblies and the Convention helped to foster a certain kind of eloquence and a form in which, to make themselves understood, all had to speak in a single tongue.

Some progress had already been made, before Napoleon's arrival, with the far more difficult task of reducing France's four hundred different codes of civil, feudal and canon law to a manageable system of justice. The rights of women, however, were as neglected as they had been under the Salic Law.

Education took several steps forward, towards a free, non-religious, politically independent, universal and compulsory system of teaching and the proposals of Antoine-Nicolas de Condorcet, Permanent Secretary of the Academy of Sciences (who incidentally gave the name Lycée to the nine advanced study centres which he proposed to set up in various parts of the country), could well serve as a guide to any state setting up a system of national education. Condorcet later committed suicide to escape the guillotine.

Inventors (some of them at any rate) benefited from a Patent Law passed in January 1791 which recognized a contract between the inventor and the State. This protection made it possible for details of new inventions to be published, which in turn led to further advances. But not all were as fortunate as they deserved to be. Philippe Leblanc, a chemist, discovered in 1786 how to produce soda ash commercially from salt (and also greatly improved the methods of producing soap by adding caustic soda to fats). But he had been set up in business by the Duc d'Orléans and for political reasons, his discoveries and his factory were seized in 1791 and he died in poverty.

Abraham-Louis Bréguet, the inventor of the automatic mechanical governor for chronometers and other precision instruments, was compelled to flee from Paris to Switzerland during the Terror.

Nicolas-Jacques Conté was more fortunate. When the war cut off supplies of Cumberland plumbago (used at that time for making lead pencils), Conté hit on the notion of mixing clay and graphite together and enclosing them in a cedarwood casing to make the modern pencil. He afterwards became Chief of Napoleon's Balloon Corps on the expedition to Egypt.

Pierre-Simon Laplace from Normandy, the son of a village

farmer, whose brilliant analysis of the laws of gravitation and celestial mechanics accounted for so much in the cosmos that had previously been considered to be inexplicable, was also fortunate. In 1785 he had already become a member of the Academy of Science, and his career was never interrupted. In his early days while Examiner at the Royal Military School he had interviewed young Bonaparte and was responsible for admitting him to the Artillery Corps.

Most revolutionary governments sooner of later concern themselves with the culture of the past—provided that it is non-political —as if to show that they care for the eternal verities and are in sympathy with all men of culture. In France a decree passed in June 1793 awarded a sentence of two years in irons for anyone destroying works of art in national property. A commission charged with the duty of preserving National Monuments was set up in August 1793 and this was followed in October by a further measure by which it was forbidden to mutilate or destroy monuments on the pretext of destroying the relics of royalty or feudalism, whether in libraries, museums or collections.

A Commission of Fine Arts was established in 1794 for, as Abbé Grégoire, one time President of the Convention said, 'We must show people that marble breathes, that canvas lives.' A Museum of Natural History was set up and, attached to it, a zoo containing the beasts from the royal menagerie at Versailles together with animals seized from three travelling circuses.

But this hardly compensated for the kind of things that Paris had lost. Even a year after Thermidor the Faubourg St-Germain, where the nobility had lived, was of course deserted and mansions that the Government had not already taken over were marked 'National Property: For Sale'. Most of them had been sacked and stripped. Even in daytime few carriages were to be seen, and after dark, once the theatres had closed, all signs of life vanished. Open-air black markets at which people bartered their most precious possessions for food existed round every corner, and took the place of shops.

Neither liberty, nor fraternity, nor equality could be said to exist. Hereditary nobility had been abolished, but trade unions were still curbed. The right to vote was restricted. And despite new laws of divorce and inheritance which broke up some of the Estates, it was largely property owners who benefited most from the Revolution. The middle-class lawyers who had conceived and carried through the Revolution remained relatively poor. The age of free-enterprise industrial capitalism was about to begin. The leaders of the Revolution had tried to find out what befitted 'man' without taking account of his true nature.

And the final verdict? Who can say today whether the Revolution was violent mainly because the rich refused to give up the possession of that to which they were not entitled or whether its horrors were due to the short-sightedness and rivalry of the leaders in whom the people were induced to place their trust? Who can say whether its failures ensued only because its work was left uncompleted?

Some of the French aristocrats who emigrated to the gloomy palaces of Germany, the manors of Britain, Venice, Austria, Russia and to the United States even, might have described the French Revolution as a pageant of assassins.

But for those who remained in France perhaps it would be more reasonable to recall the words of the Comte de Ségur who wrote with but little exaggeration his final summing up:

> Finally, I blame no one for the evils of this revolution, for at first everyone wished for it; everyone tried to play a part in it within his limitations and capacity; from the King to the least of his subjects all worked for it to a greater or less degree.

What a pity it was that they had not all started working a generation earlier.

Appendix Two

A NOTE ON SOURCES

JAMES M. THOMPSON, former fellow of Magdalen College, Oxford (and predecessor of Dr A. J. P. Taylor), at the beginning of his absorbing study *The French Revolution* begged the reader of any historical work to bear in mind that wrong 'facts' and prejudiced views have been passed on, unchallenged for centuries, from one historian to the next and to ask himself the simple question, 'Is it likely that people would behave as they are said to have done?' He listed fifty best books on the French Revolution but refused to be drawn into giving his opinion of their merits, insisting that the reader must ultimately determine the reliability of the authors from his own experience.

Though I agree with this line of argument, which converts every historical work into a challenge to the reader's powers of criticism, my approach is from another angle. In these notes I have given preference to books most likely to awaken the further curiosity of the average reader—especially if he can read French—about the facts of the Revolution, since I believe that this kind of book list is preferable to an inventory of all the works that could be useful to

241

the scholar. Not all 'my' books are easy reading and some cover an extremely restricted field of more or less limited historical importance. Yet I would not like to leave out any of them, or to refer to them without comment.

At the top of the list comes one of the most unreadable yet fascinating books to be encountered—namely Pierre Caron's *Manuel Pratique pour L'Etude de la Révolution Française* published by A. et J. Picard et Cie of Paris. This work surveys the wide range of sources open to the historian. Thus apart from printed books there are studies carried out by learned societies, by national commissions, and in periodicals; records of Government ministries and of municipalities. Caron lists bibliographies and guides one's path through the treasure house of the French National Archives, through the series of manuscripts to be found in national and provincial libraries and even to private collections of autographed letters held in France and abroad.

Caron's book makes one realize the debt owed to French scholars who have devoted lifetimes of study to the Revolution, but for me it also contains the implicit warning that one of the most difficult tasks for any historian is to perceive those things which the people of former times took for granted and therefore *never* mentioned even in their most intimate writings or discussions with one another.

The latest pieces of research, presented with considerable discretion and insight, are to be found in that interesting quarterly *Les Annales Historiques de la Révolution Française*, published by the Société des Etudes Robespierristes, 304 rue de Belville, Paris, which contains the latest gossipy gleanings as well as solid studies, and of course reviews of the newest books.

Those who like their raw material in large draughts can find it in *A Documentary Survey of the French Revolution* by John Hall Stewart (the Macmillan Company, New York 1951); in *Select Documents Illustrative of the History of the French Revolution* edited by Wickham Legg (Clarendon Press, 1905) and in *The Principle Speeches of the Statesmen and Orators of the French Revolution* edited by H. Morse Stephens, two vols. (Clarendon Press, 1892). Works such as these do not age much.

Among general histories it is impossible to overlook the highly compressed but invaluable *French Revolution from Its Origins to 1793* by Georges Lefebvre translated by Elizabeth Moss Evanson

and published in London by Routledge and Kegan Paul and in the
U.S. by Columbia University Press. In fact none of Lefebvre's
works should be missed.

A well-planned and extremely thoughtful book was published in
1963 as No. 36 in the series *L'Histoire et Ses Problèmes* produced
by the Presses Universitaires de France. This is *Les Rèvolutions
(1770–1799)* by Jacques Godechot, which, as its title suggests,
argues that the French Revolution forms an integral part of a
world-wide movement of unrest not confined to France or to the
years most commonly applied to the French Revolution. Even
those who, like myself, remain only partly convinced will find their
critical faculties stimulated.

Memoirs of the French Revolution, I find, are often more useful
as a clue to the character of those who wrote them than as a record
of what happened. Many were composed—and in some cases
rewritten—with the aid of fading powers of recollection long
after the events that they describe, or in political circumstances
when self-justification was of more importance to the author
than an exact account of the part he or she had played in the Revolution.

Among the more detached commentaries are those of Gouverneur
Morris who was American Minister to Paris during some of the
critical moments of the convulsion. His diary, though incomplete
and scrappy, is penetrating in its analysis despite the fact that
Morris was necessarily excluded from taking part in the momentous
conspiracies being hatched around him. A useful edition of the
diary is that edited by Beatrix Cary Davenport and published by
George G. Harrap & Co. Ltd in 1939. The British point of view
comes in *Dispatches from Paris* selected from the Foreign Office
archives, edited by Oscar Browning, and published by the Camden
Society in London in 1910. There are a number of useful eye-
witness anthologies such as *The French Revolution as Told by Contemporaries* by E. L. Higgins (George G. Harrap & Co. Ltd, 1939);
Histoire Racontée par Ses Temoins by J-B. Ebeling (Librairie Plon,
Paris 1929) and the more recent work *The French Revolution* by
Georges Pernoud and Sabine Flaissier in the *History in the Making*
series of Secker and Warburg. One might also perhaps include here
La Révolution Française Vue par Ses Journaux by Gérard Walter
(Tardy, Paris 1948). Arthur Young's *Travels in France* in the early
days of the Revolution and immediately before it have been the

subject of a number of productions, including one edited by Constantia Maxwell and published by the Cambridge University Press in 1950. Young is still freely quoted by the French themselves as a reliable witness of the condition of the French farmers and peasants in the late seventeen-eighties.

Those with a taste for artistry in detail (such as for example the information that Marat's bath is still to be seen in Paris and that the shop building where Charlotte Corday bought her knife—177 Palais-Royal—is still standing), will like to read the works of G. Lenotre—particularly *Paris Révolutionaire* (Librairie Académique, Perrin et Cie, Paris 1916) and *The Guillotine* (Perrin et Cie, Paris 1927). Another work by Lenotre *Le Drame de Varennes* (Perrin et Cie, 1921) is a historical reconstruction of the highest order. *La Vie Quotidienne au Temps de la Révolution* by Jean Robiquet (Librarie Hachette, 1938), throws a number of sidelights on manners and customs of the day.

Almost every aspect of the Revolution has been studied at one time or another. *The Origins of Totalitarian Democracy* by J. L. Talmon (Secker and Warburg, 1952) is a fascinating work for anyone interested in plotting the line of communication linking the French Revolution with modern dictatorships. *The Crowd in the French Revolution* by George Rudé (Clarendon Press, 1959) analyses the social make-up of the mobs that took part in the mass risings of the Revolution. *La Crépuscule de la Monarchie* by Louis Madelin (Librairie Plon, Paris 1936) sketches in bold strokes the inevitable failure of royalty to preserve itself from the guillotine. *Les Suspectes* by Louis Jacob (Librairie Hachette, 1952) describes the ordeals of those under suspicion before and during the Terror.

The Revolution's greatest artist and his contribution to the festivals of the Republic are preserved in David Lloyd Dowd's *Pageant-Master of the Republic: Jacques-Louis David* (University of Nebraska Studies, June 1948).

The recently published *Paris in the Terror* by Stanley Loomis (Jonathan Cape, 1965), a highly readable account of the bloodiest days of the Revolution, has reverted once more to the highly critical attitude formerly in vogue towards Robespierre and, though I agree in many ways with this assessment, readers anxious to hear the case for the defence might consider *Etudes sur Robespierre* by the great scholar Albert Mathiez of the Société des Etudes Robespierristes (Editions Sociales, Paris 1958).

An unusual topic is dealt with in *Les Origines du Système Métrique* by Adrien Favre (Presses Universitaires de France, Paris 1931) and the war chants, cabaret skits and political anthems of the Revolution are tastefully displayed in the *Histoire de France par les Chansons* volume IV by Pierre Barbier and France Vernillet (Gallimard, Paris 1957).

Albert Soboul has maintained the highest standards of French scholarship and interpretation in his *Précis d'Histoire de la Révolution Française* and other works.

It is hard to bring any selection of books on the French Revolution to a close. But one thing is certain. Anyone who wants to read about those great times soon makes his own special list according to his own preferences. And it is sure, like this one, to be incomplete.

INDEX

247

DATE DUE

6/2 ptv		
NOV 1 1 1970		
NOV 2 6 1970		
NOV 2 4 1971		
NO 7 '72		
GAYLORD		PRINTED IN U.S.A.